Language Online

In *Language Online* David Barton and Carmen Lee investigate the impact of the online world on the study of language.

The effects of language use in the digital world can be seen in every aspect of language study, and new ways of researching the field are needed. In this book the authors look at language online from a variety of perspectives, providing a solid theoretical grounding, an outline of key concepts, and practical guidance on doing research.

Chapters cover topical issues including the relation between online language and multilingualism, identity, education and multimodality, and then conclude by looking at how to carry out research into online language use. Throughout the book many examples are given, from a variety of digital platforms, and a number of different languages, including Chinese and English.

Written in a clear and accessible style, this is a vital read for anyone new to studying online language and an essential textbook for undergraduates and postgraduates working in the areas of new media, literacy and multi-modality within language and linguistics courses.

David Barton is Professor of Language and Literacy in the Department of Linguistics at Lancaster University, UK and Director of the Lancaster Literacy Research Centre.

Carmen Lee is Assistant Professor in the Department of English at Chinese University of Hong Kong.

Language Online

Investigating Digital Texts and Practices

David Barton
Carmen Lee

Routledge
Taylor & Francis Group

LONDON AND NEW YORK

First published 2013
by Routledge
2 Park Square, Milton Park, Abingdon, Oxon OX14 4RN

Simultaneously published in the USA and Canada
by Routledge
711 Third Avenue, New York, NY 10017

Routledge is an imprint of the Taylor & Francis Group, an informa business

British Library Cataloguing in Publication Data
A catalogue record for this book is available from the British Library

Library of Congress Cataloging in Publication Data
Barton, David, 1949– author.
    Language Online : Investigating Digital Texts and Practices / David
    Barton and Carmen Lee.
        pages cm
    Includes bibliographical references.
    1. Communication—Technological innovations. 2. Language and
languages—Usage. 3. Human-computer interaction. 4. Technological
innovations—Social aspects. 5. Social media. I. Lee, Carman, author.
II. Title.
    P96.T42B37 2013
    418.00285—dc23   2012039540

ISBN: 978–0–415–52494–0 (hbk)
ISBN: 978–0–415–52495–7 (pbk)
ISBN: 978–0–203–55230–8 (ebk)

Typeset in Sabon and Scala Sans
by Swales & Willis Ltd, Exeter, Devon

CONTENTS

LIST OF FIGURES   vii

PREFACE   viii

1   Language in the digital world   1

2   Ten reasons why studying the online world is crucial for understanding language   15

3   Acting in a textually mediated social world   23

4   Hello! Bonjour! Ciao! Hola! Guten Tag! Deploying linguistic resources online   42

5   Taking up the affordances of multiple languages   55

6   'This is me': Writing the self online   67

7   Stance-taking through language and image   86

8   'My English is so poor': Talking about language online   107

9   Everyday learning online   124

10   Language online as new vernacular practices   137

11 Language online and education 153

12 Researching language online 164

13 Flows of language online and offline 178

APPENDICES 184
BIBLIOGRAPHY 194
INDEX 205

FIGURES

2.1   Ten reasons why studying the online world is crucial for
        understanding language   15
3.1   A Flickr photo page   37
7.1   Look at me in the eye   97
7.2   *cjPanda*'s photo page 'handwritting'   100
10.1 Abraham Lincoln with photo album   143
13.1 '4 UR Convenience', a convenience store in London   180
13.2 Fitness centre in Hong Kong   181

PREFACE

Like any other academic endeavour, the study of language develops in hops and jumps. Sometimes, it goes steadily forward with ideas developing in an incremental manner. At other times, there are sudden bursts of activity and movement in all directions, with steps backwards and sideways as well as forwards. At these times when disciplines and sub-disciplines shift and regroup, it is necessary to question existing ideas, to read outside one's discipline, to rethink, and to tear up existing lectures and notes.

The study of language has reached such a point, especially within sociolinguistics where researchers are challenging existing concepts and exploring new ideas. People talk of 'languaging', of 'translingualism', of 'superdiversity', with much of the interest coming from the study of multilingualism and migration. This questioning and rethinking is going on elsewhere, such as in the study of world languages and lingua francas, and in studies of multimodality. It affects all areas of language study, from socio-phonetics and spelling through to semiotics and pragmatics. This all makes the study of language at this point in time exciting, demanding and ultimately rewarding.

Our particular approach is to focus on the implications of the online world for the study of language. This book is aimed at two distinct audiences. First, for linguists it argues that understanding the online world is essential for the study of language. Second, to social scientists studying and researching the internet, it argues that an understanding of the role of language is essential. In the book, we explore language online from a range of perspectives. In brief, the first three chapters set the scene, providing a strong theoretical framework and introducing key concepts that are needed when examining language online. Then there is a set of chapters investigating specific language issues and drawing on extensive data. They start from studies of multilingualism, and then explore identity, stance, multimodality and metalinguistics. This is followed by chapters concentrating on learning, the significance of vernacular practices and implications for education. Next, ways of researching texts and practices online are outlined and a final chapter examines online-offline interaction.

Special features of the book include clear reasons for studying the online world and explanations of a set of key concepts. It provides many detailed authentic examples. Worked examples of analysing language and image are provided and there are contrasting biographies demonstrating the role of technology in people's lives. Rather than extensive screen shots and other illustrations, there is an accompanying page on the Routledge website which contains a list of internet links to some of our data and examples.

The discussions and illustrations cover a wide selection of examples from young people and adults with diverse linguistic backgrounds from various parts of the word. We draw upon an extensive range of online platforms. As befits a book about language, we provide examples from different languages, in particular Chinese and English. These two languages provide different affordances for people to draw upon, at all levels of language, especially, as we will show, in terms of the written language.

Our aim has been to complete a book about language online that is written in a clear and accessible manner. We are aware of the range of possible readers of this book and have in mind the novice, student readers as well as the experienced researcher in this developing field of the study of language. The book was written across time zones in England and Hong Kong. One particular rhythm of collaboration that has sped up the writing of this book is the way in which, as co-authors, one of us could finish a section in the evening and save our work on Dropbox. Meanwhile, the other author would be waking up across time zones and could go through the work and return it all in the same day. Our writing practices reflect the affordances of the technologies available to us.

Many people have supported and encouraged this work and we are pleased to acknowledge their varied contributions. First, we would like to thank the many people who participated in the studies which are drawn upon in this book and who patiently answered our questions and provided us with data. At both Lancaster University and the Chinese University of Hong Kong, we are pleased to acknowledge the many discussions and ideas from colleagues, especially Julia Gillen, Mary Hamilton, Greg Myers, Uta Papen, Diane Potts, Karin Tusting and Johnny Unger. We are grateful to Claire Coulton, who read and commented on the whole manuscript, and to Mary Hamilton, Diane Potts and Karin Tusting, who read parts of the manuscript. We would also like to thank our research assistants in our Flickr and Web 2.0 projects, especially Dennis Chau, Corah Chiu, Joey Li, Pierre Lien, Kelvin Lui, and Xavier Tam. Colleagues at the conferences where we have presented our work have provided invaluable questioning and probing, especially at the Language in (New) Media conferences and at Sociolinguistics Symposiums.

We thank the Faculty of Arts and Social Sciences and the Department of Linguistics at Lancaster University for financial support, which aided the smooth completion of the book. Some of the studies reported in the book were funded by the Hong Kong Research Grant Council General Research Fund (Ref: 446309) and the Chinese University of Hong Kong's Direct Grant for Research (Ref: 2010342).

We are grateful to Louisa Semlyen and Sophie Jaques at Routledge for their constant support and encouragement.

David Barton, Lancaster
Carmen Lee, Hong Kong

1

LANGUAGE IN THE DIGITAL WORLD

- Contemporary change
- Approaches to language online: three key directions
- Some overarching issues when discussing language online
- Language online as texts and practices

CONTEMPORARY CHANGE

The idea that technological innovations can change life in a fundamental way and that these changes reach into every aspect of life has been associated with many innovations throughout history, including the development of the printing press, newspapers, cameras, the postal service, radio and telephones. It is becoming central in how we think about contemporary change in digital technologies. This was well expressed by Marshall McLuhan more than 40 years ago in relation to television:

> The medium, or process, of our time – electric technology – is reshaping and restructuring patterns of social interdependence and every aspect of our personal life. It is forcing us to reconsider and re-evaluate practically every thought, every action, and every institution formerly taken for granted. Everything is changing – you, your family, your education, your neighborhood, your job, your government, your relation to 'the others'. And they're changing dramatically.
>
> McLuhan (1967: 8)

These changes identified by McLuhan continue apace with newer technologies. Now it is more accepted that all aspects of life, including everyday activities, workplace practices and the world of learning, are transformed by digital technologies. To give an example, practices of photography have been largely digitized – digital cameras and online photo sharing have taken over the place of film cameras and printed photo albums. Instead of sitting together at home leafing through photos in an album, nowadays people are more likely to share photos with friends and relatives on the internet either on social networking sites such as Facebook or photo sharing sites. Another example of contemporary changes is academic practices. As the authors have experienced, academic writing has been reshaped in many ways with the rise of new technologies. Very few people would handwrite a full manuscript of a book before typing it out on the computer. Students have assumed handing in an essay means handing in a typed, word-processed essay. At work, we receive far more emails than handwritten notes or letters. Other interesting examples of digitally transformed everyday activities include meetings, reading, note-taking, form filling, booking trips, map reading and shopping.

Technology is part of people's lived experiences across all contexts, ranging from engaging in a plethora of social networking sites with friends, through to studying and working or engaging in family life. In fact it is hard to find an area of life that is unchanged. People have gradually taken digitally transformed everyday activities for granted. This is often referred to as the domestication of technology (as in Berker *et al.* 2005), a concept that captures the process through which technologies are integrated into and mediate people's lives; while at the same time, technology users reappropriate technologies to facilitate their everyday activities. This has all been happening in a relatively short period of time and has become naturalized and unnoticed by people in their lives. There are certainly many issues of access and differences between people and groups of people. Nevertheless, technological change is affecting people everywhere and transforming all domains of life.

These technology-related changes in life are embedded in broader social changes. Contemporary life is changing in many ways which impact on language and communicative practices. Technology is a central part of this but it is just one among a set of interconnected factors. Lankshear and Knobel (2011) have drawn attention to changes that are occurring in the nature of institutions, media, the economy, and general processes of globalization. Kress (2003) further identifies four simultaneous change processes: changes in relations of social power, in the direction of abolishing existing settled hierarchies and remaking new ones; changes in economic structure, with writing taking on different roles in an economy in which information is increasingly important; communicational changes, with a shift from writing to image as the dominant mode, altering the logic of our communicative practices; and changing technological affordances, with a shift in media from page to screen (as in Snyder 1998). As we can see, it is this combination of changes in different areas of life that contribute to changes to our communicative practices and landscape.

It is important to make clear that technologies themselves do not automatically introduce changes in life. In other words, new activities in life are not technologically determined but technology itself is also part of broader social changes. And different people would adopt technologies differently to suit their own purposes in different contexts of use. Thus, in this book, and in understanding the relationship between technology and life more generally, our point of departure is *what people do* and how they draw upon resources to make meanings in their everyday activities.

The centrality of language

Language has a pivotal role in these contemporary changes, which are first and foremost transformations of meaning making and communication. Language is essential in shaping changes in life and our lived experiences. At the same time, it is affected and transformed by these changes. Many studies of language have been based on a set of fairly stable concepts, which are now rather strained as people's lives go online. For instance, on a website which combines images and words, basic concepts like *text* have to be redefined. The core units of sociolinguistics such as *variation*, *contact* and *community* need to be reassessed. Many researchers are aware that the central notions of interaction like *turn-taking* and *face-to-face* work differently with online data. Ideas of *author* and *audience* become even more complex. When to refer to language as *written* or *spoken* is not clear-cut and the activities of *reading* and *writing* are being redefined. This book is about understanding this contemporary change and the central role of language in it. Part of the book is also devoted to examining new data and methods in linguistic research, and new views of language more generally with respect to online spaces.

Starting from a view of language as situated practice, this book investigates how people's language use is changing as they participate in online activity. Covering a broad selection of online environments, it examines both online texts and people's practices around them, both how they create and how they use online texts. This book also focuses on specific language issues including language choice, language and identity, stance-taking, multimodal relations of language and image, and discourses of language and learning. Overall, the book demonstrates the importance of situated language analysis for understanding the dynamics of textually mediated online spaces. It shows how people integrate online and offline practices. The approach taken in this book focuses on how practices are located in the detail of people's everyday lives. For linguistics, it provides a theoretical framework of key concepts for researching online spaces.

The book covers the broad array of digital platforms that people use, examining sites where language is important in different ways and where the writing spaces have distinct affordances. These include primarily the platforms that we have researched and observed extensively such as Facebook, Flickr, and instant messaging. To understand what these tools mean in people's everyday lives and language use, we explore their 'technobiographies'. These are detailed life histories and narratives of people's relations to technologies, how technologies are part of their lived experiences across their lives, and how such relations shape their language use online through different phases and domains of life. We also move beyond these three key platforms and draw on existing research from the emerging fields of digital literacies and computer-mediated discourse, which covers: studies of websites and discussion forums; mobile texting; blogging and microblogging such as Twitter; wikis, online dictionaries and encyclopedias such as Wikipedia; search engines such as Google; and multimedia sharing such as YouTube.

This opening chapter introduces readers to the general approach taken by this book to language, literacies, and the internet, focusing on what happens to language and practices when they move online. The next section starts with an overview of research that has been done on language online. Then we turn to the specific approach we draw upon. This is a social practice view of language and literacies with specific attention to writing done online, which explores what happens to texts and practices when people participate in online activities. The next chapter provides a set of 10 reasons why those interested in language need to pay attention to the internet. These two chapters are closely related to Chapter 3, which consists of an overview of the key theoretical concepts adopted throughout the book.

APPROACHES TO LANGUAGE ONLINE: THREE KEY DIRECTIONS

New online media have generated much multidisciplinary interest in recent years, from information science to media studies, psychology and sociology. Two areas that place emphasis on writing activities online are linguistics and digital literacies. Over the past two decades or so, works by linguists and literacy theorists have developed two seemingly separate yet complementary traditions of research, with their own sets of terminologies, theoretical frameworks and methodologies. These bodies of work have introduced new research methods, while at the same time reappropriating traditional theories and concepts in response to the changing affordances of new media. This section identifies and describes three key approaches to language online within linguistics. Traditions from literacy studies will be outlined in a later section.

(i) Structural features of computer-mediated communication

One of the earliest and perhaps most dominant traditions of language-focused online research is the identification and description of linguistic features and strategies that are not commonly found in other modes of communication. A topic of great interest within this early tradition was to compare language strategies in online media with existing modes of communication. A key topic under this strand is whether text-based computer-mediated communication (CMC) should be treated as speech or as writing, or whether it is a hybrid of *speech and writing* (Herring 1996; Baron 2003). Thus the starting point of CMC research was to draw upon the existing concepts of linguistics to understand language online. In relation to this, another direction attempted to describe CMC as a 'new' variety of language that is characterized by features such as:

- acronyms and initialisms (e.g. GTG for 'got to go', LOL for 'laugh out loud'),
- word reductions (e.g. gd for 'good'; hv for 'have'),
- letter/number homophones (e.g. U for 'you' and 2 for 'to'),
- stylized spelling (e.g. I'm *soooooooooo* happy!)
- emoticons (such as :-) and :( ),
- unconventional/stylized punctuation (e.g. '!!!!!!!!!!!!!', '...................').

As a result, many other labels have been given to describe the set of peculiar discourse features identified in CMC such as *emailism* (Petrie 1999), *Netspeak* (Crystal 2006), *interactive written discourse* (Ferrara *et al.* 1991), and other publicly recognized terms such as e-language, chatspeak, textspeak, cyber language, and internet slang, to name just a few. This body of work however took a somewhat deterministic view that it was primarily the new technological affordances that naturally foster new forms of language in CMC. In the beginning, there was almost no discussion of the contextual and social factors that might have also contributed to these linguistic features. Large quantities of publicly available online data (e.g. IRC chat rooms) were often randomly collected and analysed without considering their immediate discursive and social contexts. Generalizations were made out of statistical analyses of the distribution of different features in corpora. At this point, corpus data were combined with discourse analysis. The umbrella term 'computer-mediated discourse analysis' (CMDA) also emerged to describe discourse analytic approaches to CMC (Herring 2001). For example, Ko (1996) compares structural features of a corpus of synchronous CMC data collected from InterChange, an online educational platform, to existing spoken and written corpora collected in offline contexts. Findings from this body of work did offer important theoretical insights and opened up new opportunities for language research. However, there was sometimes a tendency to overgeneralize the findings from such studies, and to imply that there are static and predictable conventions across all CMC language. In fact, in real life what may be referred to as Netspeak features are not employed in all types of CMC and all contexts of use. There are varieties across individual users as well as across different online platforms.

(ii) Social variation of computer-mediated discourse

Written genres are not separable from their users and social contexts (Hyland 2002). CMC researchers began to realize that CMC language is shaped by various social factors and is situated in their specific contexts of use (Herring 2002; Giltrow and Stein 2009). This direction of research acknowledges that, on the one hand, regular similarities and differences occur within and beyond one single mode of CMC; on the other hand, in reality, users do not apply the same set of CMC features to all contexts; but they constantly reappropriate their ways of writing in different modes of CMC to suit different purposes. In view of this, studies of social variation in CMC language began to emerge. There have been detailed discourse analyses of particular types of CMC including blogging (Myers 2010a) and SMS texting (Tagg 2012). A growing body of work focuses on language and identity online, notably studies of gender differences in CMC (e.g. Herring 1996; Danet 1998), and how social identities are performed through adopting certain linguistic features and styles (Bechar-Israeli 1995; Nakamura 2002). Seeing social network sites as spaces for everyday storytelling, Page (2011) takes a narrative approach to identity performance in social media and examines how new narrative genres emerge as a result of people reshaping traditional ones in new media. Following this socio-cultural trend, another group of researchers has been investigating CMC features across cultures and linguistic backgrounds. Instead of examining CMC from a solely monolingual, usually English, perspective, a growing body of research is interested in how speakers of various languages have adopted such new forms of writing to different extents (e.g. chapters in Danet and Herring 2007). This tradition is often informed by pragmatics, sociolinguistics and, especially, discourse analysis – areas of linguistics that begin to take into account the effect of context and web users' perceptions of what they do online. While corpus-based analyses are still an important method in researching CMC, researchers started to realize the importance of drawing on online users' perspectives through methods such as interviews (e.g. Cherny 1999).

(iii) Language ideologies and metalanguage

A more recent strand of linguistic research takes a more critical approach to new media language data. Much of this work draws upon concepts from sociology and language ideology (for example Blommaert 1999). Studies within this approach are not only interested in micro-level features of language online, but also how ways of communication are shaped by social ideologies, and how such ideologies are discursively constructed in new media. This work has often developed on from discourse approaches to language and traditional media such as newspapers, film and TV (as in Johnson and Ensslin 2007). One recurring theme is how language is talked about online or what is often referred to as *metalanguage*. Folk linguistic theories about language in new media are often represented in mass media (Thurlow 2007). Because this research direction is relatively recent, researchers tend to be interested in Web 2.0 media, especially those involving user-generated multimodal content, such as Flickr (Thurlow and Jaworski

2011) and YouTube (Chun and Walters 2011). One salient feature of this approach to research is that some researchers deliberately take a critical gaze and problematize their data in their discussion. An important issue of this direction of research is how the researcher's stance is expressed through their specific analysis and interpretation of data. (See Chapter 7.) This line of research has moved beyond seeing language as a tool of communication, but is more concerned with understanding how language is represented, or perhaps misrepresented, online and in society more broadly. Alongside these approaches to the academic study of language online, the impact of new media has always been at the centre of public discussion. A set of moral panics come together when new media are discussed, including concerns about 'young people'. These techno-panics revolve around uncertainty and worry about newness and constant change, along with fears about falling standards of language and literacy. (These topics are pursued in more detail in Thurlow 2007.)

We have identified these three key approaches to studying language online. They can also be viewed as stages of development with each building on the earlier approach. We are beginning to see a fourth phase where traditional concepts of linguistics are jettisoned in favour of new framings where concepts such as superdiversity (Blommaert and Rampton 2011) and supermobility reveal new insights into language online and contemporary change. These will be explored in later chapters.

SOME OVERARCHING ISSUES WHEN DISCUSSING LANGUAGE ONLINE

Problems of terminology

The notion 'online' itself is first explained here. In the book title, *Language Online*, 'online' is used as a convenient term and a shorthand for all forms of communication carried out on networked devices. Having said this, this book does not assume a strict online-offline dichotomy. When we say online and offline, we are referring to the different situational contexts where communication takes place. We are not suggesting, however, that people's lives are either carried out online or offline, nor are we implying that the online is replacing the offline. As will be seen throughout the book, many contemporary social practices seamlessly intertwine online and offline activities and they cannot be separated. As Wellman (2001: 18) points out in his discussion of social networks,

> [t]he cyberspace-physical space comparison is a false dichotomy. Many ties operate in both cyberspace and physical space. [. . .] Computer mediated communications supplements, arranges and amplifies in-person and telephone communications rather than replacing them. The Internet provides ease and flexibility in who communicates with whom, what means they use to communicate, what they communicate, and when they communicate.

In this book, a range of terms and concepts are used to refer broadly to the context, the tools, and the reading and writing activity associated with the theme of language online. These terms are not without problems themselves and one has to be cautious when interpreting them. In the context of this book, they do serve as useful descriptors at different points of the discussion.

- When we use the words 'online', 'internet', and 'the web', we are referring to the broad context and domain where online communication takes place.
- When we use 'computer-mediated communication', 'digital media', 'digital communication', 'new media', 'new technologies', or 'digital tools', 'sites', and 'platforms', we are referring to the tools that people use to carry out their online communication. In this respect, SMS texting is also included in our study as a form of computer-mediated communication since a mobile phone is basically a portable computer and is clearly a form of digital communication.
- When we say 'digital literacies', 'new (media) literacies', and 'new vernacular literacies', we are broadly referring to the everyday reading and writing activities online. The plural 'literacies' is preferred to capture the fact that literacy is not skills-based but there are many different sorts of literacy that people draw upon for different purposes.
- When we use the expressions 'language online', 'online texts', 'writing online', and 'computer-mediated discourse', we are referring to the linguistic processes and products resulting from online communication. This is referred to by Crystal (2011) as linguistic 'output'.

The question of the 'new'

New technologies are no longer new and email and instant messaging are referred to as old media when considered alongside Web 2.0 sites such as Facebook, which itself is no longer new. The idea of communicating online and participating in virtual activities was new in the 1990s, but a generation of people are growing up taking digital media for granted. In the same way as somewhere called New College may have been established in 1379, so new technologies and new literacy studies are only new by name. Whilst there is always a cutting edge, we can no longer speak of technological advances in themselves as being new.

Rather than fixing on a particular new activity, the idea of constant change is now more accepted. To draw on a linguistic concept, literacy and what it means to be literate can be seen as *deictic*, that is, it points to a current situation (Coiro *et al.* 2008: 5–7). However, it quickly goes out of date. Any description of what people do online is situated in the present and is likely to change. In the time it takes for a book to be published or a university course to be completed, people's practices have changed and the book and the course have become out of date.

Nevertheless, it is worth identifying where there are continuations of existing practices and where there are practices that can be regarded as new. In our research we have observed that people's online participation changes over time. When first using a site, often people bring old practices with them, that is, they do old things in new ways. So for example a person using a photo site to share photos of family birthdays or weddings may initially see this as the continuing of an offline practice. Over time this changes as they see the new opportunities. And they participate in activities that are new for them, so they may be aware that the photos are seen by a broader range of people.

When discussing 'new' language-related phenomena in CMC, Susan Herring makes it clear that not all linguistic phenomena on Web 2.0 sites are new. She provides a three-way distinction. She characterizes discourse practices in convergent media or what she refers to as convergent media computer-mediated discourse (CMCMD) as follows:

> phenomena *familiar* from older computer-mediated discourse (CMD) modes such as email, chat, and discussion forums that appear to carry over into Web 2.0 environments with minimal differences; CMD phenomena that adapt to and are *reconfigured* by Web 2.0 environments; and new or *emergent* phenomena that did not exist—or if they did exist, did not rise to the level of public awareness—prior to the era of Web 2.0.
>
> (Herring, 2013a)

We return to the idea of newness when contrasting *literacy studies* from *literacies studies* below.

The Web 1.0–Web 2.0 dichotomy

We are focusing primarily on Web 2.0, that is, web-based applications that allow users to create and publish their own content online. Creators of applications such as Facebook provide a strong framing with the layout and affordances of their applications. Within these structures, the content which users provide is relatively unregulated, although there can be forms of moderation and conflicts over censorship. Weblogs and Twitter are common examples of Web 2.0, where within a given framework people publish their own texts to share with others. Further examples include Wikipedia and other online encyclopedias and dictionaries that rely on user-generated data. Another central idea of Web 2.0 is that of social networking, that is, participating and collaborating in communities of users. Often this is achieved in the form of people interacting by writing, but it also includes uploading images and videos. Social network sites such as Facebook and Twitter are platforms for people to interact with each other and connect through the written word and other multimodal content. Users of these sites often exchange views on their everyday interests and experiences, evaluating and reacting to music they have heard, books they have read, and hotels and restaurants they have visited.

Another important feature shared by Web 2.0 spaces is their commenting systems. On YouTube, for instance, people interact through leaving comments about one another's uploaded content. Commenting is an important act of positioning oneself and others, that is *stance-taking,* as will be discussed in Chapter 7. Such activities are highly textually mediated (Barton 2001) and they all provide new affordances, that is possibilities and constraints, for people to act within. (See chapter 1 of Knobel and Lankshear 2007 for more discussion of the distinctive characteristics of Web 2.0 literacies.) In this book, Web 2.0 is not a label given to just a certain set of sites, nor should it refer to sites that are developed at a certain point in history. Rather, when we use the term Web 2.0, we are referring to particular features of web site design such as self-generated content and interactivity that tend to be more common in 'newer' media. We are also aware that older sites are adopting Web 2.0 features and because of that there is no clear-cut boundary between Web 1.0 and Web 2.0.

The concept of digital natives

The idea that young people are particularly adept at using new technologies and can be characterized as 'digital natives' has been around for some time (Prensky 2001). The idea is that they were brought up surrounded by digital media and can be contrasted with 'digital immigrants', that is older people who were brought up on print media and have had to move – or migrate – to new technologies (Prensky 2001). This division may have been useful for a while around the year 2000 when there was a generation of people not involved with the internet and for a time researchers who had lived through changes from print to screen were studying younger people who had been brought up with new technologies. Much research on language and new technologies is on young people's – usually students' – online activities and often their uses of social media. It is important not to stereotype internet use as consisting primarily of young people's activities on social media sites. In fact the idea of digital natives, and a digital divide, masks the variety of knowledge and experience in young people (Hargittai 2010; Bennett *et al.* 2008), and older people alike. In addition there is no clear age for marking a difference in people's technology use. Rather, every year brings differences in people's familiarity with new media. It is better to think of this deictically, as pointing to a particular situation and where there is constant change. That is why this book takes a situated approach to language online. Studying people's technobiographies serves as a way of understanding the impact and ongoing changes of language use online, which we are all part of.

The problem of moral panics

Since the beginning of the internet there has been a strand of public criticism associated with certain linguistic features that are often found in online communication such as word reduction and stylized spelling commonly used in texting. These public discourses, or moral panics, that are largely reinforced by mass media are centred on how the language adopted by young people in their online communication may negatively affect their literacy skills. Claims are made about how people are reading fewer books or have lower reading abilities and concentration skills because of increasing use of new media (e.g. Carr 2010). Labels have been given to what may seem to be a genre of texting language such as 'textese' and 'textspeak'. Indeed, such techno-panics have existed for a long time throughout history when earlier technologies such as radio, TV, and telegram writing style were invented, as Crystal (2011) has pointed out. These claims tend to be unfounded opinions based on brief observations and often contrast with scholarly research on new media language discussed above. This has developed into growing tension between academic and non-academic understandings of language online.

Related to this is the problem of predictions about the influence of the internet on language use. One prediction is that English will dominate the internet. This might have been true for a short while in the 1990s but now the internet and its users are becoming increasingly multilingual to the extent that people who used to be labelled as monolinguals now inevitably engage in certain kinds of translingual practices. (See Chapters 4 and 5.) Another prediction is that 'Netspeak' features threaten standard English language. However, as Crystal (2011) points out, only a small proportion of English vocabulary has been modified for internet communication. Short forms existed before the internet. Besides, the basic grammatical structure of the language has not changed because of the internet. Academic studies have begun to emerge as a reaction to these misconceptions. For example, Plester and Wood's (2009) research reveals a positive relationship between texting and spelling abilities among British children.

LANGUAGE ONLINE AS TEXTS AND PRACTICES

The approach taken in this book is to combine the study of practices with the analysis of texts in order to understand language online. Our particular background and starting point is work in literacy studies investigating language practices. The social practices which language is embedded in are particularly salient when examining language online not least because of the constant change, the constant learning and the fluidity of texts. A crucial part of the context of texts online is locating them in the practices of their creation and use. We move on to an overview of the approach of literacy studies as a way into examining texts and practices online.

Literacy studies is an area of research which has come into being in the past 30 years. It is a 'mid-level' socio-cultural theory of reading and writing that starts out from what people do with written language in their lives. It examines in detail people's broader social practices, noting that many of these involve texts of some sort, and that we live in a textually mediated social world (see Chapter 3), where texts are part of the fabric of social life.

In this socio-cultural approach to written language, literacy is a social activity and can best be described in terms of people's literacy practices. These practices are drawn upon in literacy events that are mediated by written texts. The notion of *literacy practices* is central to literacy studies. There are common patterns in using reading and writing in a particular situation where people bring their cultural knowledge to an activity.

The other key concept is *literacy event*. The notion of literacy event and the methodologies of literacy studies have their roots in the sociolinguistic idea of speech events and the ethnographic approaches associated with Dell Hymes (1962). For literacy studies this provides both a link to and a divergence from the mainstream of sociolinguistic thought. Rather than focusing on spoken language practices, literacy studies emphasizes the materiality of written language, through the physicality of texts. An early researcher in literacy studies, Shirley Brice Heath defines literacy events as 'any occasion in which a piece of writing is integral to the nature of the participants' interactions and their interpretative processes' (1982: 50). Crucially, literacy events are about the interaction of the written and spoken, as a literacy event can have talk around a text. To bring the two terms together, literacy practices are the general cultural ways of utilizing literacy that people draw upon in a literacy event. Examples of literacy events and practices can be found throughout life, online and offline. For example, going online to comment on a news story, to book a ticket, to play a game or to arrange to meet a friend all involve negotiating written language and are all *literacy events*. In deciding where and when to do these things, along with what styles of language to draw upon, the participants draw upon their literacy practices. (This social practice approach to literacy has been laid out in more detail elsewhere, for example in Barton 2007.)

There are many ways of reading and writing, and not one set of literacy practices. Where different practices cluster into coherent groups, it is very useful to talk in terms of them as being different *literacies*. A literacy is a stable, coherent, identifiable configuration of practices such as those associated with specific workplaces. Historically, literacy studies has identified different literacies being associated with different domains of life such as education and work. These are different places in life where people act differently and use language differently. However, especially when considering life online, the reality is more fluid. And people may move seamlessly in and out of different domains of activity.

In particular domains of activity, such as the home, or school, or workplaces, we see common patterns of activity and we may wish to contrast the ways literacies are used in these different domains. Starting from particular domains has been a useful way for then seeing how different domains interact and overlap and how there is much hybridity and fusion. The borders, transitions and the spaces between domains then become very salient. Literacy studies often has the *everyday* as the starting point and enables a discussion of the blurring of the domains of work, education and everyday life.

The view of literacy as being part of social practices that are inferred from events and mediated by texts requires a certain methodology. It is a methodology of attention to detail and it draws heavily on ethnographic approaches. It involves the examination of particular events in order to understand broader practices. Researchers integrate a variety of methods including observation, interviews, the analysis of texts, the use of photography and more. This is an ecological approach accepting that all activities are situated and that people's actions both affect and are affected by the environment they are in. There is no simple causality and rather than talk of 'effects' of technologies it discusses the affordances which technologies offer for action, as pursued in Chapter 3. This provides a way of moving on from technological determinism when discussing change.

The range of studies, the developments of theory and methodology and the links to practice over the past 20 years are evidence of the success of literacy studies. (For an overview, see, for example, Baynham and Prinsloo 2009, who identify different generations of literacy research.) These studies have been used to challenge deficit theories and myths about literacy. At the same time, the approach offers a set of concepts, such as *networks, brokers* and *sponsors*, which are useful in understanding the language-based dynamics of interaction. The approach of literacy studies is close to data, but at the same time it is theorizing by providing concepts and by linking to broader theories.

Literacy can be a powerful lens for examining changing social practices. This includes the impact of new technologies, since engagement with texts of various kinds is central to life online. As stated elsewhere:

> By examining the changing role of texts we uncover the central tensions of contemporary change: new literacy practices offer exciting possibilities in terms of access to knowledge, creativity and personal power; at the same time the textually mediated social world provides a technology of power and control, and of surveillance.
>
> (Barton 2009: 39)

In relation to globalization, the examination of literacy practices provides a way of tracing links between local and global practices and documenting local forms of appropriation and resistance. It can also show the ways in which new literacy practices are generated out of existing ones (Barton and Hamilton 2012). This largely uncharted area needs the empirical work of understanding people's practices if we are to understand and have some control over these competing possible futures.

In taking account of the online world, literacy studies has experienced a 'digital turn' (Mills 2010) and research is increasingly examining language online and the associated 'digital literacies' (as in Gillen and Barton 2010). To emphasize the online focus, some researchers identify the plural *new literacies* and distinguish this newer *literacies studies* from the more established *literacy studies* (as in Lankshear and Knobel 2011; Coiro *et al.*

2008). Literacies remain central as much of the internet is mediated by literacy activities: it is written and it is read. Often activities involve writing and reading, whereas the linguistic forms are closer to what has been thought of as spoken language. There needs to be a rethinking of the relation between written and spoken. Again it is deictic, and what is true today may not be in the future with a shift towards using spoken instructions to phones and computers, and where the talking may not be to real people or by real people. We prefer to refer to language practices online and not highlight a distinction between writing and speaking.

As shown earlier when discussing different approaches to researching language online, analysing discourse has been central to this research. Studies have followed a wide range of approaches of discourse analysis and critical discourse analysis. One approach that explicitly locates the analysis of discourse in activities is the mediated discourse analysis approach associated with Ron Scollon and colleagues (Scollon 2001). The basic unit of analysis is the mediated action, which is effectively the practice where the text is used. Seeing practices as important for understanding context, Rodney Jones argues that discourse analysts need to develop new ways of seeing social interaction, 'ways that encompass multiple modes and make use of multiple methods, ways that begin not with texts but with people's actions and experiences around texts' (Jones 2004: 31).

In other work moving beyond the text, Ruth Wodak and colleagues have developed a discourse-historical approach to critical discourse analysis (Wodak and Meyer 2009) where the researchers collect texts to develop an understanding of the context, as well as drawing upon their background knowledge. A strand of work that aims to bring together discourse analysis with ethnographic approaches is Androutsopoulos' 'discourse centred online ethnography' (DCOE) (2008). This approach has developed from his work on German-based web environments. For example, one of his projects looks into sociolinguistic styles and identity constructions on sites devoted to hip-hop culture. In doing DCOE on these sites, Androutsopoulos starts with systematic observation of the discourse of the sites, moving on to inter-viewing internet actors to elicit insiders' perspectives. When working with both texts and practices, literacy studies tends to start from practices and from this work identifies salient texts for analysis. Discourse analysis often starts out from the texts and then uses empirical methods to provide further information. Researchers are finding many ways to bring these approaches together.

The centrality of language in online research is reinforced in the next chapter, where we present 10 reasons why linguists and those who are interested in the digital world should pay attention to language issues online.

2

TEN REASONS WHY STUDYING THE ONLINE WORLD IS CRUCIAL FOR UNDERSTANDING LANGUAGE

1. The world is increasingly textually mediated and the web is an essential part of this textual mediation.
2. Basic linguistic concepts are changing in meaning and a new set of concepts is needed.
3. New multilingual encounters online shift the relations between languages.
4. Linguistic resources are drawn upon to assert new identities and to represent the self in online spaces.
5. People combine semiotic resources in new ways and they invent new relations between language and other modes of meaning making.
6. The internet provides spaces for reflection upon language and communication.
7. Language is central to the constant learning in online spaces.
8. Vernacular language practices are becoming more public and circulated more widely.
9. Language is central to new forms of knowledge creation and new forms of enquiry.
10. New methods for researching language are made possible.

Figure 2.1 Ten reasons why studying the online world is crucial for understanding language

Linguists have long been interested in investigating language as either speech or writing. As we have seen in Chapter 1, the internet and its related new media have brought about changes to language and its use in unprecedented ways. There are new forms of interaction and everyday activities are transformed in a fast-moving semiotic landscape. New media provide different relations of people and technologies, giving rise to new affordances. There are new and emergent forms of mediation of language, with machines using language, and there are even challenges to the basic distinction between human and machine. Although language-focused online research has gradually gained currency, there remain many unexplored issues. To reinforce the urgency of attending to this area of inquiry, this chapter provides 10 reasons why researchers and others need to take account of language online (Figure 2.1). In presenting these reasons, we introduce a set of specific language issues that arise in the online world, thus highlighting the key features of the book. In this way the themes of the chapters are also outlined.

1. THE WORLD IS INCREASINGLY TEXTUALLY MEDIATED AND THE WEB IS ESSENTIAL TO THIS TEXTUAL MEDIATION

There is a growing importance of writing in contemporary life. Written language is crucial in the vernacular activities of everyday life. It is also central in the learning endeavours of education. And it is fundamental in most workplaces. Written language is woven into these activities, often unnoticed. For instance, in all these areas, notes and records are kept of activities; rules and regulations are followed; texts are used to communicate. In this way, written language holds activities together. People's activities in all areas of social life, in everyday life, in education and in workplaces are textually mediated (Barton 2001). Increasingly, new technologies are the medium of this textual mediation. These technologies provide new and distinct writing spaces, as illustrated in the next chapter. People explore the affordances of these writing spaces and literate forms are being renegotiated. There is an explosion of new genres and proto-genres, which are the beginnings of future genres. The textually mediated nature of new media is first elaborated in Chapter 3 and is further explored throughout the book. Understanding writing activities online is crucial for discourse analysis and the study of written language.

2. BASIC LINGUISTIC CONCEPTS ARE CHANGING IN MEANING AND A NEW SET OF CONCEPTS IS NEEDED

For linguistics and the study of language more broadly, a set of stable concepts that have been developed in the past few decades are now overturned. The word 'text' is an example. First of all, *texts* can no longer be thought of as relatively fixed and stable. They are more fluid with the changing affordances of new media. In addition, they are becoming increasingly multimodal and interactive. Links between texts are complex online and *intertextuality* is common in online texts as people draw upon and play with other texts available on the web. New media have also introduced new relations between the traditional notions of speech and writing. More hybrid genres are identified on the web. As another example, established media studies notions such as 'audience' also become more complex and the concept of 'author' and 'authorship' is changed. The boundary between author and reader is also fuzzy with the rise of self-generated content on the web. Domains of language use are more fluid, as are notions of groups and communities that are significant for language use. In these ways people are responding to new affordances of language use. This provides challenges to the existing understanding of fields of linguistics such as pragmatics, morphology and grammar, and of the boundaries between them. At different points of the book, we revisit some traditional notions of linguistics, such as politeness, and explore how they fit it with new media data.

3. NEW MULTILINGUAL ENCOUNTERS ONLINE SHIFT THE RELATIONS BETWEEN LANGUAGES

New multilingual encounters that were not possible before are common in many online spaces. In this way the internet provides people with new opportunities for language contact. Multilingual participants are able to negotiate language choice and deploy their languages strategically. There are also new spaces available for minority languages.

It is important for multilingualism research to investigate how people participate in new multilingual encounters. Multilingual issues are pursued in Chapters 4 and 5. Chapter 4, 'Hello! Bonjour! Ciao! Hola! Guten Tag! Deploying linguistic resources online', begins with the classic debate of whether the internet fosters the use of English only or multilingualism. The chapter then discusses the rich array of linguistic resources that online participants draw upon for their online writing. In particular, we demonstrate how multilingual online participants negotiate language choice. Language choice is an important lens for understanding language use more generally and it is often where we can see more general language issues most clearly. We show that such multilingual encounters are common in many online spaces including instant messaging, Flickr, YouTube, and Facebook. In Chapter 5, 'Taking up the affordances of multiple languages', we begin with a discussion of how people take up the action possibilities of different linguistic resources when participating in the online world. It presents a set of ecological factors affecting people's language choice; these also apply to language use online more broadly. Chapter 5 broadens existing understanding of multilingualism and discusses new issues related to multilingual encounters online. For example, people who used to be considered mono-linguals now inevitably come across and work with different languages when participating in online spaces. Although we do not cover it in detail, there are dramatic changes in the translation of languages that affect what one can know of something originally written in an unknown language. Translation is now often an activity undertaken by machines and then checked by people. It is becoming increasingly possible for translations to be instantly available. In online communication we can also see how people use and standardize minority languages, and forms which were earlier only available in spoken language are increasingly being written down. These are all important *translingual practices* introduced and reinforced on the internet, an issue dealt with in Chapter 5.

4. LINGUISTIC RESOURCES ARE DRAWN UPON TO ASSERT NEW IDENTITIES AND TO REPRESENT THE SELF IN ONLINE SPACES

How people talk about and represent themselves in the online world is an important issue for language and identity research. This is dealt with throughout the book, especially in Chapter 6, "This is me": Writing the self online'. In the chapter, we first provide an overview of ways in which online participants represent themselves through language in new media. We introduce the concept of people's techno-linguistic biography, people's technology-related lives where language plays a central role. This is used as a major source of research data and provides a method for researching language and identity online. It is also an important means for understanding the relationship between people's lived experiences with technology and their language use online. We argue that language choice is one of the most salient practices for identity performance. We show how participants on various online platforms represent the self through particular ways of choosing language and deploying their linguistic resources such as different scripts. In particular, we discuss how writing in multiple languages in the same space can widen participation, thus allowing people to negotiate between their more local and more global identities.

5. PEOPLE COMBINE SEMIOTIC RESOURCES IN NEW WAYS AND THEY INVENT NEW RELATIONS BETWEEN LANGUAGE AND OTHER MODES OF MEANING MAKING

People draw upon available semiotic resources to make meaning and to assert their relationships to the meanings expressed. In particular, people combine images and other visual resources with the written word online. There are new relations of language and image developing. Image is not replacing language; but we are seeing new ways of these modes working together in powerful ways. The intertwining of language and image has also drawn renewed interest in the developing field of linguistic landscape research (Shohamy and Gorter 2009; Shohamy *et al.* 2010). Looking into instances of multimodality in online media broadens methods and approaches of linguistic landscape research, which can be moved from outdoors in the public sphere of city streets to public spaces online.

Multimodality is a crucial concept and it is first introduced in Chapter 3. We concentrate on language and image as two powerful forms of meaning which are often used together. Making meaning through multimodal means is a way of positioning the self and others. These issues are pursued in detail in Chapter 7, 'Stance-taking through language and image', where multimodality is investigated as one of the resources for stance-taking. Stance refers to the positions people take and express through particular forms of language and other resources. Various stance-takers, resources, and objects can be identified in different writing spaces online. We focus on image here from the dimensions of the image producer, the image and the viewer. The concept of stance is used to draw attention to the positioning of the researcher in online research. Worked examples of analysing multimodal texts from the dimensions of the image producer, the image, and the viewer, and the researcher are also provided in the chapter.

6. THE INTERNET PROVIDES SPACES FOR REFLECTION UPON LANGUAGE AND COMMUNICATION

With new ways of participation and dialogue, people can be more reflexive; they can be more aware of language and more tolerant of language varieties. They are also more playful and creative with language, exhibiting metalinguistic awareness. This creativity relates to the internet being a space for language change. Reflection and discussion about language lead to development of the affordances of language and how people can draw upon them to act in the world. This is important for studies of reflexivity and language awareness and is pursued in Chapter 8, '"My English is so poor": Talking about language online'. Here we move to the metalinguistic level and consider how people actually talk about language in relation to their online participation. Drawing upon examples from participatory web spaces such as Flickr and YouTube, we show the ways in which Web 2.0 sites provide a platform for people to publicly reflect upon and discuss language-related topics through self-generated writing, such as personal profiles and comments, thus revealing their vernacular theories of learning, which is pursued in Chapter 9.

Understanding how language works online is also important so that linguists can contribute to public discussions of the social significance of new media, providing alternatives to deficit theories, challenging moral panics about language, and getting beyond technological determinism. This can help people develop a critical awareness of how to use online spaces effectively.

7. LANGUAGE IS CENTRAL TO THE CONSTANT LEARNING IN ONLINE SPACES

Participating in rapidly changing online activities involves constant learning, much of which is informal. People learn in new and different ways; they reflect on their learning and they undertake intentional projects of learning. Chapter 9, 'Everyday learning online', shows how online spaces are important sites of learning of all sorts, especially languages. It starts with conceptualizing ways of learning online and how people draw upon and develop language practices. We focus on a particularly powerful way of informal learning online – deliberate learning. Starting with theories of adult learning, the chapter moves on to examples from Flickr to show how key aspects of these theories, which were developed before the existence of the internet, nevertheless apply to learning in new media. The chapter points to the importance of participation in learning and the role of other people and networks in supporting learning. It then links up with a set of issues around reflexivity, identity and discourses of learning that have been raised in other chapters. The chapter also shows how informal language learning takes place in various online spaces. Later, in Chapter 11, 'Language online and education', we briefly provide an overview of the educational implications of vernacular theories of learning. Two practical issues are covered in this chapter: first, we make recommendations as to how educators, and language teachers in particular, can utilize the internet and digital technologies as pedagogical tools; and second, we briefly outline how new technologies change educational practices more broadly.

8. VERNACULAR PRACTICES ARE BECOMING MORE PUBLIC AND CIRCULATED MORE WIDELY

Understanding everyday, or 'vernacular', practices has been important for literacies research. Reading and writing activities in everyday life involve different types of literacy practices and serve a wide range of purposes. While many of these activities, such as filling out tax forms or paying utility bills, are carried out in response to external demands, much of the reading and writing that people do, and the ways in which they do them, are not imposed externally; for example, activities like reading novels and magazines, writing down recipes, shopping lists, keeping in touch with friends are often done voluntarily. And it is important for language and literacy researchers to note how many of these writing activities are now carried out and transformed online. These issues are pursued in Chapter 10, 'Language online as new vernacular practices'.

Chapter 10 revisits the concept of vernacular literacies and examines general changes in literacy practices that have been taking place in the past 20 years. The chapter starts with a specific vernacular practice, popular photography, providing a brief history and examining how it has been transformed by new media, specifically photo-sharing sites such as Flickr. Further examples from Facebook and elsewhere are drawn upon to illustrate new characteristics of vernacular literacies in Web 2.0 spaces. We show how they are now more valued as people participate in more global spaces.

9. LANGUAGE IS CENTRAL TO NEW FORMS OF KNOWLEDGE CREATION AND NEW FORMS OF ENQUIRY

Language has often been construed as being the vehicle of communication, where communication is thought to be the passive sending of messages as fixed objects and where there is a unidirectional idea of influence of sender on audience. The field of media studies started out with this unidirectional idea of influence, and the notions of audience that were used came from theatre and TV. And this view still existed in early Web 1.0 views of online communication. However, it is crucial to have a more active view of communication when examining how people are creating new forms of knowledge and new forms of enquiry online, in everyday activities as well as in activities such as cloud computing, citizen science and citizen journalism. By naming, sorting, classifying and categorizing in different ways, people are using language to create new knowledge. Language is central to knowledge creation and knowledge organization as well as to communication. These two aspects of language come together in the act of communication and it is important to focus on the meaning making aspects of language online.

Also central to such new forms of inquiry is the increasingly superdiverse nature of communication practices and the social world as a result of globalization and flows of people, objects and ideas around the world. An important indication of language being more diversified is multilingualism online, which is dealt with in Chapters 4 and 5. At the same time, language features that used to be confined to the online world have made their way to offline contexts. Chapter 13, 'Flows of language online and offline', considers how globalization presents new relationships between the online and the offline.

10. NEW METHODS FOR RESEARCHING LANGUAGE ARE MADE POSSIBLE

Investigating texts and practices online provides new possibilities for linguistic research methodology. Crucially the internet provides large amounts of freely available textual data. New links across areas of linguistics are possible, such as discourse analysis and corpus linguistics. Studies of texts and practices as discourse analysis can be combined with detailed ethnographic approaches. New links across disciplines are possible as the approaches of language and literacy studies complement other socio-cultural, technical and sociological approaches and media studies. People's active participation means auto-ethnographic approaches can be incorporated into the range of research tools available to investigate language online. This is pursued in Chapter 12, 'Researching language online', which provides an overview of major methods of researching online texts. The chapter covers both traditional methods (including observation and interview) and newer methods (such as auto-ethnography and techno-biography) adopted in the research on IM, Flickr, and Facebook that we have covered in the book. Other important methodological issues are discussed, including the ways in which we combine texts and practices in our research approach, developing a responsive methodology, the researcher's roles in online research, and challenges of carrying out research on the internet.

To sum up, this book brings together ideas and concepts related to language online, examining both theory and methodology. Theoretically, it investigates a set of specific language issues arising from online media. These include new multilingual practices, how multiple identities are performed through textual means, linguistic acts of stance-taking, how online users talk about their language use, as well as discourses of learning. It also provides new understanding of the vernacular and how new textual practices emerge as a result of everyday uses of new media. Methodologically, the book provides empirical data and case studies that present new ways of understanding texts and practices online. As well as using examples from other scholars' work, we draw upon authentic examples from our own research on different sites in the past decade.

The next chapter provides explanations of key concepts that need to be introduced and clarified when discussing language online. These are terms that are potentially confusing by being used differently in other works or left undefined. It describes four key online sites in terms of their writing spaces and affordances. They are Facebook, Flickr, IM, and YouTube, and they will be used as the main examples throughout the book.

3

ACTING IN A TEXTUALLY MEDIATED SOCIAL WORLD

- Practices
- Writing in a textually mediated social world
- Affordances
- Multimodality
- Stance
- Affinities and other groupings
- Globalization
- Writing spaces online
  - *Flickr*
  - *Facebook*
  - *YouTube*
  - *Instant messaging*

In this chapter, we introduce a set of seven key concepts that are brought to the fore when considering how people use language online. First, the concept of *practices* reflects our fundamental orientation to language as meaningful activity. Texts are central to language and literacy practices and people act within a *textually mediated social world* utilizing the *writing spaces* available. In online writing spaces, people perceive and draw upon the *affordances* in order to act according to particular purposes. Language exists as one set of resources people utilize to create meaning in a *multimodal* manner. A prominent aspect of how people make meaning online is expressing *stance* towards what they are saying, including views about language. When using language people act in relation to other groups and communities in many ways, including the *affinity groups* in which they participate. Finally, *globalization* provides an important context for understanding language online. At the end of the chapter, we introduce the key online sites and tools, which we draw upon for examples to facilitate our discussion throughout the book.

PRACTICES

Everyday life is infused with reading and writing. Planning a holiday, for instance, is a common activity for many people, one which can involve a great deal of language, both written and spoken. This includes spoken language such as when discussing with others where to go and when to go. This talking is often around texts, online and offline, and there can be much reading of guides and timetables. Planning a holiday is a recognizable social practice and many aspects of it, such as checking train or flight timetables and booking tickets, can be seen as *literacy practices*. These are literacy practices because there are common patterns in using reading and writing in the context of planning a holiday. People bring in their cultural knowledge to this activity. In other domains of life there are also identifiable social practices where literacy is important. In the domain of education, for example, activities such as writing an assignment or preparing a presentation involve a wide range of literacy practices. Similarly, in the domain of work, whether it is a doctor or a claims clerk, most people's work day involves using reading and writing. Even in seemingly less text-based jobs, such as cleaners and security guards, people often have to keep records of their activities; they follow written instructions and they deal with written issues of health and safety, as well as records of their pay.

Literacy practices has been a key concept for researchers of *literacy studies*. The concept encompasses the practical ways of utilizing reading and writing but crucially it also includes the meanings that underlie practices. The notion of practices is important in that it is both empirical and close to data and at the same time it invokes a theory and helps link activities to broader concepts. Literacy practices are made up of specific activities and at the same time are part of broader social processes, as in the examples above. Here we start from the more general notion of social practices and view literacy practices as being the social practices associated with the written word. Literacy practices may be supportive of other aims, as with the example of travelling. Elsewhere the literacy is central to the activity, as with an assignment where the outcome is a written text, and this can be seen as a certain sort of literacy practice: *text-making practices*. The field of literacy studies has been important in documenting literacy practices in various domains of life. Researching practices highlights certain methodologies, and within literacy studies detailed qualitative approaches have been invaluable.

Social practices such as planning a holiday are being transformed as many areas of life are moving online. The associated language and literacy practices are part of this transformation, so the actual booking of tickets and searching for places to stay involve online literacy practices, such as filling out a hotel booking form on a hotel website, or comparing across different websites for the lowest fares. This is also true of the other examples above, that writing practices such as an assignment or keeping workplace records have a strong online component. Social practices are changing, and this is achieved through the new reading and writing activities that constitute the practices.

Practices is not a simple word and it is not a lightly chosen word. It is the key concept that underlies literacy studies and makes language and literacy studies what it is. The concept provides the route map for thinking about topics as diverse as the role of agency, and the significance of the body, objects and texts. It clarifies the relations of action and discourse. When language is viewed as a set of practices, it provides the framing for locating a theory of language in a theory of life. On the one hand, language activity can be seen as a set of practices, and literacy practices in particular have been studied extensively. At the same time, practices is a key concept elsewhere across the social sciences. We can see human life as made up of social practices. That is the reason why we emphasize people's lived experiences and everyday relations to technologies, or what is referred to as techno-biographies, when researching language use online (see Chapter 6).

These are all issues that become particularly salient when considering language online, which in reality is about practices online. The term helps us locate literacy studies in broader philosophical traditions and therefore link up with other socio-cultural research. Such 'practice theory' has its roots in the work of Ludwig Wittgenstein and is pursued in contemporary philosophical enquiry such as Reckwitz (2002) and Schatzki (2012). As different new media get used people gradually develop agreed ways of utilizing such media. These agreed ways, or what Gershon (2010) refers to as 'idioms of practice', are developed through interacting with others on the web. And as a medium gets used by different groups of people, different sets of idioms of practices can be created to define these groups, as discussed below in relation to communities of practice. The broader social links to practices will be a thread throughout the book.

WRITING IN A TEXTUALLY MEDIATED SOCIAL WORLD

The notion of *texts* is central to the study of language, and most social practices involve language in some way. We need to be clear what we mean by text, as the term is used in quite different ways in different disciplines. To some, especially in media studies or literature, a text can be a film, a novel, a TV programme or a newspaper article. To the linguist, a text can be any coherent piece of language under discussion. It usually refers to written language. Spoken language becomes a text by being transcribed. As with other terms, like 'practice' and 'discourse', the term can vary in scale. A single word headline can be a text, a paragraph can be a text, a chapter can be a text and a whole book can be a text. Texts are situated in time and space. Texts are created and can be written in many ways. They have been sprayed on to walls, or are published in newspapers, or written in diaries. Texts are then used; they are read and acted on or responded to.

Text is often treated as a product of language. It has the idea of stability and fixedness. A text can act as a fixed point in an interaction and can be a starting point for analysis. By acting as a reference point, texts such as a letter, a novel or a newspaper can then move across events, changing in function and value. They come from somewhere and they move on to somewhere else.

As people's social practices have moved online, many texts in our contemporary life have also moved online, and in doing so they take on different properties. First, the materiality of text has changed. A letter, a novel and a newspaper exist on a page or a piece of paper. When they move online they are located on a screen. This shift *from page to screen* has been examined extensively (as in Snyder 1998). One difference is the relationship between texts. A simple Twitter post on a screen is a short text. It is located within a set of messages or tweets earlier and later. At the same time, it is located within a page of other writing. A tweet on a page may be an original post of the author or it can be a reposting of a tweet (a 'retweet') written by another member of Twitter. These relationships between texts are particular to Twitter and on other sites such as Facebook, weblogs or Wikipedia, there will be different relationships between texts.

Texts are central to the online world. This shift to a digital world means that texts and text-making are more pervasive in all domains of life. The everyday activities mentioned at the beginning of the chapter such as planning a holiday or writing an assignment are all highly textually mediated. The online world is constantly being written, be it in the form of single-authored websites, collaboratively written wikis, or just a short comment on a social network site. By writing, people leave records everywhere and create information that other people can use, that informs search engines, and that is the saleable product of companies like Google and Facebook. Google has indeed become the largest language corpus in the world. Both online and offline texts are located in a world of other texts. Part of their meaning comes from their intertextual links, their links to earlier texts, and this is stronger and more dense in the online world.

Online texts are no longer stable, acting as fixed reference points. Rather, they are more fluid than print-based texts and there is constant change. And many people can contribute to this change. Newspapers are a good example of the difference between the physical offline world and the equivalent virtual online news sites. The physical daily newspaper has a fresh new edition every day, but it is fixed for the day and one can keep a physical archive of a daily newspaper. Online a separate daily edition does not really exist and news stories online can be constantly updated and changed second by second in the form of Twitter feeds. Users can also add comments at any point.

Another way in which texts are no longer fixed is that readers have more control over a text in the online world. For a book, say a novel, the original author of the content decides how we read it, with a clear table of contents assuming the linear order of different parts of the book; for a website, although the site designer may decide how we will view a site, the user has relatively higher control over their reading path. For some sites, users may even have some control over layout, and they can change their minds about it. This leads to different users seeing a text quite differently, which is something they may or may not be aware of.

The underlying assumption about these changes in the nature of text is that most social practices contain elements of language and literacy and that we live in a *textually mediated social world*, where texts are part of the glue of social life. Texts are central to social interaction and much spoken language is performed in the context of and taking account of written language. Language and literacy are at the heart of much of current social change because it is language and literacy that structure knowledge and enable communication. This is especially true when examining the contemporary online world. More language and more interactions are mediated and the web of links between them is greater.

To understand language in this textually mediated world there are some useful concepts for examining the dynamics of language use. First, texts are always situated. They are in spaces that provide the possibilities and constraints of what can be written, and what is likely to be written. In the physical world, the pages of a newspaper, a novel and a diary all provide different possibilities for writing. And of course not all physical writing is on pages: some is on clothes and some is on scrolls, and there are different sorts of pages with different dynamics, so a newspaper page works differently from the pages of a novel. Online the spaces will have different constraints and possibilities, as we will see in the next section.

AFFORDANCES

Affordances are the possibilities and constraints for action that people selectively perceive in any situation. *Perceived affordances* become the context for action. To understand the significance of this term, it is important to stress that its origins lie in an ecological approach to perception. This emphasizes that people do not focus on the intrinsic properties of an object; rather, they perceive what is of value to them in a particular situation when they have particular purposes (Gibson 1977, 1986). When it comes to perceiving action possibilities in online spaces, this means more than providing a list of the features originally intended by the designers. There is a long history of the mismatch between designers' original expectations and the ways people bend technologies to their own purposes. The mobile phone is an often-cited example, where it was originally designed for business uses as a portable talking device, with no expectation that it would be used largely for other purposes such as photo-taking and texting. As another example, Facebook was first introduced as a means for university students to develop social networks and that is still an important use. However, its uses are much more diverse and nowadays many schools and universities have adopted Facebook as a learning platform, even though it was never designed as an educational tool. Screen-based affordances are often compared to those of paper. While there are speculations about the computer replacing paper-based materials, Sellen and Harper (2003) pointed out in *The Myth of the Paperless Office* that at that time the use of paper was actually on the rise and computerized office work still relied heavily on paper. This is due to some of the unique affordances of paper that the computer screen cannot offer, which people still value in their day-to-day activities.

Since affordances are not pre-determined, there is a limit to the usefulness of trying to list the 'properties' of a technology. A smart phone has certain properties, such as internet connectivity and software installation. But the uses it is then put to by people cannot be read off from these properties. Any list of uses is provisional and changing. Ultimately what is important are the actual uses which are made of it. This is where a social practice approach is significant in identifying what people actually do, and how they make sense of their environment. It is another aspect of an ecological approach that the environment is not a given and it is not fixed. Rather, people both create and are created by their environment. In this way affordances are socially constructed and change as people act upon their environment. Affordances affect what can be done easily and what can be done conventionally with a resource. Creativity is in part seeing new affordances and going beyond existing possibilities. Affordances are emergent, and new possibilities are created through human creativity. So, for example, on Facebook the structure of the software creates likely activities and likely pathways, but human ingenuity leads to the wide range of uses it is put to.

The whole environment provides resources to be drawn upon as affordances. Practices take place in a world full of objects and technologies. Different modes, such as speech, writing, layout and images, can be drawn upon, as can different devices, such as touch screens and keyboards, and different platforms, such as Wikipedia, Facebook and Tumblr. As we will demonstrate, different languages can also be perceived as meaning-making resources offering different action possibilities. Languages differ in what you can do easily with them, and this is true of all levels of language. Taken together, the structures of the online world provide a remarkably rich set of affordances for people to act within. In the context of language online, new language and literacy practices emerge as a result of people perceiving and taking up new affordances on the internet.

The concept of affordances has been taken up in the study of multi-modality by Kress (2004), and by scholars of digital literacies, such as Jones and Hafner (2012), as a way of describing how people draw on new possibilities. What a literacy studies approach in particular offers is an insider's perspective of people's actual practices in response to what they perceive of as the possibilities and constraints in particular situations. In terms of methodology, if we are to understand why and how online users use language in a particular way, it is important to first consider what they think about what is available online, and what they make of what they do. This needs to be understood against ethnographic insights, and is not determined by the media alone. It is clear throughout our research that people from similar backgrounds who share the same linguistic resources may take up the affordances of resources in different ways according to their situated purposes. As we show in Chapter 5, multilingual online users often see ways in which a certain language affords more expressive powers than others in different situations.

The internet is not limitless and that is why looking at affordances is essential. Affordances work closely with the concept of *design*. The metaphor of a 'blank sheet' is relevant, as in some senses a platform such as a blog is like a sheet of paper, as boyd (2006) has pointed out, and it can be put to many uses: it can be used as a diary, a story, a work of fiction or a newspaper, utilizing specific genres. But it differs from a blank sheet in that, like all websites, a blog site is highly structured, in that bloggers are required to write within a template that has been pre-designed by the site designer. This structuring means that blog posts are always arranged in reverse chronological order, for instance, and that there are not many options as to where on the site one can write the blog post or post a comment. It is the ways in which people can act within the affordances of designed spaces that create different possibilities for writing. That way, a site such as a blog is not one coherent genre. It is a *designed space* with many potential uses. Political blogs, travel blogs and book review blogs may develop specific genres, but a blog itself is not a genre: it is not a form of language – rather it is a space for language.

MULTIMODALITY

In understanding language online, we are also trying to understand how different *modes* work together to form coherent and meaningful online texts. Modes, which are also known as communicative modes or semiotic modes, broadly refer to systems or resources that people draw upon for meaning making. These include spoken language, written language, image, sound, gesture, etc. In our everyday lives, multimodal texts, especially those that combine the verbal with the visual, are ubiquitous. Multimodal practices are not new and have been an essential meaning-making strategy throughout the history of written language. In print-based materials such as magazines, newspapers, and advertisements, the design of the visual often shapes how viewers interpret the verbal, and vice versa. These visual effects may involve specific decisions about the use of colours, font size, and typeface of the words (so that a text printed in **bookman old style**, for instance, may appear more serious and formal than one in **Comic sans ms**). In school textbooks, pictures and diagrams are often used to complement written descriptions. The layout of different items on a page is also designed for meaning to be taken in particular ways.

With traditional printing, the reader has little control over layout or fonts. However, when it comes to multimodality on the computer screen, it is relatively easy for anyone to produce multimodal texts. Users can mix together language, images and videos and have a great deal of control over colour, layout and font. Websites are not just web pages with content from different modes of representation; hyperlinks are often added to words and images to create intertextual links across multiple multimodal web pages. In text-based interactive computer-mediated communication such as email and instant messaging, because of the lack of physical and contextual cues, emoticons are often attached to utterances to mark the writer's intention and tone. For example, writing 'I love my job :-)' with a smiling emoticon is likely to evoke a more positive interpretation than writing 'I love my job! :-(' which may be intended to convey the opposite. What is crucial here is that because affordances of semiotic modes are perceived, as we have discussed, when combined in different ways, they can offer many meanings to different viewers, and thus action possibilities. This is evident on the photo-sharing site Flickr, where the same photo may on the one hand receive comments that are closely related to what is shown in the image; on the other hand, some comments may point to the photographic technique behind the scene, or just the photographer.

Multimodal texts in many print-based media (and even websites) are relatively static and are created by a single author. In Web 2.0 spaces, by contrast, multimodal content can be co-created and constantly edited by multiple users. The convergence of writing spaces in new social media presents new opportunities for easy creation, posting, and sharing of multimodal texts such as sharing a video from YouTube with a self-generated written description posted on Facebook. Despite these multimodal possibilities, as we show throughout the book, the written word still plays a central role in meaning making on these new sites. On Flickr, for example, images are often surrounded by titles, descriptions, and tags, thus forming a cross-modal cohesion throughout the page. People also talk around a photograph through written comments. As we show in Chapter 7, these opinions are shaped by particular ways of seeing multimodal resources. Because the creator of a text is making decisions about layout, choice of images and other modes it may be useful to describe the online writer as a designer. Although the layout of different writing spaces is often predetermined by the site designer, when reading through a web page, different viewers can have different starting points. On a YouTube page, we may decide to watch the video first, while others may want to read the comments first. In pursuing these different reading paths, people take different meanings from the text.

STANCE

Stance has been a very useful concept in linguistics, bringing together a wide range of work that has been concerned with understanding how utterances' meanings are expressed and how speakers (or writers) address their audience. Stance can be broadly defined as a position taken by a speaker in relation to what is said and to whom the utterance is directed. Linguistic studies of stance range from examining the grammar and lexis of utterances through to critical discourse analysis of stances embedded in political speeches, for instance. At a micro-level, a speaker's stance can be understood by looking into specific linguistic features such as the choice of verbs and sentence structures. For example, the clause 'I think' is often used to introduce a statement in which an opinion is embedded. This is not a random choice. When one says '*I think* I know what I am doing', the speaker is expressing a certain degree of certainty, which could have been weakened by introducing the statement with 'I *guess*'. Cognitive verbs such as 'think' and 'know' are thus a key marker of what is called *epistemic stances*, stances that assert certainties, beliefs, and knowledge. For an illustration of this, see Myers' analysis (2010b) of how cognitive verbs are used on blogs. Epistemic stance can be contrasted with *affective stance* where speakers express their attitudes and feelings about what they utter, as in '*I love* the way this chapter is written!' (See chapter 1 in Jaffe 2009 for a more detailed overview of the area.)

We see stance as a central concept that frames our understanding of how opinions are expressed in online media. Many Web 2.0 sites and social media are *stance-rich* environments. The perceived affordances of the writing spaces encourage the production, sharing, discussion, and evaluation of public opinions through textual means. YouTube is an excellent example of a platform that is rich in stance and acts of stance-taking. The video posters may express their opinions on a certain topic through speech in their videos; at the same time, viewers can evaluate the videos by giving them 'likes' or 'dislikes', or by leaving written comments. Commenting is indeed a key site of stance-taking in many popular Web 2.0 sites including Flickr and Facebook. On these sites, stance is not taken by one single speaker or writer, but is constantly created and renegotiated collaboratively by a networked public. Another salient feature of stance in new media is that, unlike traditional communicative contexts such as a face-to-face conversation where either speech or writing becomes a sole resource of stance-taking, multimodal stance-taking is made possible in many global online sites. On Flickr, people may focus on a particular genre of photos (e.g. black and white self-portraits) with written tags such as 'me' to present a particular sense of self to their target viewers. Multilingual users may choose to switch between languages. All these are practices and resources of stance-taking that were certainly not common in the pre-Web 2.0 era. Thus, at a broader level, understanding acts of stance-taking is crucial in understanding how identities are constructed in new online spaces. It also becomes clear that stance-taking is not just a linguistic act but a situated practice that should be understood in the context of communication. In Chapter 7, we illustrate these features of stance further with worked examples from various writing spaces online.

AFFINITIES AND OTHER GROUPINGS

Language is made and remade in relations between people. This takes place at the micro level of two people interacting and at the macro level of whole communities. There are many sorts of groupings of people and they are important in maintaining language, shaping language practices and in language change. People use language to interact with each other and specific forms of language develop, such as the adjacency pairs of question and answer in conversations and the part initiation, response and evaluation (IRE) of a typical classroom interaction between teachers and students. It is through interaction with other people that language changes and develops, and genres and styles solidify, break up and reform.

Seeing people acting within groups, small and large, has been foundational for the development of sociolinguistics. At the more macro level, one such grouping is the notion of 'speech community'. This concept is widely used to understand linguistic variation. Speech communities are seen as stable entities, with people sharing particular norms of language use; there are strong notions of membership, and density of the networks between people are measured in terms of language use. Language differences within speech communities can index relations of gender, class and other social factors. And when people act within these speech communities, they act within a particular socially constructed discourse, a particular way of using language, together with a repertoire of genres and styles, which is generally recognized. A *discourse community* is another enduring concept. Academic discourse, for instance, exists because there are generally accepted ways of using language by the people who use it. These people, in other words, are members of a specific discourse community. A discourse community is a group of people having shared texts and practices, whether it is a group of university students writing assignments or the readers of a teenage magazine.

A further grouping, that of people acting within a 'community of practice', has been taken up enthusiastically in the study of language. Coming from socio-cultural theory and the work of Jean Lave and Etienne Wenger (Lave and Wenger 1991; Wenger 1998), the notion of community of practice has been well articulated. It is defined as a grouping of people sharing three characteristics: there has to be mutual engagement between people; they need to be involved in a joint enterprise; and they need to draw upon a shared repertoire. People can have different forms of participation in such groupings. Wenger's work set out from a fairly stable workplace team where people have a common endeavour. It has since been applied much more broadly, including to educational sites, as well as to management learning in workplaces. To bring language use into this, for a community of practice to develop people have to be working with each other and have a common goal and they develop shared ways of interacting, including specific ways of using language. This can be seen, for instance, in work by Eckert (1999) on communities of practice and a study by Mendoza-Denton (2008), who examines whether the language dynamics of youth gangs can be analysed more fruitfully as speech communities or as communities of practice. More generally, see Swales (1998) on the usefulness and limitations of thinking in terms of discourse communities and the notion of 'community'.

Like other areas of language study, the field of literacy studies has seen people as located in physical communities, as in Barton and Hamilton (1998). Alongside this, literacy studies early on talked of people being located in networks of support. Researchers have examined the ways in which people support (or hinder) each other as language brokers, mentors, mediators and scribes. Often there is reciprocity in these relations. (See Baynham and Prinsloo 2009.) Looking more broadly, the language of such dyadic – or two-person – relations have been studied across linguistics, ranging from child language research of adult and child through to studies of service encounters, doctor-patient interactions and other unequal encounters. Other relationships between people have included interviews and interrogations. There are in fact all sorts of networks and groups, as diverse as a sports team, a family, neighbours, an academic department, or a class, each with different dynamics. TV audiences and the readers of a novel or a newspaper have certain bonds and affiliations but may never meet or interact with each other. All these diverse groupings have implications for language use.

Turning to learning and education, it is common to gather in groups to learn, whether it is voluntary or enforced. People come together in classrooms and colleges. They learn from other people and they learn in groups. These concepts, such as communities of practice, have been important in relation to learning, and a coherent theory of learning as changing participation in practices is outlined in Wenger (1998). Questions are raised about when they become 'learning communities' and whether and how classrooms can become communities of practice. At the same time the reciprocal relations studied by literacy studies have also been identified as significant for learning.

Once we turn to the internet, we see some of these same groupings and forms of participation, and the same queries and cautions arise. We also see other forms of participation and people participating in other groupings. James Gee (2004) pointed out that the dynamics of young people interacting through video gaming could not be simply regarded as participating in communities of practice because in a community of practice membership is relatively static and is defined by a specific set of requirements; rather, he analysed them as 'affinity groups', grouping which people joined because of a specific interest and moved easily in and out of such groupings. See Gee and Hayes (2011) for more detail on affinity groups and Gee (2005) on comparisons with the notion of communities of practice. Some of these issues are pursued in Chapter 9 in relation to learning online.

There are other groupings on the internet that can be identified as having some of the characteristics of communities of practice, but it is a new situation. Often they are more fluid. The internet supports many sorts of relationships and forms of interaction, including affinity groups, but going beyond them. People can be interacting without physical presence and without clear or rigid roles. They can be participating with anonymity, using invented identities, and with new notions of audience. All of these factors can lead to different and new forms of participation. Additionally, as we have already made clear, it is not really possible to separate online and offline activity and people may have existing strong offline bonds in any online site. People may be contributing to common endeavours such as giving tags collaboratively or contributing to ratings without being aware of their participation. At the micro level there are different sorts of encounters, and interactions like commenting on a blog or website are likely to be different linguistically from well-studied phenomena of turn-taking. We should be looking for new groupings of people and accept that there are many ways of interacting with new media offering new possibilities. For our purposes, we need to be aware of different forms of participation and different purposes when theorizing language-related issues online.

GLOBALIZATION

With a focus on language online we see technological change as being a central part of this but it is important to realize that it is one among a set of interconnected factors which are transforming many aspects of contemporary life. Interacting with technological change there are political and economic changes, contributing to general processes of *globalization*. All these changes impact on language and communicative practices. The relationship between language and globalization has been widely discussed by linguists (including Crystal 1997; Wright 2004; Phillipson 2004; Canagarajah 2007; Blommaert 2010). The term 'globalization' itself is complex and is used in different ways across different disciplines. Within the study of language there are two different aspects that are focused on: one is based on the homogenizing aspects of the internet, where it is seen as creating uniformity in language use. The other one, which we have seen in our data, is a culturally and linguistically diversified one, which allows space for different cultures and languages to develop simultaneously. In this way people want to be part of the global world without giving up their existing local identities.

Clarifying the relation between the local and the global has always been important for understanding language and literacy practices (as in Baynham and Prinsloo 2009, for example) and in relation to education (as in Barton 1994a; Block and Cameron 2002). When discussing language the relation between the global and the local is probably best understood in terms of *glocalization*. Koutsogiannis and Mitsikopoulou (2007) utilize this concept in their study of online language use in Greece, where they define glocalization as 'a dynamic negotiation between the global and the local, with the local appropriating elements of the global that it finds useful, at the same time employing strategies to retain its identity' (143). To date, much attention has been on local appropriation of the global, as when global hip-hop culture is localized through local languages. This is best seen as a two-way process: it is not just how the global affects the local, but how the local shapes the global. Global language practices are localized, and at the same time local practices are becoming globalized. In our research on language online, we are seeing both and in particular how people are using the local to write the global. Within literacy studies, drawing on concepts from Actor Network Theory, it is possible to identify literacy practices that act as 'localizing moves' and others that act as 'globalizing connects' (Barton and Hamilton 2005: 31). In a sense all interaction is local. In our data we see how people deploy multiple languages to project both local and global identities.

An important aspect of globalization is the way in which the social world is speeding up. There have always been flows of people, objects, and ideas around the world, but the patterns of activity have changed significantly. The physical flows of people from place to place include migration, tourism and travel for work. The flows of objects take place through trade and commercial networks, whilst information and knowledge flow through mass media and the internet. Language has a role in all these and they are all aided by the internet. At the same time, languages themselves flow around the world. There are many new opportunities for interaction and for the development of new genres and styles. Many aspects of this mobility are being studied by sociologists (such as Urry 2007), but less attention has been paid to the flow of languages. We see this 'supermobility' as capturing the flows and fluidity of language.

One aspect of this movement, coming from studies of migration, is the 'superdiversity' (Vertovec 2007) seen in the movement of people. Migrants have many different reasons for travelling and have varying backgrounds in terms of religion, language and ethnicity. They have a variety of life histories and they also travel to and from many different countries. As Vertovec (2010: 83) explains,

> more people are now moving from more places, through more places, to more places . . . today newer, smaller, transient, more socially stratified, less organised and more legally differentiated immigrant groups comprise global migration flows . . . .. Super-diversity is a term intended to capture a level and kind of complexity surpassing anything many migrant-receiving countries have previously experienced.

Existing concepts of multilingualism such as 'speech community' cannot capture this diversity. Linguists (such as Blommaert and Rampton 2011) are taking up the concept of superdiversity to rethink the concepts and terms of sociolinguistics, primarily in the study of multilingualism but also in other areas. Much of the rest of this book is about language online in a supermobile and superdiverse world and we pursue issues of globalization and superdiversity in several chapters.

WRITING SPACES ONLINE

With these seven key concepts that characterize language online in mind, we now turn to the spaces online where these features are manifested. We want to call these spaces 'writing spaces', as they are spaces that provide the possibilities and constraints of what can be written, and what is likely to be written. We are particularly interested in writing spaces because no matter how multimodal online texts are, the written word is still central to all forms of online interaction and content creation. YouTube, for instance, is essentially a video-sharing site but most forms of participation are mediated by written language, from video titles and descriptions through to searching and user comments. In the following, we provide an overview of the writing spaces on the four main sites drawn upon in the book: Flickr, Facebook, YouTube, and instant messaging.

Flickr

Flickr is a popular photo-sharing site which allows people to upload, display and share photos. First launched in 2004, it has over 50 million active users and over 6 billion photos have been posted as of August 2011 (Flickr Blog 2011). Although photographs are often perceived as the central element of Flickr, members of Flickr frequently interact through various writing spaces, such as giving titles, captions, and tags (or keywords) for their photos, as well as commenting on one another's photos. These writing spaces form a cross-modal cohesive tie between the photo posted and the words around it. Flickr is basically a public space (though users can control privacy of their photos) and it is a global online platform, so its users vary geographically, culturally and linguistically. Our research on Flickr has focused primarily on the interaction between the photo posted and the writing around it, that is, the titles, descriptions, tags, and comments. These can be seen in Figure 3.1. Here we offer more details of Flickr to illustrate the differences between possible writing spaces, and because readers may be less familiar with Flickr than with the other sites.

To describe how the participants in our research used the writing spaces mentioned above, first the people we studied all used titles, though they did not give a title to every picture. Many titles were similar to the titles of novels or paintings; they might be explanatory or descriptive, such as names of people and places, *on the road, teatime* or *class of 79*. Many were playful. Often they were intertextual to other photos or to the wider world, such as drawing on popular culture with song titles, such as '*Wandering eyes*', '*Singing in the rain*' and '*Common people*'.

The captions, or what Flickr calls descriptions, can be of any length. Usually they provided further information about the picture and the person's

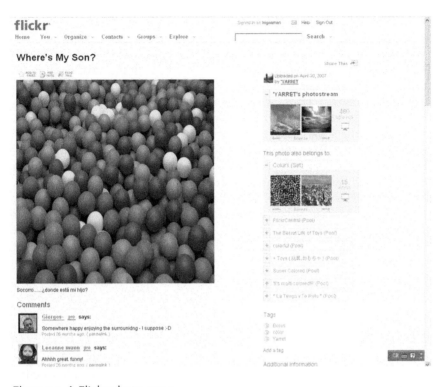

Figure 3.1 A Flickr photo page

relation to it. *Tags* provide another space for writing and originally appeared as a vertical list on the right-hand side of the screen but is now set out as left-to-right text. They are categorizations provided for individual photos and they were used extensively by the participants in our study. These ranged from conventional classifications – *beach, summer, blue, door bell* – shared by other people through to innovative, idiosyncratic ones, such as *disappear, heartbroken, desire*. Some would require insider knowledge and would only be recognizable to other Flickr users, such as the tag *365* or *365Days*, meaning that the photo has been uploaded as part of a common photo project where the person is taking one photograph a day for a year. We discuss this activity later on. Other people used tags to write poems and to provide idiosyncratic comments on their photos. The names for tags result in taxonomies created by people, often referred to as 'folksonomies'. It is worth noting that whilst some of the categories which people used as tags were taxonomic, sometimes they seemed just to be adding descriptions of particular photos without making general categories or linking to their other photos or those of other people.

Profiles are the next writing space we examined. In a separate screen Flickr users can write what they want, and people used it in many different ways, varying in how much they put in. Often they wrote a short paragraph or mini biographies about themselves such as where they come from, what cameras and lenses they use, and their passion for photography.

Finally, the comments area is the most interactive writing space on Flickr. The comments, which appear beneath the photos with the most recent ones at the bottom, were commonly evaluative – usually positive, as in *amazing shot of an amazing view.* Some comments may be questions about the photos, such as where the photo was taken or what the person in the photo was doing. Others were less clear, as in *Hey baaaaby! Don't hate me! =).* It was in the comments space that people were most likely to use emoticons, abbreviations and creative punctuation. Sometimes people would respond to comments and this might gradually develop into an interactive 'conversation' between the photographer and their contacts, some of whom they already know in their offline lives. As such, Flickr has become a space for socializing and maintaining friendships. Throughout the book, data from Flickr will be used as examples illustrating themes such as multilingualism (Chapters 4 and 5), stance-taking (Chapter 7), metalinguistic discourses (Chapter 8) and informal learning (Chapter 9).

Facebook

Facebook was first launched in 2004 in the US. Originally started as a site to facilitate communication among college students in Harvard, it then spread globally and rapidly. As of April 2012, it has over 900 million active users from different parts of the world (Hachman 2012). Although still popular among college students, it is reported that it is most popular among people aged between 26 and 34 (Burbary 2011). Like many other social network sites, Facebook is structured around user profiles (now called timelines). The layout and functions of the site have been modified and redesigned many times over the years. However, its major spaces for writing are still available. A key writing space that we have investigated into extensively is *status updates* (or simply called posts now), which was originally designed as a space for micro-blogging like Twitter. Micro-blogging refers to the writing of short messages on the web designed for self-reporting about what one is doing, thinking, or feeling at any moment. This can be performed on stand-alone micro-blogging platforms like Twitter or on social network sites such as Facebook.

The status updates feature on Facebook is similar to that of Twitter in that it works mainly with a prompt (What's on your mind?) and a text box (Publisher box) that appear at the top of a user's homepage and personal profile. Lee (2011) notes that Facebook participants use status updates to achieve a wide range of discourse functions, from expressing opinions (e.g. Ariel thinks that no news is good news) to reporting moods and other feelings (e.g. Amy is in a good mood). Status updates were once entirely text-based with an imposed word limit of just 420 characters. Since late 2011, their limit has been increased to 5,000 characters, and more multimodal content is allowed to be attached to the status updates, such as photos and videos.

Facebook exhibits a collocation of online spaces where a number of traditional synchronous and asynchronous forms of CMC interaction take place in one space. In addition to posting status updates, there is a commenting feature that sometimes acts as a site for mini discussion forums. People can share photos and create photo albums; but photo sharing works quite differently from that on Flickr due to their different perceived affordances. On Facebook, photos are often shared with a known audience, while on Flickr, photos can be showcased to a much wider and global audience, who may be strangers. Friends can also communicate privately through Facebook's private email or its chat function. Facebook is one of the best representatives of convergence culture. Users can easily connect to external sites, for example a newspaper article, by clicking the 'LIKE' button. This immediately creates intertextual links between texts and resources available online. Examples from Facebook will be used throughout the book to illustrate various issues of language online, such as multilingual and translation practices (Chapters 4 and 5) and ways of performing identities through textual means (Chapter 6). A case study is also discussed in Chapter 10 to illustrate how status updates are situated in a pregnant woman's lived experiences.

YouTube

The third site of interest is the video-sharing site, YouTube. Established in 2005, the site has gained immense popularity with over 800 million visits to the site per month and 72 hours of videos being uploaded every minute (YouTube 2012). It is often seen as a social network site rather than a site for only uploading videos (Burgess and Green 2009). This is due to the unique relationships developed between video uploaders and their viewers, which did not exist before YouTube. These relationships are often developed through multimodal means. A key type of videos that best demonstrates this specific feature of YouTube is video blogs (vlogs) or first-person vlogs. These videos feature the vlogger facing the camera and talking about their first-person experiences. Seeing their viewers and subscribers as their social capital, vloggers tend to perform playful identities in order to attract more viewers and subscribers. For example, the effect of humour and irony is often created through adding written annotations that contradict with what is said in the video (Lien 2012).

Although primarily a video-based site, YouTube is rich in writing spaces. In addition to subtitles and annotations, which can be easily added to the video screen using YouTube's built-in video editor, *commenting* is the key interactive writing space on the site. YouTube comments appear below the video. As with the videos, comments can also be rated by users (vote up or vote down). Throughout the book, we show how commenting on YouTube serves as a site for promoting translingual practices (Chapter 5) and meta-discourses about language and the learning of it (Chapters 8 and 9).

Instant messaging (IM)

IM is defined as an 'Internet-based synchronous text chat, with point-to-point communication between users on the same system. A window is dedicated to the conversation, with messages scrolling upward and eventually out of view as the conversation ensues' (Grinter and Palen 2002: 21). With its increasing popularity, especially with enhanced IM technologies on mobile devices, IM has become a major part of people's everyday lives. Many people use IM to stay in touch with friends on a daily basis for a range of purposes, such as talking about homework, setting up weekend events, interacting with colleagues in the office (America Online 2005; Nardi *et al.* 2000). Although multimedia features are available, IM is largely used as a text-based communication tool. Such everyday use and exchange of text messages foster the development of IM as a social practice associated with sets of values that influence people to use texts in specific ways. Although largely text-based, IM is also used in conjunction with other forms of communication, such as video chat (or what is often referred to as VoIP), for example Skype.

The reason we include IM here is that while it is not typically labelled as a Web 2.0 site, it shares many of the characteristics of Web 2.0. First, it is interactive; second, it is rich in self-generated text; third, it supports multimodal messages; fourth, it generates new forms of creativity as well as new learning opportunities, as we will show in later chapters. In our discussion of multilingual practices online in Chapter 4 and identity performance in Chapter 6, we will discuss examples of IM chat logs collected from a group of bilingual college students in Hong Kong, where one of the authors is based. We also show how IM is a crucial platform in many people's technology-related lives, and an important site for many of our informants to establish and transform their linguistic practices online.

These platforms are chosen as the key sites of discussion in this book for various reasons. First, we are active users of these sites, which means we can draw upon our insider knowledge when researching them. Second, these are some of the most popular computer-mediated spaces that comprise different modes of meaning making and different dynamics of interaction. For example, Flickr and YouTube are based on the visual and include a great deal of interaction with strangers, while on Facebook and IM people tend to communicate with friends they already know in the offline world. Third, these sites represent different eras of online activities – IM is considered as an older form of synchronous CMC that has been transformed from time to time, while Facebook, YouTube, and Flickr are typical examples of Web 2.0 sites. Fourth, while much research has been about young people's and students' uses of social media, Flickr and YouTube have a broader age profile of users and wider functions than social networking. While focusing on these four key sites, in the course of our discussion, we also look into other sites partly for the sake of comparison; but at the same time, we want to acknowledge the interrelation between text-making practices that people draw upon when participating on different sites in different areas of their lives. In the next chapter, we begin our discussion of language online by exploring the rich array of linguistic resources that online participants can deploy in multilingual encounters in the global internet.

4

HELLO! BONJOUR! CIAO! HOLA! GUTEN TAG!

Deploying linguistic resources online

- English and other languages online: an overview
- Deploying multilingual resources in online writing spaces
  - *Code-switching practices on instant messaging (IM)*
  - *Multilingual practices on Flickr*
  - *Language choice in micro-blogging*
  - *Languages on YouTube*

ENGLISH AND OTHER LANGUAGES ONLINE: AN OVERVIEW

More than 80 percent of the content posted on the Internet is in English [. . .] Whether we consider English a "killer language" or not, whether we regard its spread as benign globalization or linguistic imperialism, its expansive reach is undeniable and, for the time being, unstoppable.

(Fishman 1998: 26)

Not only does it [the web] offer a home to all linguistic styles within a language; it offers a home to all languages.

(Crystal 2006: 229)

Back in the 1990s, a number of scholars predicted that English, having achieved global status (Crystal 1997), would remain to be the dominant language on the internet, as shown in Fishman's observation above. For one thing, the internet started and first became popular in the United States, where English is the primary language. This early dominance of English online is also supported by statistics from surveys and media reports. For example, in 1998, over 80 per cent of internet content was written in English (Fishman 1998). The 1990s was the time when our society was largely shaped by discourses of the 'hyperglobalizers' (Held and McGrew 2001), who believed that globalization would lead to the homogenization of the world. In view of these beliefs, concerns were expressed as to whether the growth of the internet in the US would result in English linguistic imperialism (Phillipson 1992), that 'the dominance of English is asserted and maintained by the establishment and continuous reconstitution of structural and cultural inequalities between English and other languages' (47). This discussion also extended to the public sphere, especially in the form of news reports and editorials, as Specter's (1996) comment in his *New York Times* article suggests:

> [I]f you want to take full advantage of the Internet there is only one real way to do it: learn English.
>
> (1)

While English may continue to be the common language for intercultural communication, recent years have seen rapid changes to the distribution between English and other languages online. Daniel Dor (2004: 99) argues that with changing economic relations between nations, '[t]he Net is going to be a predominantly non-English-language medium'. This seems to be happening. In 2012, English web content dropped from 80 per cent in 1998 to 55 per cent (W3techs.com 2012). And according to Internet World Stats (2010), about 73 per cent of internet users in the world have a first language other than English and the proportion is continuing to grow. The survey also shows that among these other languages, Chinese and Spanish are the two most popular user languages on the internet. Although the methodology adopted by such public surveys are questionable as they only count one language per user, a growing number of academic studies also emerge to support the presence of multiple languages online and multilingual internet users. The publication of the volume *The Multilingual Internet* (Danet and Herring 2007) marks a significant transitional phase in linguistic research on computer-mediated communication. The book covers studies of a wide range of languages and geographical locations. A number of studies focus on the co-existence of English and other languages, and how internet users often write in languages which are normally restricted to spoken contexts. For instance, Warschauer *et al.* (2007) demonstrate the extensive use of romanized Arabic in informal email and chat messages in Egypt; Lee (2007a,b) examines creative forms of written Cantonese in Hong Kong-based instant messages; and Androutsopoulos (2007) discusses code-switching in German-based Persian and Greek diasporic discussion forums. Since then multilingualism or mixed language writing on the internet has also become a key research direction in the field of digital discourse (Sebba *et al.* 2012). This emerging area provides important evidence that the global spread of the internet gives rise to not only English but other major languages like Chinese and Spanish, and, for different reasons, smaller languages such as Catalan (Block 2004). With the advent of social media and Web 2.0 technologies, we expect that self-generated content in social media such as YouTube and Flickr to further encourage and reinforce multilingual writing online. Even David Crystal, who once acknowledged the global status of English in his book *English as a Global Language* (1997), began to question his earlier conclusion and has suggested that the web indeed 'offers a home to all languages' (Crystal 2006: 320). This chapter and the next chapter together explore what people do with multiple linguistic resources on the internet and how working with multiple languages has become an important literacy practice online for all web users.

DEPLOYING MULTILINGUAL RESOURCES IN ONLINE WRITING SPACES

The background discussed in the previous section seems to suggest that both the user and the content of the web are becoming more linguistically diverse than before. What then happens to literacy practices if the web and its users are multilingual? To answer this question, one needs to move beyond the old question of whether the web leads to linguistic imperialism or pluralism. In the age of Web 2.0, new online media are easy to get started on and ordinary web users have unprecedented power of choice and creativity, which is quite different from traditional web sites in the so-called Web 1.0 generation, where the choice of website language lies with a single web author. Because of this changing nature of authorship in new web spaces, it seems reasonable to look into the actual social activities and practices surrounding such multilingual writing online, so as to understand better *how* and *what* people write online and *what they do* with their texts. (See Lexander 2012, who provides a model for understanding multilingual SMS as literacy practices.) In the subsections that follow, we present cases of people's experiences with multiple languages on four different web spaces: Flickr, instant messaging, Facebook, and YouTube. Most of these are a result of our research projects, while at times we bring in examples from other scholars' work. The discussion starts with issues related to language choice; we then gradually introduce other new multilingual practices online. We take a broad view of multilingualism in this book. When referring to people as *multilingual,* we mean they have more than one language to draw upon or that they switch between two or more languages in their everyday lives; when we use the term multilingual practices, we are referring to a subset of literacy practices that involve people doing things with two or more languages.

Multilingual practices on Flickr

In the study of Flickr the focus has been on the ways in which people creatively deploy multiple linguistic resources when interacting with one another in globalized networks, and how new multilingual practices shed light on current understanding of vernacular literacies (which is followed up in Chapter 10). We first examined the photostreams of 100 Flickr users who were members of a major English language-based group, FlickrCentral. The writing spaces in these 100 photostreams initially show that Flickr is a linguistically diverse space, as shown in the following observations:

- In addition to English, 10 other languages were identified: Chinese, Spanish, German, Italian, Portuguese, French, Tagalog, Arabic, Dutch, and Russian.
- English, Chinese and Spanish were the most common written languages used by these people, which coincidentally are the three most common languages online, as suggested by the statistics we presented earlier.
- 65 per cent of the people we surveyed come from a country where English is not spoken as a primary language.
- Languages other than English were found on 49 per cent of the sites, of which 4 per cent contained more than two foreign languages. Seventy-five per cent of the users had their profile in only English; a further 12 per cent had a bilingual profile including English. A small number of them (7 per cent) had it in a language other than English.

Although these figures may keep changing over time as Flickr gets used by different groups of people, they do allow us to view Flickr as a multilingual environment. We were also struck by the high degree of multilingual writing found on the photo pages we observed. For a more in-depth view of the production and use of these texts, we turned to a different group of Flickr users and selected active users who have written in at least two languages on their sites, Chinese and English or Spanish and English. (See Chapter 12 for details about the methodology adopted in this study.) In the following, we provide a more detailed discussion of multilingual practices involving different writing spaces on Flickr.

Multilingual writing practices on Flickr can start with a person's *screen-name* and *profile*. Screen-names are nicknames people create to identify themselves in online spaces. For the Spanish participants, most had screen-names that related to their real names in some way, such as *Caroline* being called *Carolink*, whilst others had completely invented names. Several had part of their first name along with an invented part – presumably their first names had already been taken. For the Chinese participants, many of them have the additional resource of two standard writing systems to draw upon, the traditional Chinese characters (used in Hong Kong, Macau, and Taiwan) and the simplified characters (used in mainland China). Two of the Hong Kong participants had bilingual and biscriptal screen-names. One of them, *tiong* (小吞), had the Chinese characters for his nickname 'little tiong' in brackets. In some bilingual screen-names, the two languages express rather different contents. In *Kristie* 遊牧民阿靜, *Kristie* is the user's English first name, and the Chinese words literally translate as 'Jing the Nomad', in which *Jing* is her Chinese first name. Other bilingual screennames reflect the user's current location. One of our mainland Chinese informants called herself *Looloo@北京*, which means the user 'Looloo' is currently in Beijing (@北京). As can be seen, online nicknames are often used as initial identity markers. Combining different languages and scripts in a screen-name is a key strategy that allows users to visually display who they are to others.

On their *profile* pages, many users included a bilingual biography or they code-switched when introducing themselves. Some bilingual profiles are sentence-for-sentence literal translations, while some other people used different languages to convey different kinds of content. For example, the profile of *Looloo@北京*, who later changed her name to *LoolooImage,* was predominantly in English, providing details about her cameras, interests, and personal philosophy; however, the Chinese version is much briefer and reads 'a 22-year-old Beijinger, loves traveling and photography. More information can be found on my Sina blog'. Where they used two languages, they tended to put the Chinese or Spanish first, with English below, as with our Spanish participants *Carolink* and *Erick C.* These practices may change over time, as we later noticed that *Erick C*'s profile was only in Spanish.

Another writing space on Flickr where multilingualism is central is photo *titles and descriptions.* Our Chinese informant, *Tinn Tian*'s site is a good example illustrating how multilingual resources are carefully deployed in titles and descriptions. *Tinn Tian* is a student from mainland China and has limited knowledge of English. Over half of his photos were described in Chinese only. Although, according to him, English is not a language he would use in everyday life, some of his other photos had either English only or Chinese-English bilingual descriptions, such as the title '爆米花 Popcorn'. Some of the English captions are partial translations of the original Chinese description such as 鸚鵡貝 as 'shell' instead of 'parrot shell' as specified in the Chinese title. Another case of bilingual writing is where a Chinese title is annotated with a longer explanation in English. For example, one of his photos features a local dish called *Maoxuewang*, and he chose to describe the dish in English:

> 毛血旺 Maoxuewang, a dish of boiled blood curd and other stuff with another name: Duck Blood in Chili Sauce.

The Chinese characters express only the name of the dish, while the English caption gives further details about the ingredients. In this case, English is used as a medium for translating local cultures to the non-Chinese-speaking world. We return to this example in Chapter 7.

Tagging is another important writing space where multilingualism is displayed on Flickr. All the Spanish users in our study had tags in more than one language, and some used several languages. For example, *Marta* had tags in mainly Spanish and Catalan, but also ones in English and a few French ones, such as when tagging a photo with *playa, platje, beach* and *plage*. Similarly, *Carolink* used Spanish, English and French. She said:

> I try to fit all the tags both in English (universalism) and in Spanish (my immediate Flickr public) and, since I know a little French, I put the French word when I remember it.

> *(Carolink)*

Almost half of the Chinese sites in our study had tags in Chinese characters. For example, on *cjPanda*'s site, approximately 45 per cent of her tags were written in Chinese, and about 16 per cent of the Chinese tags were also tagged with their English equivalents or translations; for example, one photo was tagged in English 'umbrella', in simplified Chinese character '伞' and in romanized form 'shan'. In some cases, even if a photo was described in English only, its tags were likely to be in both English and Chinese. For instance, a Hong Kong participant, *HKmPUA*, showed a photo of McDonald's in Sai Kung (a district in Hong Kong). The caption for this photo is in English only: '*I'm lovin' it, McDonalds in Saikung*'. However, when tagging the location of this photo, both traditional and simplified Chinese characters were included in addition to the English ones: 'Saikung, 西貢 (traditional Chinese), 西贡 (simplified Chinese), Hong Kong, 香港'. Tagging in different languages is, on the one hand, an act of speaking to different audiences; on the other hand, this is also a way of enhancing Flickr's search engine, that the photo would show up when the search keyword is in either Chinese or English. This not only ensures that his photos can get more 'views', it also shows that *HKmPUA*, like many Flickr users, sees himself as belonging to an affinity group of active and global Flickr members who want to maximize their participation as much as possible through multilingual writing.

An even more interactive multilingual writing space is the comments section underneath the uploaded photo. As one of our Chinese participants, *sating*, pointed out:

> I like Flickr because commenters on Flickr, especially my own contacts, all make comments in an objective and polite manner. If my photo does not receive any comments, that shows it isn't a popular one. But that's alright. I enjoy such an authentic and harmonious atmosphere.

> *(sating)*

Although the user can control who can make comments on their photos, the people in our study generally welcome comments from any Flickr members regardless of the language used. This implies that they are likely to receive comments in languages that they are not familiar with. When responding to comments in different languages, many users wrote their replies according to the languages used by the comment posters; if they did not know the language concerned, they would respond in English, as illustrated by the comments on one of *Carolink*'s photo pages:

fr1zz:	and where did the tattooed folks went to – set to private?
carolink:	Sorry, fr1zz. . .what do you mean?
fr1zz:	weird, the newest images you just posted, for a while they disappeared
	. . .this image:
	[a small photo embedded]
carolink:	I was trying to maintain some "logical" order, and I erased them to upload them again. . .Well, there they are. The girl just was there playing with the wind, and happy to pose!
fr1zz:	thanks. a beautiful girl. :)
	. . .
Migue A. Yuste:	Mucho tiempo sin verte, me gusta el gesto de esta mujer. *Translation: I haven't seen you for a while, I like this woman's gesture.*
carolink:	Gracias port u visita, Miguel A. Aqui seguimos, poco mas o menos :) *Translation: Thanks for your visit, Miguel A. We're still here, more or less :)*

In this chain of messages, *Carolink* writes to *fr1zz*, a German speaker, in English but switches to Spanish when responding to *Miguel A. Yuste's* comment. Similarly our Chinese informants also adapt their responses to the language used by their commenters. Multilingual encounters on Flickr are quite different from those found on IM in that on Flickr, users often find themselves speaking to an unknown group of people, who they may have never met in their offline lives. In IM, by contrast, it is rare to find people chatting with different audiences in different languages in a single conversation. By accommodating their language choice to different audiences, Flickr members we have studied would actively present themselves as global citizens through their constant switches between languages and selecting the most suitable form of language for their intended viewer (see subsection 'Who the intended viewer is' below), even though not all of these languages are used in their offline lives. We also observe that when interacting with people from all over the world speaking different languages, Flickr members generally see strategically deploying language as a crucial practice in becoming a legitimate Flickr member and in their relationship with other Flickr members. Further details of the multilingual aspects of this study can be found in Lee and Barton (2011).

Code-switching practices on instant messaging (IM)

As already introduced in Chapter 4, IM is largely used as a text-based communication tool. Such everyday use and exchange of text messages foster the development of IM as a social practice associated with sets of values that influence people to use texts in specific ways. In a study of the text-making practices of MSN Messenger (or what is now called Windows Live Messenger) in Hong Kong, one of the authors, Carmen, looked at how a group of bilingual university students deployed their range of linguistic resources available to them. IM was reported to be the most popular online activity in Hong Kong (comScore 2009). The multilingual background of Hong Kong people opens up an interesting area of research, particularly in terms of people's choices of language and use of writing systems online. Cantonese is the main spoken language in Hong Kong and people are brought up learning to read and write Mandarin Chinese. Most educated people such as the participants in the study can also read, speak, and write English.

The participants in the study used IM almost every day, mostly at home, after school. Their chat partners were mainly friends or other people with whom they often interacted in face-to-face contexts such as family and relatives. Within such a social practice, in which texts play a central role, these chat participants gradually developed specific ways of using texts within IM. First, the participants drew upon a number of linguistic resources in their IM chat. Five categories of linguistic resources available to Hong Kong IM users can be identified:

(i)   standard English;
(ii) standard written Chinese;
(iii) Cantonese in characters;
(iv) Romanized Cantonese; and
(v)   morpheme-by-morpheme literal translation.

The first two types, standard English and Chinese, are the standard written varieties that are commonly used in offline contexts and are the written varieties taught in school. Cantonese, which is the students' primary spoken language, has never been standardized as a written language. The study found that these IM users have created interesting and innovative ways of representing Cantonese in their IM chat, including borrowing characters from standard written Chinese, spelling out Cantonese words as Romanized words, or even using English transliteration (types iii to v above).

An interesting example of transliteration is the phrase 'sky and land lessons', which was used in the IM data. It is a common phrase among university students to mean a long period of spare time between a lecture in the morning and another one in late afternoon. It is a literal translation of the Cantonese expression 天地堂 . What is particularly intriguing in this data is not just the wide ranging and creative forms of linguistic resources, but how and why these codes are deployed differently for different purposes by different IM users. The study noted that not all of these forms of language were drawn upon in any given chat session. Sometimes the participants would use one code only while at other times they would mix linguistic codes. And there seems to be no fixed pattern in using or choosing such codes.

The following example chat log (Extract 4.1), provided by one of the student participants, Snow, illustrates how these language resources are carefully and strategically deployed in IM. At the time of the research, Snow was a postgraduate student in linguistics. Like most people in Hong Kong, Cantonese is her first language. Being educated in English too, Snow can read and write in both standard written Chinese and English. The extract is taken from one of her chat sessions with her friend Shu, a Hong Konger who was also educated in English and at the time was studying in Germany. Here they are talking about the different McDonalds they have been in around the world. Their primary language in the chat session is written Cantonese, but note their insertion of English words from time to time:

Extract 4.1: An IM chat session between Snow and Shu

1. Shu: 都好耐冇食過呀 ~~~~~~~~~~~~~~~~~
   (Yeah, I haven't been there [McDonald's] for a while.)

2. Snow: 喂我果時 o 向 freiburg 好似冇見過 m 記 ....
   (Hey I don't remember seeing a McDonald's in Freiburg when I was there.)

3. Snow: 果時見到 london 果 d 好多沙津囉 ....
   (I also remember there were many kinds of salad in the McDonald's in London . . .)

4. Shu: 係呀 ~ 不過都唔跟餐
   (Yeah, but they don't do set meals.)

5. Snow: 係呀係呀 我果時 only 食左個 muffin .... 1 euro, 已經好抵咁 ....
   (Oh yeah, and once I ordered a muffin [in Freiburg], and it was 1 euro, seems quite reasonable really.)

In addition to Cantonese written in characters, Snow draws upon other linguistic codes in this extract. Several words that have Chinese equivalents are written as English words ('freiberg', 'london', and 'only', 'muffin', and 'euro'). Another use of different codes is in turn 2, where the letter *o* is combined with 向 to form o 向 which means the locative preposition *at*. Turn 3 exhibits the use of Romanized Cantonese: The letter *d* is used to represent the Cantonese classifier 啲 (similar to the meaning of 'some' in English), which is an exact homophone of the letter *d*. In turn 2, 'm 記' refers to McDonalds, which is composed of the initial letter of McDonalds, followed by the Chinese suffix 記 which generally means a shop. These instances of code-switching may be completely incomprehensible to non-IM users or to those who are not used to the practice of code-switching. Nonetheless, it is exactly such complex deployment of linguistic resources that characterizes linguistic practices in IM among multilingual users.

Using spoken Cantonese-English code-switching has long been a common linguistic practice among educated Hong Kong people. Throughout history, Cantonese-English code-switching has been confined to spoken contexts. However, mixed language writing is not encouraged in school or other official situations. The strong presence of mixed language writing in the above extract shows that IM has provided a conversation-like platform, a specific kind of writing space, for students to freely express themselves in any linguistic form of their own choice. However, in the above excerpt, Snow does not automatically transfer her code-switching practice in speech to her IM writing. The way Snow writes in this excerpt seems to suggest a rather different case of code-switching compared with switching in everyday talk. For example, the research noted that the insertion of 'only' in turn 5 was rather unusual because adverbs are rarely said in English in a Cantonese-English mixed language utterance. This was taken up in a face-to-face interview, where Snow explained specifically her code-switching practice in turn 5:

Interviewer:	Here [referring to turn 5], you write "我果時 only 食左個 muffin" Would you talk like that?
Snow:	Oh no, never! That sounds awful. How can I say that [in speech]?
Interviewer:	Why not?
Snow:	Ok, I would say 'muffin' in English. But I wouldn't say 'only' when I talk [in mixed code]. I wrote 'only' [in the message] because it was difficult to type '淨係' [Chinese equivalent for 'only'] but 'only' was easy to type.

Apart from the fact that Snow considers some code-switching practices unacceptable in an offline context, as in 'That sounds awful', her case demonstrates clearly that code-switching is indeed a situated practice. Inputting Chinese characters involves rather complicated decoding processes and requires extra effort to learn and type. Indeed a number of other participants expressed similar concerns, thus preventing them from chatting in Chinese. Because of certain technical constraints imposed by Chinese inputting methods, in this particular chat session, Snow deliberately replaces '淨係' (the Cantonese expression for *only*) with its English equivalent 'only', even though she usually expresses this word in Cantonese in other contexts of communication. These creative linguistic practices are not commonly found in people's offline speech or writing. Snow's case certainly illustrates multilingual online users' abilities to reappropriate their linguistic resources and practices for different situations of use. Further details of this study can be found in Lee (2007a).

Language choice in micro-blogging

Posting short messages on a regular basis, or micro-blogging, on social network sites has gradually become a key social practice. As of April 2010, over 100 million user accounts had been created on Twitter (*The Economic Times* 2010), attracting people from all over the world, including many parts of Asia and Europe (Semiocast 2010). Like other global websites, in addition to English, many languages are found on Twitter. However, at the time of Honeycutt and Herring's (2009) study Twitter was still a largely English-based platform. Part of their study collected samples of tweets posted at four time periods of a day, covering major time zones. Although over 13 languages (including Japanese and Spanish) were recorded over these four periods, English was still the dominant language in all these four periods (ranging from over 35 per cent to as high as 68 per cent). However, what is not included in Honeycutt and Herring's study is *who* posted these tweets. As we will demonstrate in the next chapter, who the poster is shapes practices in significant ways.

Micro-blogging on Facebook seems to provide a different picture of multilingual practices. The status updates feature on Facebook is similar to that of Twitter in that it works mainly with a prompt (What's on your mind?) and a text box (Publisher box) that appear at the top of a user's homepage and personal profile (wall). Status updates have also become a major writing space on Facebook. Another study collected two sets of status updates from a group of Hong Kong Facebook users before and after Facebook changed the prompt and compared their communicative functions and languages used. This study found that language choice in Facebook status updates was very much influenced by the question in the status prompt, which Facebook changed several times. In late 2007, the prompt was 'What are you doing right now?', and users had to begin the post with their first name and then the verb *is* appeared automatically (e.g., 'Carmen *is writing*'). Later, however, Facebook removed the 'is' to offer greater flexibility; in March 2009, the prompt was also changed to 'What's on your mind?', which seems to have led to some changing practices in language choice. Comparing the two samples of status updates, it was found that the use of Chinese increased significantly from 34 per cent to about 58 per cent, while English posts dropped from about 60 per cent to just under 40 per cent. More mixed code messages were also identified in the more recent corpus, such as:

Peggy: 點解我句 status msg 會自動消失？ ('Why has my status message disappeared?').

Kate: 大埔海濱公園好靚呢 Congratulations, my dear fd~
(Tai Po Waterfront Park is so beautiful ~~~ Congratulations, my dear friend~)

The status update authors were interviewed regarding their linguistic practices on Facebook. Among Chinese, English, and mixed code, it was almost impossible for the participants to single out any of these resources in their linguistic repertoire when writing their status messages. A number of participants referred to the expressiveness of their language resources, suggesting that Chinese allows them to freely express themselves on Facebook.

The changing design of the status update's function, the availability of Facebook in various languages, as well as the easier processing of and access to non-roman writing systems on the web are all important factors that contribute to the increasing use of languages other than English on Facebook. All this echoes findings about the reduced use of English on Twitter (Semiocast 2010). Similar to language choice on other platforms, the language used to write status updates on Facebook is also very much embedded in the immediate context of communication as well as in people's lives. Ariel, for example, is one of the few bilingual Hong Kong participants who writes almost all of her posts in English only. Ariel's tendency of writing in English on Facebook has to be explained in conjunction to her lived experience. Ever since she graduated from university in Hong Kong, Ariel has been away from her hometown intermittently to further her studies in different countries including Australia, France, and Belgium. Many of her contacts on Facebook are friends she has met from different parts of the world, with whom Ariel communicates in English only. Factors such as expressiveness of language and target audience will be discussed in the next chapter.

One might also expect that the dominant practice of Cantonese-English code-switching on IM would be carried over to Facebook. However, contrary to what was found on IM, the proportion of mixed code status updates is extremely small in the data in the Facebook study (less than 10 per cent in either corpus). This may be explained by the synchronicity of different forms of CMC. Status updating, unlike IM, is essentially an asynchronous, i.e. delayed mode of communication, like email and online forums. Since instant replies are not expected, bilingual users do not feel the need to speed up their interaction by mixing languages as strongly as they do in face-to-face talk or online chatting. Although we have already pointed out that linguistic practices online are not technologically determined, the changing multilingual practices on Facebook seem to suggest that language use online is still more or less shaped by the changing design of the platforms. Further details of this study can be found in Lee (2011).

Languages on YouTube

Over the years, many YouTube users have perceived the affordances of commenting as a platform for critical debates and discussions, not only on the video per se, but on other topics arising from the original discussion. YouTube, being a major Web 2.0 site, attracts users from all over the world, who also bring with them their own linguistic practices and repertoires in their videos and written comments. As of July 2011, the YouTube interface is available in 34 languages, suggesting its global reach. Many YouTubers also make use of the video sharing possibility on YouTube to 'teach the world' languages that they speak. One Canadian YouTuber *carlosdouh* became a celebrity after he posted his first video in his *Learning Cantonese with Carlosdouh* series, in each of which he introduces a new Cantonese expression using both English and Cantonese. Researchers have started to pay attention to the presence of non-English languages on YouTube, despite the limited published scholarly work on the subject.

This global video sharing site also offers potentials for second language education (see Chapter 11). Phil Benson (2010), for example, carried out an interesting case study of one YouTube video in which a secondary schoolgirl from Hong Kong called Ruby criticized the spoken English of an invigilator in a public examination. Benson's data included video responses (mostly remixes and parodies) to Ruby's original post as well as a corpus of comments. He noted a range of translingual practices, including Cantonese-English code switching, especially when other YouTubers discuss the English used in Ruby's video. (We return to this video in Chapter 8.) In another study of informal language learning on YouTube, Benson and Chan (2011) analysed a corpus of comments made on three English-subtitled versions (or fan-subbing) of the Beijing Olympics theme song. These comments, in addition to the presence of multiple languages, exhibit significant evidence of language teaching and learning discourses among the commenters. This body of research usefully points out how social media can serve as important platforms for critical discussions, language learning, and cultural exchanges across borders.

This chapter started with the traditional debate of whether the global internet reinforces the global status of English or gives rise to linguistic pluralism. Although both seem to be happening at the same time, there is evidence that the web and its users are increasingly multilingual. With examples from four online platforms, this chapter demonstrates ways in which new media provide important writing spaces for web users to creatively deploy their multilingual resources for different purposes. This is a result of taking up not only the affordances of the sites, but also the affordances of languages, which is the theme of the next chapter.

5

TAKING UP THE AFFORDANCES OF MULTIPLE LANGUAGES

- Taking up affordances of multiple languages
- New multilingual encounters and translingual practices online
  - *Translating content online*
  - *Using language in a mobile world*
  - *Maintaining minority languages online*

TAKING UP AFFORDANCES OF MULTIPLE LANGUAGES

Throughout the book, we take a situated approach in understanding language online. The argument in the previous chapter thus also goes beyond the debate over whether the internet leads to linguistic imperialism or pluralism; in fact, the evidence from our research shows both are happening, but for different reasons. A more revealing approach is to observe people's actual practices and how they perceive and take up affordances of what is made available to them in different episodes of technology use, and this is what we pursue in this chapter. Towards the end of the chapter, we outline a number of new multilingual encounters and translingual practices that have become salient in the global online world.

The case studies and examples discussed in Chapter 4 demonstrate that online users know very well how to deploy their linguistic resources in different contexts for different purposes and to different people. This is a result of taking up and acting upon the affordances of different languages. And in working out what different languages can or cannot do, online participants take into consideration a number of ecological factors. These are primarily: who the user is, who the intended viewer is, what is posted, and how the medium is used. These then effectively become four aspects of language and literacy practices to focus on when studying not just multilingual practices, but the important factors that shape all sorts of linguistic practices in online spaces and how changes in practices regularly take place.

Who the user is

The immediate factor that shapes language choice online is who the user is or what we call the situated language ecology of individual users. This ecology includes the individual's geographical, educational, linguistic, social, and cultural backgrounds. For example, our Chinese participants for the Flickr project come from a range of Chinese-speaking regions including Hong Kong, mainland China and Taiwan, where they speak different varieties of Chinese but may share similar writing systems. Our Spanish informants live in different parts of Spain, in Argentina, and in Mexico and may have different levels of access to the internet. People in these different communities may have different levels of exposure to English, thus having different attitudes towards their linguistic resources. In the interviews, these bilingual Flickr users agreed that English is the 'universal' language, which they would use to communicate with people who do not speak their local languages. There are many instances where people also consider the expressiveness of a certain language. For example, one of our Spanish participants, *Saski*, has used the English word 'breathe' because he found the word more 'evocative than the Spanish term "respirar"'. In this case, English is preferred as it is shorter and more phonetically appealing than the Spanish equivalent. There are parallel examples where people prefer a Spanish or Chinese term rather than an English one. Likewise, on IM, the bilingual Hong Kong participants would prefer to code-switch as that is how they speak with their friends in their offline lives.

Who the intended viewer is

As with any writing activity, web users often consider who is going to view the written content they create. There are three main groups of intended audience or viewers in online spaces: the general 'unknown' audience on the web (especially on Flickr and YouTube); 'friends' who are listed as contacts (especially on Flickr and Facebook), and friends in 'real' life (especially on instant messaging). The Flickr participants usually select their language according to what language the primary target audience speaks. Our general observation of the various sites reveal that, even though language choice varies in different instances, there is a tendency that people would write in their shared language if they know each other in real life; English, not surprisingly, is often used to an unknown audience, or to someone who only speaks English. Bilingual writing may appear in either of the two main forms, as described by Sebba (2012): it can be a literal translation from one language to another, that is 'parallel' bilingual texts targeting monolingual audiences; or it can be as 'complementary' bilingual texts containing different information, which only bilingual people can fully understand. An example of complementary bilingual texts is when Flickr users write a photo title in one language, and the photo description in another. Elsewhere, we have noted examples where people provide partial translation of what they have said in their profiles.

On IM and Facebook, it is relatively easy to accommodate to the 'reader', that is, to use a language that the target reader understands, as most contacts are known to the writer. But in more public networks such as Flickr and YouTube, how do web users find out what language another user speaks if they have never met in the offline world? One Hong Kong Flickr user, *contradiction*, told us that looking at the language they use in captions, titles, and comments can provide some clues of the linguistic backgrounds of other Flickr members. As they get to know what language their intended audience speaks, users switch between languages accordingly. For example, *Loolooimage* received an English comment from *dans*. Later on, from *dans'* photo site, *Loolooimage* found out that *dans* came from Taiwan. *Loolooimage* then wrote back in Chinese which began like this '*dans, I know you are from Taiwan, so let me respond in Chinese.*' *dans* then also wrote back in Chinese in their subsequent exchanges. Some of the Spanish speakers, such as Madelena Pestana, checked people's profile to work out what was 'the author's mother tongue'. This is in many ways a new form of multilingual practice that some people had never encountered in the pre-internet era. What is happening in this example is how people frequently engage in some practices of linguistic negotiation in the form of publicly available conversations (e.g. commenting on Flickr or YouTube). At other times, people may want their comments to reach a wider audience in addition to the specific commenter and so they would write in English instead of the local language that they share with their commenters. These examples also suggest that the practice of code choice keeps changing as people's relationships with their intended audience change. These multilingual practices are markers of identity as well. Multilingual Flickr participants choose their language not only according to who they are, but who they want to be to others. (See Chapter 6 for more on identity performance online.) This factor of considering intended audience often co-occurs with the previous factor, as they both constitute the meaning of identities in online spaces, i.e. who you are and who you are to others.

What is posted

The subject matter of what is posted also shapes language choice online. On IM, the Hong Kong chat participants would prefer to write in Cantonese or code-switch when chatting about in-depth and complex topics that can only be vividly expressed through their most familiar language. On Flickr, we notice that photos that denote a particular culture tend to be described bilingually and tend to trigger multilingual comments. Bilingual Flickr participants are willing to switch to English if the photos are of general interest such as music and other popular global cultures. However, when it comes to photos that express local cultures or refer to the photo posters' families, they would use languages that are closely associated with those local cultures. *Saski* said:

> When I post thinking about someone, a close friend or a known follower, I tend to post in Spanish. . .. If I tag in Spanish, it has to be for a local (or personal, e.g. 'torollo') non-translatable term.

However, there are instances where the local culture in an image is annotated in great detail in English. For example, *zfz0123^_^* displays an image of the Chinese character '福', which means 'good fortune'. It is also a common Chinese new year greeting. Underneath the image, she provides a detailed explanation for people who do not read Chinese as follows:

> Nowaday, "福" in chinese means "fortunate". . . but when you come to visit a traditional chinese family in the spring festival, you will notice that this "福" is written in another style which has a big difference with the one we use everyday. so do you know why chinese write "福" in this way? what's it mean?
>
> (zfz0123^_^)

*zfz0123^_^* told us that 福 is 'a character with rich culture', so she would like the photo to reach as many people as possible. With such a mixture of intended audiences, the best way to reach them is to provide descriptions in both Chinese and English. With the English description, she would be able to introduce this word to the rest of the world who may not understand Chinese language and culture. She added:

> I tried my best to share all these information i found with all my flickr friends who might have interests in that. However, of course, only the friends who know both language will enjoy the most.
>
> (zfz0123^_^)

Another example of multilingual practices is where *SMeaLLum* from Argentina has provided the words of a tango in Spanish under a picture. He has also included a note in English linking to his *personal English translation* and to another link explaining that the song is written in Lunfardo, a non-standard Spanish dialect used in Argentinian tangos.

How the medium is used

Language choice is tied in closely with the perceived affordances and action possibilities of the medium. How a site is used is not predetermined but is based on different purposes for different communicative situations. For the IM participants, the site is primarily used as an informal and social communication technology. Such an informal, personal, and sometimes private environment allows users to decide what languages to use and how they use them. This can be illustrated through a range of non-standard and creative varieties of language, including both spoken and written forms. An example in point is the use of mixed language, as shown in the previous chapter. At other times, student IM users may stretch the affordances of IM and use IM as a learning tool. One informant told us that she once chatted with her classmate entirely in English in order to practise English writing for her A-level examinations. And a few other participants also shared similar experiences of practising English writing on IM with their peers. These different ways of seeing the functions of the same medium are important in deciding what linguistic resources to draw on in online writing.

To our Flickr participants, Flickr is not just an online photo album. As Flickr gets used more, many new purposes and functions emerge. Some Flickr participants aim to have their photos viewed by as many people as possible. To achieve this, it is important to deploy their languages strategically to maximize the accessibility of their photo sites. This is why English, the perceived global language, still plays such an important role here. But apart from increasing their popularity among the global Flickr world, these multilingual users also want to attract their fellow Chinese or Spanish speakers to view their sites. There has been a growth in the number of localized Flickr groups such as the 心台灣 Heart of Taiwan group, which is primarily a Chinese language group. Similarly there are some Spanish sites that are Spanish only; these link up Spanish speakers in Spain, in Latin America and those living throughout the Spanish-speaking world. This also shows how people who come from the same background but do not live in the same country can now use Flickr as a diasporic forum to interact with one another. However, for some Flickr users, their activities are not primarily around language, but they prioritize their photographs. Our Hong Kong informant *tiong* (小吞) decided not to choose any particular language for Flickr and humorously made an explicit bilingual statement about this in his profile:

> *my english is so . . . .. . poor !*
> so, i take photos. . .
> 唉，中文都一樣 .... 不見得是好！ *('sigh. . .my Chinese isn't good either!')*
> 都是拍照算了 *('so I should better take photos')*

Although claiming that he has not mastered Chinese or English, the fact that the English text is placed above the Chinese writing indexes his code preference, that language serves the function of marking his identities. English seems to be the language that *tiong* (小吞) prefers to display on his profile page and the language that he expects the world to see first on his Flickr site. This humorous comment, which can only be fully understood by people who are bilingual in Chinese and English, shows that the use of the two languages is not necessarily to translate from one language to the other.

The above factors show that language choice online is not primarily related to the user's familiarity with their linguistic resources or their every-day exposure to a particular language. Someone who is fluent or educated in English may not necessarily use more English than someone who only knows a few English words; likewise, someone who knows little English can participate actively. For example, *cjPanda* from mainland China told us that she did not have to use English in her out-of-school life, but she was willing to describe her Flickr photos in simple English, which she described as *'very ABC'* and *'no longer than 8 letters'*. When it comes to describing photos that convey complex ideas, she would switch back to Chinese. In contrast, *HKmPUA*, who is an English-educated Hong Konger, often includes Chinese tags for his photos alongside the English ones. All these, together with the examples discussed before, show the ways in which new digital media have provided a new platform for new multilingual encounters to take place. People who may or may not be multilinguals in their offline lives have become used to working across different languages in order to participate as global members of the web.

NEW MULTILINGUAL ENCOUNTERS AND TRANSLINGUAL PRACTICES ONLINE

The central idea of this chapter is that new media offer new possibilities for multilingual interaction. On the web, anyone (including people who see themselves as monolinguals) can experience or do things with different languages. The multilingual internet has gone beyond the question of which language dominates the internet or how users code-switch. It is now a question of how people act differently as they take up new possibilities offered by the different languages on the web. To cite a few examples of changing multilingual practices: Many people have developed a habit of using online translators to maximize their access to online information, or even have a view about how reliable or terrible online translators are; people teach and learn languages on YouTube and engage in discussions about languages by leaving written comments online; in a Flickr or YouTube comment chain, it is not uncommon to find people participating in multiple conversation topics written in different dialects and languages. These new *multilingual encounters* online are part of people's *translingual practices* (Pennycook 2008; Blackledge and Creese 2009).

This idea of translingual practices focuses more on communicative prac-tices across different groups and communities of people rather than within a specific speech community defined primarily by the geographical locations of speakers. It is also concerned with the *process* of working with different languages rather than the product of it. In some cases, translingual inter-action does not necessarily involve more than one language. A relevant example is cited in Davies (2007) – on a Flickr photo page, a photo shows an American user, *Saffron*, wearing a 'throw' (as written in the photo description) given to her by her grandmother. A Norwegian Flickr user, *Astrid*, comes across this photo page and asks *Saffron* what the word 'throw' means in her photo description. *Saffron* then explains:

> Hi astrid, yep like a small blanket i guess . . . a pashmina is also used as a wrap and a chunky scarf. this is about a metre and a half long knitted wrap. i guess my grandmother would call this a shawl. I would think a poncho refers to material with a hole in the centre so you slide it on rather than wrap it. aaah such confusion.

The whole communication is delivered in English only. From the view of learning, this translingual interaction is packed with discourses of language learning and can be seen as a 'mini-English lesson' (Benson and Chik 2010: 68). In other words, translingual practices can be understood as *the ways in which groups and communities of people experience and do things that involve more than one language.* Web users with different linguistic and cultural backgrounds discussing languages online has become an increas-ingly common practice, especially on sites that facilitate public commenting such as Flickr and YouTube. These are just some of the new practices that we never found ourselves doing before the age of digital media. In the follow-ing subsections, we present some key issues related to new multilingual and translingual experiences online that require more extensive research.

Translating content online

Administrators and developers of many new sites have become aware of their global market, and have translated their site interfaces into multiple languages. Flickr, for example, is available in 10 languages to date. This may partly be a result of constant negotiation between the web users and the web developers. Flickr was available in English only when it first launched, which generated a great deal of debate regarding how this would hinder partici-pation and accessibility of the site; many members thus requested that the site should have been available in more languages. Flickr developers seemed to have responded to these views by translating the site interface into several other languages, including Chinese, Korean, Italian and a number of European languages. We also come across translation-related groups on Flickr. There is a group called 'Translate Me', whose purpose is described by the group administrator as follows:

> This group is for anyone who is curious about linguistics. Have you photographed something written in a foreingn [sic] language and wondered what it meant? Are you

> bilingual or multilingual? Then this is the group for you. Lets post photos in all alnguages [sic] and invite each other's translations!
>
> [. . .]
>
> Discussions should please include talk of ambiguities and friendly critiques of existing translations.

Apparently, web users are given increasing amount of power to take charge of their language choice, with the dominance of self-generated content. This, however, does not mean that all languages are welcome. Wikipedia is one example providing evidence that Web 2.0 sites are still relatively controlled by web administrators who still favour well-known languages. If we want to propose a new language for Wikipedia, we have to ensure that the language proposed:

> has a sufficient number of living native speakers to form a viable community and audience. (Wikisource wikis are allowed in languages with no native speakers, although these should be on a wiki for the modern form of the language if possible.)
>
> [. . .]
>
> If the proposal is for an artificial language such as Esperanto, it must have a reasonable degree of recognition as determined by discussion (this requirement is being discussed by the language subcommittee).
>
> (http://meta.wikimedia.org/wiki/Language_proposal_policy)

The above information is an extract of the 'Language proposal policy' on Meta-Wiki, a sub-part of Wikipedia that discusses anything related to the development of Wikipedia. This policy is drafted by Wikipedia's Language Committee who are in charge of language issues of the site. The fact that this proposal seems to ignore smaller languages has generated some debate on the 'Discuss' page. Many commenters draw upon their own understanding of 'big' and 'small' languages when discussing this seemingly 'unfair' policy. For example, one user *Rickyrab* points out: 'Why is English given special treatment with a "simple" wiki? Why not allow "simple" language wikis in languages other than English?'. Another user (ةيبانريدمجعلودبحلاوبع) is also sceptical of the policy by using his knowledge of the relationship between standard Arabic and Egyptian Arabic. He commented: 'any Arab can understand the Egyptian dialet [sic] and any Egyptian can understand the standard arabic. the standard arabic wikipedia is a general wiki for all of Arabs, and there is no need for other wikipedias.'

Advances in free online translators have also presented new translingual practices and change the way people engage in translation activities in society. As a result of media convergence, online translators can be incorporated into social network sites. For example, Facebook now allows users to view foreign language posts in their native language. Facebook has added the link 'See Translation' underneath a post that is not written in the user's native language so that the user can click through to see a translation powered by Microsoft Bing. But the best-known online translator to date is possibly Google Translate. According to its original creator Franz Josef Och (2005), Google Translate does not adopt a grammar rule analysis in their translation method, but a statistical machine translation method. This means that instead of teaching the machine some basic grammatical rules such as word order of the target language, the translation results are based on analysing bilingual text corpora (e.g. frequency of certain strings of words that appear together in a sentence). This also means that the programme only gives the translation that is more frequently occurring in the corpora, which is believed to be a more accurate and reliable method of machine translation. Indeed, many of our Flickr participants told us that their English writing on Flickr is a result of Google Translate. While being as reliable as it can, statistical translation can still cause mistakes, sometimes even creating some humorous effects. A classic example that has been widely circulated on the web is when a Chinese sign '请在一米线外等候' (Please wait behind the one-meter line) is translated into 'Please wait outside rice-flour noodle'. This is because 米线 without the pre-modifier 一 (one) in Chinese is more commonly known to mean 'rice noodle'. The result is believed to be generated by either Google Translate or Babel Fish, another popular online translator. This example is discussed in greater detail in *Language Log*, a blog maintained by an American linguist.

While machine translation of some languages may still be far from reliable, what is known as 'cloud translation' seems to be a good (and cheap) solution to the problem. The idea of cloud translation is to involve ordinary web users in the translation of web content, thus gradually teaching the web their native language. The 'translations' application on Facebook is an example of collaborative translation on the web. It is an application that users can add to their Facebook profile page. Once the 'translations' application is added to a profile, the user can then join the 'community of translators' and become a translator of any language of their own choice. Translations of any content on Facebook can be submitted to the community of translators, who will then review and approve of the translations through a voting system. The original aim of the application is to make Facebook available to everyone regardless of language and ethnicity. All these raise interesting questions as to whether users really benefit from such forms of multilingual affordance. Lenihan (2011) argues that the Facebook transla-tions application is perhaps just one of their marketing strategies, for a number of reasons. First, its translation page interface is available in English only; second, translations can only be submitted via the US English site; third, Facebook administrators can only receive and answer feedback/ questions in English. This reminds us of the way Flickr greets us in a new language every time we log on, from English, Chinese, to smaller languages such as Māori, an indigenous language in New Zealand spoken by just a few thousand people. Certainly, how social network sites discursively construct their global image through multilingual translations, whether artificial or natural, would be one of the key future research directions in understanding web-based linguistic practices.

Maintaining minority languages online

While concerns are expressed over the possible decline or death of minority languages due to the dominance of English, globalization may in fact help minority languages to regain their status. Although larger languages, especially English, still enjoy higher status than smaller languages on the web, a great deal of research has provided evidence that the web also provides a space to maintain minority languages in the form of writing (Paolillo 2007). A successful case is the presence of Assyrian in English-based CMC, reported in McClure (2001). Assyrian is spoken by a small minority group in the Middle East. When participating in English-based chat rooms and newsgroups, McClure found that Assyrian participants would write their greetings and closings in Assyrian. Code-switching to Assyrian is also noted when the participants discuss issues related to their ethnicity. This not only helps maintain the language, but writing in a local language online is also clearly an act of self-positioning so as to strengthen their Assyrian identity.

Written languages that are no longer used in offline lives have become more visible in online platforms. For example, in their study of language choice online in Egypt, Warschauer *et al.* (2007) discovered a new written form of romanized colloquial Egyptian Arabic. In Egypt, classical Arabic is the language having high prestige and is widely used in books, newspapers, speeches and other formal contexts. Colloquial Arabic, by contrast, is used in informal spoken situations only, and it rarely exists in writing. Warschauer *et al.* (2007) surveyed and interviewed a group of young professionals in Cairo regarding their language choice in formal and informal online contexts. Their findings suggest that colloquial Arabic, which used to have very limited use in offline contexts, is used extensively online, alongside English.

An emerging direction for future research is how small languages are also represented discursively, metalinguistically, and ideologically in new social media such as YouTube and Facebook. Horner and Krummes (2011) present a case study of the representations of Luxembourgish on YouTube. The status of Luxembourgish is similar to that of colloquial Egyptian Arabic in that Luxembourgish is mostly used for spoken communication in Luxembourg. However, with the rise of the internet, written Luxembourgish is gradually gaining importance, at least in online contexts. Horner and Krummes have looked into the written comments made on some Luxembourgish language lessons on YouTube. A major topic that commenters often discuss is the status and categorization of Luxembourgish as a language. In doing so, the commenters also employ a number of strategies including code-switching and articulating their historically rooted linguistic ideologies. These ideologies are sometimes conflicted, due to the geographically and perhaps culturally diverse background of the commenters. It is worth noting that in the study of Flickr that within the relatively small number of people studied, there were spontaneous references to, and examples of, Catalan and Basque, as well as Asturian, a minority language of northern Spain, and Lunfardo, a non-standard South American Spanish dialect used for the lyrics of tangos.

Using language in a mobile world

We are living in an increasingly mobile world, both physically and virtually. Flows of people, knowledge, ideas and objects are all speeding up, leading to new interactions between people and new forms of learning online and offline. Language becomes an important vehicle that can support, direct, impede and channel these flows. One major linguistic phenomenon mobilities have introduced is the increasing use of local languages among diasporic community in web-based communication, leading to a truly multilingual internet. The Assyrian study by McClure mentioned above is a good example of this. Assyrian speakers spread around the world as they do not have their own nation state. In the US, many Assyrians have their families in Iraq, Australia, Canada, and other countries. However, with internet forums and newsgroups, Assyrian communities around the world are able to assert their ethnic identity through written Assyrian, thus allowing them to form a global community regardless of geographical locations. We have also seen how Flickr as a globalized network now serves as a platform for diasporic communities. On Flickr, there are photo 'groups' devoted to a particular culture, country, or language. People from around the world sharing the same background would create specific groups that belong to their own local language or culture, and interact on these sites using their home language. For example, the group * *Flickr en Español* is a group with descriptions and discussion topics written in Spanish only. This helps unite Spanish speakers who live in different countries, from Spain to Argentina. A similar story is found in Androutsopoulos (2013) on German dialects on YouTube. Although YouTube is commonly viewed as a global platform, it also gives rise to local activities, such as discussing local dialects among German speakers. As an initial observation of the situation, Androutsopoulos notes that a great deal of videos on YouTube are tagged with German dialect-related key words such as *Bairisch* ('Bavarian'), *Alemannisch* ('Alemannic'), or *Berlinerisch* ('Berlin city dialect'). These dialects are not only present in these videos but also become the theme of these videos and viewers' comments on them. This study will be further discussed in terms of metalanguage in Chapter 8.

Apart from interacting through global websites like Flickr and YouTube, there exist a large number of more localized diasporic websites, 'websites that are produced and consumed by members of diasporic communities' (Androutsopoulos 2007: 341). Androutsopoulos (2007) examines the extent to which German-based Greek and Persian migrants preserve their home languages or switch to German when participating in two German-based diasporic web forums. For example, extensive use of Persian is found in the

Persian forum, regardless of the topics of discussion. Instances of code-switching are also present in the Greek forum. Evidence from this study has shown that home languages have not only regained dominance on these forums, but have also been transformed, mainly in the aspect of Romanized writing. Similar observations of code-switching, which we will not describe in further detail here, are found in Sebba's (2007) research on English-Caribbean creole in the comedian Ali G's websites and Jaworska's (2011) study of German and Polish diasporic forums based in the UK. Certainly, these are only some of the examples showing how deploying multiple linguistic resources gives rise to new forms of participation on the web. Multilingual practices online enable people to participate locally and globally, so as to assert new kinds of identity, a topic that is further pursued in the next chapter.

6

'THIS IS ME'

Writing the self online

- Identity and language online
- A techno-biographic approach to language and identity
- Constructing glocal identities in public online spaces
- A textually mediated self in a changing world

IDENTITY AND LANGUAGE ONLINE

A Frenchwoman living in Paris has a photo on Flickr of herself smiling into the camera and holding a handwritten sign saying '23 year'. The photo is entitled 'Happy birthday to me' in English with a short description below in French explaining that today is her 23rd birthday, 'et voila aujourd'hui j'ai 23 ans'. A man wearing an England football t-shirt has a similar photo where he is holding a cake with one lit candle in the middle. There are similar photos by many other Flickr photographers from around the world. The title, 'Happy birthday to me', is playing around with the first line of what is probably the most well known everyday song in the world. What is unusual in these examples is how these photos and descriptions draw attention to the self and are shared with the rest of the world. This particular practice has probably only been carried out since the affordances of shared digital photography have made it possible. This is what Crandall (2007) refers to as 'presentational' culture, where people constantly pay attention to how to present themselves. And such 'self-centredness' has been identified as a key aspect of the online world.

New digital media offer new opportunities for people to document and display their everyday lives in the form of writing and other modes. Aspects of life are often shared to different kinds of audience, though not always publicly. Often people share information online in a 'publicly private' manner, that is, where the identity of the content poster is revealed but the access to the content posted is relatively controlled. Others may do the opposite by exhibiting 'privately public' behaviour, posting publicly available content without letting others know who the poster is (Lange 2007). These disparate new practices have changed the ways people think about themselves. Thus, identity online is not just about *who we are*, but also *who we want to be to others*, and *how others see us*. Issues of identity management are central to online research.

An important point about the notion of identity is that it is multi-faceted and fluid. First of all, in any given context of social interaction, there may be one or more aspects of our identity that we may or may not want to express or reveal. Some aspects of identity are relatively static and not easy to change, such as age, gender, and nationality; some may be defined by social domains and relationships with others such as being a friend, a family member, a student, or by occupations such as a doctor, a worker, etc. Other parts of the self may be more dynamic and can change over time, such as hobbies, interests and social networks. The plural 'identities' thus seems a more appropriate term. Second, these properties of the self are not predetermined and fixed categories, but are open to transformation and changes. Such changes may be a result of different contexts of interaction, or to whom we wish to assert our identities. Identities are thus sometimes understood as masks that can be worn and taken off in different contexts of social interaction (as in Goffman 1959). This chapter focuses on the relationship between these different senses of the self and how language functions as a crucial form of cultural capital in asserting identities.

The above conceptualization of identity provides a backdrop for understanding the dynamics of self-representation online. As text-based computer-mediated interaction supports limited physical contextual cues, there is much room for people to construct and perform different features of identities (Turkle 1995; Baym 2010), primarily through linguistic means. A number of previous studies already show how online participants may adopt non-standard typographical features or a particular form of spelling to signal themselves as part of a sub-culture, while others may switch to a language not normally used in face-to-face communication to highlight their local identity. All these are strategies people use online to write themselves 'into being' (boyd 2007), so as to carefully manage their impression to others whom they cannot see face-to-face. Linguistic performance of identity is evident in all forms of CMC. For example, Internet Relay Chat (IRC) was an early form of synchronous online chat that has been studied extensively. When people meet for the first time on IRC, the conventional practice is to introduce themselves by constructing a message in the format of A/S/L (Age/Sex/Location, e.g. 18/F/UK). There is, however, no guarantee that every participant would accurately disclose their personal particulars, especially their real names and age. A person in IRC may be '18 years old one day and 60 years old the next. Even temporary gender changes are possible, enabling one to experience being a member of the opposite sex' (Bechar-Israeli 1995).

One salient practice in some public online spaces is giving oneself a nickname or screen-name, which can be quite different from one's real name used in offline life. An obvious reason for doing so is that people do not already know each other and there may be safety issues if authentic information is given. Nonetheless, not displaying all aspects of their offline identities does not necessarily mean that people want to deceive others; the anonymous nature of text-based IRC often gives rise to creativity and playfulness. Playful and carefully designed nicknames (or 'nicks' in IRC terms) are an important means to catch other participants' eyes so as to initiate a new conversation. This is because associative meaning is embedded in a nickname such that it often signals some sense of the self (e.g. *Blondie* suggesting the user's hair colour). While nicknames in off-screen life are often given by others, nicknames online are invented by oneself as an 'extension of the self' (Bechar-Israeli 1995). The practice of not using real names is not necessarily about creating a fake identity for the virtual world. Rather, it is a way for people to 'explore their potential by "trying on" different kinds of identities' (Jones and Hafner 2012: 79). The practice of creating nicknames or screen-names varies across online platforms and also changes over time. On Flickr, for instance, more people are willing to give themselves screen-names that signal all or part of their real name. As discussed earlier, some Flickr users creatively mix languages in their screen-names to present themselves as a more global person and to speak to a wider range of audience. Elsewhere, for example on LinkedIn and Facebook, people are more likely to participate as someone who is closer to their 'offline' self, and real names are expected.

In many existing studies of language and identity online, features of identity are often quantified, for example, by measuring the average length of messages, counting certain micro-linguistic and grammatical features such as the use of personal pronouns. Gender is one well-explored area of language and identity research within the CMC literature (such as work by Susan Herring and colleagues). For example, it was found that in asynchronous CMC such as discussion forums, male participants tend to use more impersonal expressions (e.g. *It is clear that...*) and write longer messages than females, who are believed to express more personal feelings by using the first-person plural *I*. Of course, generalizations as such have to be handled cautiously. While these features may provide a snapshot of how identities are represented through the structure of a message, a more meaningful study of online identity performance should take into account *why* such features of language exist by observing authentic interactional contexts as well as the message producer's insider perspective. This is also the approach that we would like to take in this chapter. In the context of mobile phone texting (or SMS), Caroline Tagg (2012: 189) shows how gendered identity in text messages is performed through playful and 'repeated performances of brevity, non-standardness, and a speech-like informality'. These discourse features seem to confirm earlier findings in structural analyses of English-based CMC such as those reported in David Crystal's description of 'Netspeak'. Nonetheless, Tagg further argues that such descriptive features need to be understood in the context of interaction, through analysing how texters co-construct and act out their identities. In more multicultural and diasporic settings, online participants may index their identities through multiple language switching.

This chapter presents examples of identity performance in writing spaces and writing activities in various online media. It looks into ways in which identities are performed online in terms of the broader deployment of linguistic resources as well as discourse styles through the lens of situated literacies. Methodologically, a techno-biographic approach is adopted, which allows us to draw upon new media users' lived experience and their relationship with technologies through their life histories.

A TECHNO-BIOGRAPHIC APPROACH TO LANGUAGE AND IDENTITY

People do not need to be IT professionals to master new technologies. Nowadays, anyone can live by technologies. Within higher education, academics spend a great deal of time on the computer. We word-process most of our writing; our lectures and research talks are based on PowerPoint slides and other digitized materials; email is a key channel of communication with students and colleagues; our courses are facilitated by web-based course tools such as Moodle and WebCT; we do much of our bibliographic search on Google Scholar and even read e-journals and e-books more often than printed materials. Of course, this particular book that you are reading now would not have become possible without digital technologies – the authors live in different parts of the world, so much of our work discussion is carried out via email and online video conferencing. Files are shared over Dropbox; we edit each other's drafts using the 'track changes' and commenting features on MS Word. These ways of writing, or *literacy practices,* constitute what we call our *technology-related life* as academics. In other areas of our life, we may be related to a different set of technologies.

People's relationship with technologies often started with acquiring the technical knowledge required to use the computer, such as switching on a machine and logging on to an operating system, using a mouse, double-clicking, opening a browser to surf the net, or even learning to send our first email. Now, using technologies means something more than just using a set of skills – for one thing, most technologies have been domesticated, meaning that they are embedded in our day-to-day activities and the environments in which technologies are used (Berker *et al.* 2005; Silverstone and Haddon 1996). With smart phones and other mobile devices, we are always on and that certainly blurs the boundary between our so-called online and offline lives, and between our public and private personae.

The situated approach to language online taken in this book involves understanding both texts and their associated practices. It is also through studying details of people's everyday relationship with technology that we have been able to closely examine the practices associated with language use and production in online contexts. New media users take up the affordances of the media that they engage in according to their purposes in a particular situation of use. Every single technology user is unique. People develop their own set of practices in response to what they think technologies can do for them in their lives. Studies in different countries have demonstrated the significance of focusing on how exactly technology is experienced by internet users throughout their lives – from childhood through to adulthood. For example, Cynthia Selfe and Gail Hawisher (2004) studied the culture-specific literate activities, or what they call literacies of technology, in the United States through the literacy histories of 20 informants. These literacies are defined as social practices embedded in people's larger cultural ecology. And this ecology is shaped by a number of interrelated factors that affect different ways of using and experiencing technology. Cynthia Carter Ching and Linda Vigdor (2005: 3) added that 'technology experiences are . . . imbued with meaning by the motivations, social interactions, and contexts surrounding technology tools and practices'. A life history approach implies that technologies are not just about 'kids' or 'teenagers' as many previous studies have focused on. After years of experience with technologies, many adults possess their own histories of technology use, in which phases and changes are noted.

In an innovative study of the 'digital histories' of a group of teachers in the UK, Lynda Graham (2008) looks into the relationship between how the teachers first learned about technologies and the ways in which they incorporate technologies into their teaching practices now. This body of work has provided a solid foundation for our understanding of how language use online relates to people's everyday experiences with technologies. One meaningful way of carrying out such studies is through a techno-biographic approach. A *techno-biography*, in short, is a life story in relation to technologies. The notion itself is apparently inspired by the traditional narrative approach to interviews, where an interviewee tells a story about certain significant events in life. Techno-biographic interviews are highly reflexive in nature. The focus is on the participant's encounters with technology at different times and locations throughout their life histories. In her major work on women's technology-related lives, Helen Kennedy (2003) defined techno-biographies as participants' accounts of everyday relationships with technology. Ching and Vigdor's work further refines the notion and considers a techno-biography as participants' encounters with technology 'at various times and in various locations throughout their histories' (Ching and Vigdor 2005: 4).

In a techno-biographic interview, questions for the participants may range from their past experiences with technology, their current uses of technology, to their anticipated future of technology use. How people feel about what they do with technologies is also crucial in understanding possible changes in their practices. The following is a list of the key areas and questions that can be covered in a techno-biographic interview.

Current practices: What are the sites you use most often, and what are the ones you have contributed to?

Participation: Have you commented on news or products? Voted on the quality of service? Submitted a review or a wiki entry? Uploaded pictures or videos for comment?

A day in the life: Think of yesterday, what technologies did you first deal with when you woke up? How did it continue during the day?

Life history: When did you first use a mouse? Send a text message? Search Wikipedia? Start using Facebook?

Transitions: Did you change your practices of keeping people's addresses, arranging to meet friends, using maps, etc.?

Domains of life: Are there differences in your everyday life, your student life, and in any work life? Other domains, such as religion, sports, politics.

Cross-generational comparisons: Differences across generations, parents, grand-parents, children; differences across cultures, friends from other countries; gender differences, prohibitions.

We notice from the limited existing research on techno-biography that interviews have often been seen as the only source of techno-biographic data. Despite its methodological merits, the traditional techno-biographic approach seems one-dimensional, often overly reliant on participants' own recounts. Researchers may remain rather passive and uninformed when it comes to the participants' situated instances of technology use. In our ongoing research on various online platforms, we have identified other forms of techno-biography. New social media provide ample opportunities and ways for online users to write about themselves, thus allowing them to create and constantly update their own auto-biographies. Such sites allow users to retell their life stories through textual means, thus expanding the scope of techno-biographies. Here are a few examples:

- *Creating an online profile*: In late 2011, Facebook launched a new profile layout called Timeline, which has the slogan: 'Tell your life story with a new kind of profile'. This rightly illustrates the auto-biographical affordances of profiles on social network sites. Many popular Web 2.0 spaces such as Facebook, YouTube, and Flickr are structured as a collection of user profiles. A profile is a sketch of the basic information about someone. For example, on a Facebook user profile, information can range from demographic details such as name, location, date of birth, education to one's personal philosophy and favourite movies. The information uploaded immediately becomes part of Facebook's search database, allowing one to be searched for by friends and other acquaintances. These profiles are not only an entry point to social networking, but also a key writing space to explicitly express our sense of self.

- *Continuous status updating:* Another popular form of expressing the self online is writing short messages about our lives, especially feelings and activities, in social media. Many of these short messages, such as status updates on Facebook, are written in the form of short narratives serving a wide range of discourse functions. (See also Lee 2011.) An interesting example that we often find among university students' status updates is counting down the number of words left to be written for an essay.

- *Visual representation:* In addition to the written word, another important form of linguistic representation of techno-biography is *visual images*, especially photographs. On Flickr, photos can be organized into thematic sets. The names given to these sets or albums can serve as a way of telling others one's life history too. Through photography, people can express their favourites and interests, document important events, share interesting places that they have visited and so on. Photos uploaded can be annotated with meaningful titles and tags. On different sites, photos may serve different purposes and express different areas of life. (See Mendelson and Papacharissi 2011 on Facebook photo sharing among college students.)

There are certainly many other ways through which people can share their life stories with others online. These three areas we have listed above, together with in-depth interviews where online participants talk about their technology-related life, then, constitute a rich and comprehensive techno-biography. In our work, techno-biographic interviews were accompanied by a pre-interview survey, close observation of participants' profiles and what they wrote on their sites, as well as screen-recordings. This comprehensive set of data allows us to better understand how identities are performed differently through language in different areas of one's technology-related life.

Focusing on language, this chapter discusses one part of a techno-biography, techno-linguistic biography. In various areas of linguistics, including language acquisition and sociolinguistics, language biographies, that is participants' own account of their life stories where language has a central role, have been used as a method of eliciting insiders' perspectives of how language is acquired or used. (See, for example, Busch *et al.* 2006; Pavlenko 2007.) Our projects studied language online using a similar approach. The techno-linguistic biographies were explored through the following aspects: key phases in a technology-related life, online-offline linguistic repertoires, home-school online experiences, roles to play in life, and people's perceived knowledge of languages.

These themes emerged from a broader study of Hong Kong university students' Web 2.0 writing activities. The project aimed to understand participants' new media writing practices and the possible changes in such practices throughout their lives. While general demographic information about the students was identified in an initial online questionnaire survey, the core data came from detailed techno-biographic-style interviews with 20 participants. Each interview involved a screen recording session, where a student participant was asked to go online for about half an hour with their screen activities recorded using screen-recording software. This was followed by a 30–50-minute interview, centred on pre-determined themes as well as new topics that emerged as the researchers went through the screen-recording with the participant. These student participants shared a similar set of linguistic resources. That is, they speak Cantonese as their primary language in everyday life, while having knowledge of standard written Chinese, a standard written variety taught in school and used in institutional contexts. Written Cantonese may also be used for informal purposes. English is used as a second language, and mixing Chinese and English in utterances is a prevalent linguistic practice in Hong Kong. In addition to these resources, some participants reported to know an additional Chinese dialect or foreign language. In the following, we briefly describe and discuss the techno-linguistic life stories of two university students in Hong Kong.

Tony's techno-linguistic biography

Tony was a third-year undergraduate student majoring in English Language Education at a university in Hong Kong. In other words, he was training to be a teacher of English for speakers of other languages. He reported to have about 10 years of computing experience and was a regular user of email, IM, Facebook, forums, and blogs.

Tracing his life history, in the beginning, it was his elder brother who introduced him to the internet world – playing games online with strangers from other parts of the world. That was when he was about 9 or 10 years old. He said he was too little to have his own computer account. So his elder brother helped him sign up at an online game site. He recalled that all the instructions and interface of the games that he used to play were written in English only. The language was too complicated for him then, he said, but he could work out how the games were played by trial and error. Still, Tony wanted to interact with overseas gamers who he had never met. So he decided to use simple English phrases such as 'good' or 'good game' to socialize with other gamers.

Getting to his senior high school years, he started chatting with friends quite frequently on IM (MSN Messenger). That was also the time when Tony started to take up the social affordances of Chinese messages, as they sounded friendlier and could more accurately represent himself. He explained:

> I can think faster in Chinese so I can form a sentence easily . . . If I write in English (online) I have to check my grammar.

> When chatting in MSN, I use Chinese most of the time . . . Most of my friends speak Cantonese . . . We know each other very well . . . Communicating in Cantonese with them is more accurate than in English . . . I can say what I want to say in Cantonese . . . and there are 'fashionable' words in Cantonese that can't be captured in English

Different senses of the Chinese language were mentioned in Tony's techno-linguistic biography. From time to time, he would visit and post in mainland Chinese-based online discussion forums, on which most participants interacted in Mandarin Chinese, who were not used to mixing languages in their everyday communication as HongKongers would. However, Tony explained:

> I am a Chinese too . . . Chinese is my mother tongue [. . .] When I participate in Chinese-based forums, most people use Chinese . . . If you switch to English, that shows you are a Hong Kong person . . . I am not saying that I am special . . . but using English may offend the mainland Chinese forum participants.

Here, Chinese is seen as the language that 'validates' his Chinese identity. But at the same time he was well aware of his Hong Kong identity too, with a rather different historical and political background, thus a different range of linguistic resources to draw upon. This is how Tony projects his perceived national identity online, which is only one of the many aspects of identity that he performed online through language choice.

Tony's techno-linguistic life also revolved around his student identity. In the interviews, he often referred to his major subject, and how his language choice was affected by his identity as an English language major. Tony gave me this anecdote that made reference to his involvement in a student society and how that affects his attitudes towards online language choice:

> I used to be the chairperson of the EngEd [English Education] society. I once wrote a formal email to my cabinet members. One of them then wrote back a long email in English. I was so angry. The official language of the student society was Chinese, while English was just a supplementary language. I am sure he knew the policy and he also knew that I understood Chinese . . . why write back in English? I even had to look words up in a dictionary! I was offended!

From time to time, Tony explicitly restated his preferred language online:

> Although my major subject is English Language Education, my friends know that I prefer Chinese (when communicating online).

However, it seemed that this preference for Chinese was restricted mainly to private and interpersonal communication. Tony, as a pre-service teacher, kept in touch with the students in his teaching practice school on Facebook. For this particular group of audience, Tony signed up for a new Facebook account where he calls himself 'Teaching Tony'.

> I started this teacher Facebook account towards the end of my teaching practice. I was worried that if my students discovered my 'real' Facebook account, I had to reshape my identity for them.

When asked what he meant by *reshaping* his identity, Tony explained:

> When interacting with students online, I always use English. Otherwise, I can't establish my image [as an English language teacher].

Compared to his other Facebook account, Tony posted less regularly on this teacher site. He also took on a more academic discourse style and he would only share posts that are of interest to his students, such as a link to an online English dictionary, posts about the progress of his teaching and grading work, etc. He wrote almost all the posts in English, because the target readers were students and his colleagues from the school where he did his teaching practice. He said it would have been inappropriate to use Chinese there because as an English teacher, he had to stick to this medium of instruction in order to encourage students to write to him in English too.

Doing his best to maintain his image as a school teacher, Tony was very conscious of privacy issues and his level of self-exposure on his teacher Facebook wall. On his teacher Facebook, he tended to shift to a more formal, non-interpersonal style of writing:

> When I leave a comment on my colleague's Facebook page, I know that some of his students may be able to see it . . . so I pretend to sound serious and formal . . . so that our students would think that we are talking about something constructive . . . I take time to polish and edit [my comments]

As of early 2012, Tony has already graduated and teaches English at a local secondary school. He is still working hard to maintain and juggle between these different aspects of his public and private senses of self through linguistic means. His teacher Facebook account still has fewer, but more polished English posts addressing a group of student 'friends'; his other account still remains an expressive and affective site where he interacts with his 'real' friends in his non-teaching life.

Yan's Techno-linguistic Biography

Yan was a second-year History major. She was born in mainland China and moved to Hong Kong with her parents when she was around 10. Before arriving in Hong Kong, Yan spoke mostly Hakka, a southern Chinese dialect, at home with her parents and school friends, though also knew Cantonese. Ever since she moved to Hong Kong, she and her family all switched to Cantonese even at home. Yan specifically told us how surprised she was about the 'sudden' switch of language at home.

Her first memory of computer use was computer gaming around 2003. She remembered this year vividly because it was the year when the SARS pandemic attacked Hong Kong. Schools were suspended for months. She had to stay at home most of the time so playing games on the computer seemed to be the best activity to kill time. Her first real 'online' experience was actually a school assignment in which she was asked to send five emails to her Chinese teacher as a kind of self-reflection task. Since then, she started communicating with teachers and friends regularly via email, in standard written Chinese. She used to be an active blogger. On her blog, she wrote longer pieces of narratives, reflecting upon life and so on. At the same time, her younger sister introduced her to the world of IM by signing her up on ICQ, which used to be the most popular IM programme in Hong Kong before MSN took over. IM, according to Yan, was reserved for private and interpersonal interaction with close friends and family. On IM, she would still insist on writing in standard Chinese, even if her chat partners wrote in English. Now as a university student, she felt that she used IM less often than when she was a secondary school student. Facebook has become a major social network site on which she frequently posts her feelings and everyday activities.

She considered Chinese, mostly standard written Chinese, mixed with Cantonese writing, as her main written language on all these platforms. She said this was partly due to her mainland Chinese background, but the major reason behind her preference for Chinese was that she had very little exposure to English ever since she started university. As her major subjects are taught in Mandarin Chinese, she did not see the need to use English regularly. Yan also affectively attached herself to Chinese. She insisted that on her blog, she had to write in Standard Written Chinese. She explained:

> I usually blog about in-depth feelings and I want to use a serious language to express myself.

Despite her personal attachment to Chinese, Yan felt that she had to brush up her English for more practical reasons. She had never had any proper English education before she arrived in Hong Kong, where she received formal English lessons in school. She had always felt that she was lagging behind. This had not bothered her too much until one time she failed to answer questions at a scholarship interview where she was required to speak English throughout. Since then, she thought she should better equip herself. One thing that she thought would help was to listen to English songs regularly on YouTube. Yan saw that as a good way of exposing herself to the English language. At other times, Chinese still remained as her primary language online. Yan's knowledge of Hakka dialect also gave rise to creativity in her texting activities. From time to time, she would write and receive text messages written in Hakka with her friends back home in mainland China. However, Hakka itself is not a written language (at least there is no standardized written form). So Yan and her friends playfully invented a system for Hakka by using similar sounding characters in standard Chinese. At first she found some of those 'stylized' Hakka messages sent by her friends incomprehensible, but she gradually enjoyed the process of exchanging and decoding them.

The stories of Tony and Yan clearly demonstrate that technologies play rather different roles in different people's life histories. One thing that technology users do share in common is that everyone deploys their language resources according to the changing meanings of technologies in different stages of their life. There are also other important factors that enable us to characterize a techno-linguistic biography. These factors allow us to understand how people's relations with technologies change their language practices and attitudes towards language online. In the following, we describe in detail five important themes that characterize people's techno-linguistic biographies: key phrases of technology use, home-school experience with technologies, online-offline linguistic resources, extension of offline identity, and people's attitudes towards language online.

Key phases of technology use

In the 20 techno-linguistic biographies, the participants tended to narrate their relationship with technologies chronologically and could identify major turning points in their technology-related lives. These include how they first got started, how they explored and developed their online linguistic practices, and what technologies mean to them now.

- **First encounter:** The first phase of one's techno-linguistic life is also the first phase of one's broader techno-biography. Our first linguistic experiences online involve a great deal of reading and writing activities, such as trying to understand how a software is installed by reading instructions on the screen, sending our first email or text message, and for some of these young participants in our projects, their first computing experience could be related to a piece of homework for a computer class. Technology mentors, people who first introduce us to technologies, also play a crucial role in this first phase. As we have seen in the above cases, Tony's elder brother introduced him to the world of online gaming, where English was the dominant language, and Yan wrote her first email in Chinese because her Chinese language teacher told her to do so.

- **Exploration:** This is the phase in life where the computer is regularly used but not seen as essential. This is also the time when we start learning to develop our online linguistic practices according to needs and purposes. For the group of university students (who were born in late 80s or early 90s), this exploration phase started in primary or secondary school years. CMC was used mostly for entertainment and interpersonal chat with friends.

- **'Taken-for-grantedness' of technologies:** The third main phase is concerned with the participants' current practices online and how they imagine what the future of digital life would be like. In this phase, technologies are perceived as indispensible and are indeed taken for granted. These attitudes are reflected in the following comments:

> I don't know how to kill time if there's no Facebook.
>
> *(Mick)*

> Telephone talks seem weird now. I text or MSN if I want to arrange to meet my friends.
>
> *(Mark)*

> Without the internet, it would be hard to look up information for my assignments!
> *(Carrie)*

Home-school experience with technologies

The second theme is the relationship between home use and school-based use of technologies. Both Tony and Yan frequently referred to their experiences at home and in school when telling their technology-related life stories. When they first got started, their language use online was very much shaped by what their brother/sister did at home. At the same time, homework and school projects were often mentioned in relation to their early techno-linguistic lives:

> I wrote my first email to my Economics teacher when I was in Secondary Four. One day I chatted with her on icq. We talked about songs. I promised her to send her some great songs that I had heard. So I got her email address and attached a few songs in the mail that I sent her. It was a very rough email with not much editing done in terms of content and language because at that time I didn't mean to share words with her but merely songs. I enjoyed writing to her afterwards and I started bombarding her email account with lots of informal letters. I just loved writing to her.
>
> *(Yan)*

Such early home-school experiences not only introduced the participants to technologies but also changed their attitudes towards the affordances of such media, as well as their awareness of online genres. The new media platforms that they often used at home for interpersonal purposes such as IM did not always match with their technology experiences in school, which were often assessed by teachers.

Online-offline linguistic resources

The third feature that shapes participants' techno-linguistic biographies is the language resources used in offline language activities. For example, we saw that Yan's interesting Hakka background broadens the resources she could draw upon in mobile phone texting. It is thus useful to find out what language(s) research participants would prefer to use in different offline situations such as: reading a newspaper, reading a novel, writing a formal letter, writing post-it notes, form filling, talking to family at home, etc. The aim was to find out how the language they used in other contexts may carry over to online ones, like whether they would read English news online, and the language they would use to write email, blogs, text messages, Facebook status updates, and keyword searches in Google Scholar when they look up info for assignments. Such data offer a snapshot of the relationship between the online and the offline language practices in the participants' technology related lives.

Extension of offline identity

In the techno-linguistic biographies that we have studied, the student participants often juxtaposed their language use online with the roles that they play in different areas of life, such as a student of a certain subject area, a friend, a family member, a speaker of a certain language, etc. Tony's case illustrates how he manages his student and teacher identities on his two Facebook accounts through specific language choice. English allows Tony to assert a professional identity and to appear as a proficient English user to his student 'friends'. Writing in a serious style and proofreading his English carefully in his teacher Facebook account is how Tony performs 'facework' on Facebook (West and Trester, forthcoming), a way to avoid any face-threatening act caused by grammatical errors. In his ordinary Facebook account, by contrast, writing in Chinese and code-switching expresses positive politeness, thus indexing himself as a friendly classmate and a close friend. A similar story is told by another participant, Mark. In the following excerpt, Mark explains how English means different things in different online platforms:

> I would leave Facebook comments in English because most of my Facebook friends are also English majors like me . . . because we are used to communicating in English. But at the same time, it is also because I am an English major that I want to avoid using English in public forums . . . People may judge me if I make mistakes.
>
> (Mark)

Mark's language choice online demonstrates his ambivalent feelings towards his identity as an English major. When among his fellow English majors, he was happy to foreground his English major identity by maintaining the use of English where occasional 'errors' are tolerated; at other times, he would recognize his possible insufficient English knowledge, which may not fit in well with his self-concept of an English student. Mark's perception about his English is also situated within the larger context of public moral panics about university students' 'falling' linguistic standards in Hong Kong and beyond. Because of this, Mark decided to avoid using English altogether when participating in public online forums. This is nonetheless a good piece of evidence showing how people manage their impression through language online.

Another aspect of identity that is often projected through language online is people's national identity. In the project, many participants stressed their ethnicity or place of origin when explaining their language choice, as in Tony's comment here:

> I am a Chinese too . . . I want to use my mother tongue.
>
> (Tony)

Tony explicitly expresses his Chineseness when talking about his participation in Chinese-based online forums. In Yan's techno-biography, her playful Hakka text messages serve to mark her unique linguistic background as not just an average Hong Kong person, but one who also has a root in southern China. These examples also suggest the deconstruction of the traditional separation of online identities and offline identities. As we have seen, identities are fluid and the so-called online world is yet another domain where people perform their identities.

Attitudes towards language online

Finally, people's life histories with technologies are largely shaped by their perceptions and attitudes towards languages. Identity is also 'the social positioning of self and other' (Bucholtz and Hall 2005: 586). In the techno-linguistic biographies that we studied, some participants reveal their linguistic and cultural identities through aligning themselves with certain groups of speakers. For example, when Tony talked about his participation in Chinese-based online forums, he identified himself as a Chinese national who was expected to write in Chinese, while being aware that he would have used some English as a Hong Konger. Such conscious positioning and repositioning are helpful in revealing the participant's stance towards different languages (see Chapter 7).

Another key factor shaping or causing changes in the participants' techno-linguistic lives is related to the user's perceived knowledge of a certain language. In Yan's story above, we learned that her preference for Chinese was due to her limited exposure to English. A similar remark was also made by another participant, Helen:

I never write an entire blog entry in English, as my English isn't good . . . I came from a Chinese-medium school, you know.

(Helen)

Helen explained her choice of a certain language in terms of some kind of self-deprecatory comments about the languages they know ('my English isn't good'). Nonetheless, Helen pointed out that this was also due to her lack of exposure to English in her secondary education. This shows how past experience is useful in understanding people's current practices. Such meta-linguistic discourses are quite commonly expressed among the university students that we studied. In fact, we have observed that these self-evaluations of language are equally prevalent in the writing produced by users of public online platforms such as Flickr and YouTube. Talking about knowledge of a certain language not only helps declare one's linguistic identity, this also seems to have become a salient practice in many forms of online participation (see Chapter 8).

CONSTRUCTING GLOCAL IDENTITIES IN PUBLIC ONLINE SPACES

So far the discussion of identities online revolves around online interaction at a more private level (e.g. Facebook, email, and IM among close friends). When it comes to identity performance on public platforms such as Flickr, a different scene is observed. The key difference lies in their different target audience groups. On Facebook, users know and can control who reads what on their profiles and the audience ('friends') is often known to the user. On Flickr, however, audience is often 'imagined'. Like many social network sites, there exist ample opportunities to write about the self on Flickr – from textual means to visual. One of the all-time most popular tags on Flickr is indeed the first-person pronoun 'me'. We notice that pictures tagged with 'me' or even 'this is me' are not only photos of self-portraits (which can include a part of oneself like an eye), but they could be photos capturing other senses of the self. We have also seen pictures of birthday cakes tagged with 'me'. In addition, 'me' sometimes serves the purpose of authenticating the photo and asserts the authority of the photographer (i.e. this picture was taken by *me*, not anyone else).

Chapters 4 and 5 have already shown how multilingual practices are salient in public Web 2.0 sites such as Flickr and YouTube. Flickr members often negotiate their language choice by taking into account the kind of identity they wish to project to an imagined audience. Although this language-identity relationship may also be found in other forms of CMC such as diasporic websites and email (Warschauer 2002; Androutsopoulos 2006), a stronger sense of global self is frequently articulated on Flickr. Our Spanish informant *Carolink* said she had never participated in a global network like Flickr before, and yet she had gradually identified herself as a bilingual global citizen. She said that participating in Spanish only is 'too limited for these Internet times. I do not leave Spanish, but I try to use English when I can.'

This aspect is underlined by the fact that several people who do not need to use English in other areas of life are also ready to interact with other members in English.

However, the quote from *Carolink* contains the other aspect of the relationship between language and globalization, where she says '*I do not leave Spanish*'. This sense leads to heterogeneity of culture. In other words, instead of seeing the web as a culturally and linguistically unified space, a truly globalized community should be a dynamic and diversified one, which allows space for different cultures and languages to develop simultaneously. People want to be part of the global world without giving up their existing identities. This can be seen in that both Chinese and Spanish are in themselves lingua francas across a range of countries. Some Spanish users certainly identified the broader Spanish-speaking world as an important audience for them. Similarly our mainland Chinese informant, *sating*, associated her global Flickr identity with Chinese rather than with English. She explained:

> If Flickr is a global website, as a Chinese, why must I use English, a language that I am not good at? Besides, most of my photos reflect the reality of China. So Chinese has to be the most suitable tool of communication.
>
> (*sating*)

sating's view challenges the globally recognized status of English as the lingua franca on the internet. Whichever sense of the global is taken, *sating*'s self-reflection about her Chineseness and her discourse of resistance to English reveal a strong awareness of her local identity on Flickr. Such a marker of local identity is useful in that it can attract Chinese-speaking Flickr users within China and beyond, and it helps promote her cultural and linguistic backgrounds to the international Flickr community.

The tension between the local and global is also expressed by way of bilingual screen-names. For example, *Kristie* 遊牧民阿靜's explanation for her bilingual screen-name reveals a close relationship between her language choice and her sense of local:

> I want a wider group of people to know me. Not that the Chinese won't know me if I call myself just Kristie but if I attached a more 'graphic' Chinese word (that's how I always see the language), we can connect quicker and better. The name also says alot about who I am in my whole darn life.
>
> (*Kristie* 遊牧民阿靜)

This further confirms that English on Flickr does not necessarily reflect users' competence in the language, nor does it automatically reveal one's ethnicity. Language choice on Flickr, we argue, is closely related to the extent to which participants intend to project themselves as *global* or *local* members of Flickr.

The negotiation between global and local languages and identities on Flickr is best understood in terms of *glocalization*. Participating as a glocal person is an important way for multilingual Flickr members to maximize the accessibility of their sites, as where they explain their local culture to the world. Writing multilingually is utilized as one of the essential literacy practices for people to project glocal identities online. A Chinese Flickr user *cjPanda*'s profile page is a clear instantiation of her shift from a *global* to a *glocal* participant. Her profile was originally written only in English; but as she made contact with more Chinese people, she decided to spend a summer translating her profile and other English texts on her site into Chinese. Similarly, the Spanish Flickr users make strategic decisions about when to write in Spanish (or Catalan) and when to use English.

Here we see the two-way relationship of glocalization, the 'mutually interdependent processes by which globalization- deepens- localization- deepens-globalization and so on' (Urry 2003: 84). However, to date, much emphasis has been on local appropriation of the global, as when an international coffee company adapts their cafes to particular countries and cultures, and as when global hip-hop culture is localized through local languages (e.g. Alim and Pennycook 2009; Androutsopoulos 2009). However, in our study of multilingual practices on Flickr, we are seeing more of the opposite: people using the local to write the global, while striking a balance between their local and global netizenships.

A TEXTUALLY MEDIATED SELF IN A CHANGING WORLD

The dynamics presented by new media enable people to constantly display, construct, perform, shape and reshape different senses of the self online through linguistic means. This is illustrated in the examples discussed in this chapter. Here, we end the chapter by summarizing some of our observations about the relationship between language, life, and identity online:

(i)   Writing online is writing oneself into being. In other words, whenever we write a post, make a comment on another person's post, upload an image, create a profile, we are also constructing an auto-biography, a narrative of who we are and what kind of person we want others to see us. These writing practices may project new identities, or enable us to extend our offline selves. As our identities travel between on and off the screen, we are blurring the traditional boundary between the online and the offline.

(ii) When we participate in new online media, we are not just behaving as one single self. We are networked individuals (Wellman 2001; Raine and Wellman 2012), a part of a community in which people are connected to one another. Thus, when we write about ourselves online, we write for different groups of people. This target audience may be expected (for example people we already know) or imagined (as with any public web users whom we have never met). Thus, the way we manage our impression may change over time according to different kinds of audience.

(iii) For multilingual online participants, the research reported here has shown how switching between languages is a salient practice in performing identities in public web spaces.

(iv) A techno-biographic approach helps us understand transitions and changes of practices in experienced technology users' lives. A focus on past experience reveals how older practices shape newer ones. It also enables us to understand experienced online users' changing attitudes towards the language they use online. Two important factors that shape changes are the perceived affordances of the medium in use and the perceived affordances of different languages, that is, what identity work that we think a language can or cannot do for us.

(v) Paying attention to self-presentation online is a process of exploring and discovering new aspects of the self. On Flickr, for example, some participate in a project called 365, where people upload a photo a day for a year. Many people also provide quite detailed descriptions around these photos. These multimodal self-presentation acts online may be interpreted as new ways of learning in the contemporary world, which we will discuss in Chapter 9.

(vi) Last, the social practice angle of literacy taken in this book allows us to situate online literacy practices within a participant's cultural and linguistic ecology, believing that ways with technologies and languages are embedded in individuals' lived experiences, which may change at different points in time. As such, young online users, though sharing similar online activities, are certainly not a homogeneous *digital natives* generation. Every individual has a unique technology-related life, revealing how different aspects of identity are developed over time.

7

STANCE-TAKING THROUGH LANGUAGE AND IMAGE

- Expressing stance in online writing spaces
- Stance-taking and photo sharing online
- Flickr as a stance-rich environment
- Two case studies of multimodal stance-taking on Flickr
- Taking into account the researcher's stance
- Stance-taking as a powerful tool for analysing language online

---

EXPRESSING STANCE IN ONLINE WRITING SPACES

Writing spaces in new digital media not only offer opportunities for multilingual texts and self-representation, they also serve as new domains for people to express their opinions and attitudes on many topics, alongside traditional modes of communication such as face-to-face talk and written texts. Whether someone is posting a status update on Facebook, giving a caption to an image uploaded on Flickr, blogging, or leaving a comment on YouTube, they frequently articulate their opinions, feelings or attitudes towards something or someone. Here are two examples from a university student's Facebook status update:

> Ariel loves her new bed and her refurnished room! yoho ∧_∧
> Ariel knows writing is re-writing.

The first statement expresses how Ariel feels about her refurbished bedroom. This is marked by the use of a particular emotive verb 'loves'. The interjection 'yoho' and an emoticon '^_^' probably indicate her excitement and joy. In the second statement, Ariel, who was then taking creative writing courses at the time of updating her status, reflects upon what she knows about the process of writing through the use of the cognitive verb 'know'. In both statements Ariel is doing more than just making a statement about the world; in one she is expressing her feelings, in the other she is expressing her relationship to what is expressed in the statement. In other words she is expressing her *stance* towards what she is talking about. Ariel's opinion statements are constructed through the act of *stance-taking* (Du Bois 2007; Jaffe 2009). The first statement is an example of *affective stance* signalling feelings of the speaker, while her second example illustrates her *epistemic stance*, signalling her knowledge and belief towards her statement.

Stance has become an important concept within linguistics as it brings together a wide range of research on how utterances' meanings are expressed and how speakers (or writers) address their audience. Stance, in short, refers to the position people take in relation to oneself, to what is said, and to other people or objects. (See the more detailed definition in Chapter 3.) Stance is marked through particular forms of language but also through other resources for meaning making. In any given stance statement, there are three major components – the person expressing the stance, the topic being discussed and the resources being drawn upon. In the above status updates, *Ariel* is the stance-taker, the person who takes a position; 'her new bed and her refurnished room' and 'writing' would be her stance objects, that is, what her stance relates to; the verbs, 'yoho', and '^_^' are her stance resources, particular word choices and style through which her stance is expressed. As a Chinese-English bilingual, Ariel also has additional linguistic resources that allow her to express different stances. The fact that her status updates are written in English is also an act of self-positioning. Stance-taking is, however, an interactive and intersubjective act. This means that a stance statement is often directed to and interpreted by a particular audience. How the speaker and the hearer (or reader and writer) understand the stance statement may then shape further stance utterances in the interaction. Therefore, to the elements of stance-taker, stance object, and stance resources, we add a fourth component, the *addressee*, who may be the reader or the hearer in any stance-taking situation.

Stance-taking has become a key discursive act in online interaction. Not only does it signal the stance-takers' opinions, through careful choice of vocabulary and other resources, some may also want to assert a unique sense of self in order to stand out in a larger community of stance-takers. In other words, stance is also a public act. This is particularly true in public online spaces such as YouTube and blogs. Blogs, for example, are sites where opinions are expressed frequently and often explicitly through specific word choice and are therefore a good place to examine stance. Greg Myers (2010b) carried out a corpus analysis of the most frequently occurring linguistic stance markers in five public discussion blogs. He found that common linguistic strategies for stance-marking are cognitive verbs (e.g. I *think*, I *guess,* I *know*), stance adverbs (*really, actually*), and conversational particles (*ooh, hey*). As Myers points out, such stance markers should not be taken in a straightforward manner as a signal of one's own opinions; often, they serve the additional purpose of relating to other people or their comments, as in one of the examples quoted in his article:

> Mcmama, *I think* the point isn't that the curiosity itself is racist.
>
> (*Bitch PhD*)

The expression 'I think' does not serve to claim any knowledge, but to clarify that another commenter *Mcmama* has misinterpreted the original post. In addition, disagreeing indirectly can serve as a device to signal *politeness* and to avoid any possible threat to *Mcmama*'s self image, or *face.* Politeness has been an important aspect of online communication, discussed in Herring (1994). In the earlier days of computer-mediated communication, rules of 'netiquette' were proposed to govern people's online behaviour. One such rule is that people should not write their messages in ALL CAPS, which is considered as shouting and an example of *flaming* behaviour, i.e. offensive and aggressive language, often directed to a specific person (see Moor *et al.* 2010 on flaming on YouTube). Messages that flame certainly violate linguistic politeness, which makes use of linguistic devices to play down possible face threats to the addressee. *Bitch PhD*'s indirect disagreement in the above example makes use of *negative politeness* strategy, which aims to reduce any possible imposition on *Mcmama*. This example also illustrates an important point about stance-taking: stance is not just about how an individual marks their stance, but also about what communicative acts one wants to achieve by doing so, and how stance-marking facilitates interaction within a larger context, such as a community of bloggers.

What we have dealt with so far suggests that stance-taking online is largely a monomodal linguistic act. In addition to the written word, many Web 2.0 media provide built-in features that invite people to express opinions publicly through *multimodal* means. A common feature shared by Web 2.0 sites is a system of *rating* posts and comments by way of clicking a button or a link. YouTube provides thumbs up and thumbs down buttons for people to rate the videos and comments that they like or dislike. On Flickr, members can add others' photos as 'favorites' and the more 'faves' one gets, the more 'interesting' the photo is. Facebook also introduced the famous 'Like' button to allow users to 'give positive feedback and connect with things you care about' (Facebook 2012). Items that can be 'liked' include status updates, photos, links, fans pages, and sponsors' adverts. Users can also 'like' webpages from outside Facebook so that they will be shared on their Facebook newsfeed. These intended uses of the Like button, however, have been constantly reinterpreted by users. The following are some of the pragmatic functions of Facebook 'Like' that we have observed:

- to express positive stance (i.e. literally like something) but not want to leave a written comment;
- to express interest in the post or the content of it;
- to show support to the content poster;
- to agree or align with the stance of the status poster;
- to answer 'yes' to a question raised in the post;
- to indicate that the post has been read.

These different uses once again show that language alone (i.e. the word 'like') does not immediately signal stances. The action of clicking the 'like' button is packed with various social meanings and pragmatic functions. Take personal video blogs (vlogs) on YouTube as a further example of multimodal stance-taking: the content in a video, presented through motion and speech, always signals the stance of the vloggers, who align themselves with certain kinds of knowledge, attitude, or emotion. At the same time, the vloggers may also draw on written language and give the video a title, subtitles, annotations, tags and some additional information. In personal vlogs, for example, quite often the additional written information creates a humorous effect to attract viewers. And to some, humour serves to attract more subscribers to their channels. The more humorous their vlogs appear, the more likely their videos get viewed and their channels subscribed to. Humour, in this way, is seen as vloggers' social capital in their YouTube participation (Lien 2012). The 'comments' feature allows YouTubers to jointly produce their stance on various aspects of the video uploaded. Some may align with the vlogger's stance, while others may take an opposing stance. Sometimes these comments may directly refer to the content of the video uploaded; at other times the commenters may shift topics and initiate new discussion topics among themselves. YouTubers come from all parts of the world, possessing a wide range of multilingual resources. Some may choose to comment in a language that the original vlogger does not know. Such acts of multimodal-multilingual stance-taking are usually self-generated at the beginning and later become collaborative. They are a salient form of vernacular practice that new digital media have made possible. It is such dynamic, cross-modal, interactive forms of stance-taking that we highlight in this chapter.

We first describe different types of stance online. We use Flickr as our primary site of interest. It is a particularly suitable site for understanding stance-taking online because, while its primary focus is photographs, a great deal of written opinion is expressed around the photo uploaded. We then discuss stance-taking on two Flickr photo pages as case studies illustrating multimodal and multilingual stance-taking in new online spaces. We end the chapter by discussing how stance-taking provides a useful analytical tool for understanding language and meta-language online.

STANCE-TAKING AND PHOTO SHARING ONLINE

There are many approaches through which we can study stance-taking but using stance to understand language in new media is a very recent research direction. In addition to Myers' work on blogging, which we have discussed in the previous section, many scholars have been interested in a specific perspective of stance. For example, Walton and Jaffe (2011) and Chun and Walters (2011) deal with the issue of race in digital discourse. Walton and Jaffe (2011) discuss how ideologies of race and class are articulated through humour by the author and commenters of the blog *Stuff White People Like*. Also looking at race, Chun and Walters (2011) analyse discourse of Orientalisms on YouTube. We shall return to this line of research in a later part of this chapter. These previous studies have made an important point about stance-taking, that is, stance is not always explicitly asserted. It needs to be inferred and interpreted in relation to a number of contextual factors. A multidimensional approach to stance-taking is thus essential when studying what stance means to the stance-taker and the recipient. In line with our broader work on language and literacy practices online, our approach to stance-taking is grounded in a combination of linguistic analysis and ethnographic insights. Our aim here is not to start with a particular form of stance or stance marker, but to provide an overview of some major types of stance we have observed. When interpreting how stance-taking works, we situate the stance utterance in the immediate situation of use. In the case of Flickr, any act of stance-taking is situated in a photo page that we see as cohesive texts situated within the larger context of a user profile and the broader Flickr site. In our analysis, we focus on how different semiotic modes (images and words) and writing spaces (title, description, tags, comments, sets and groups) work together in an act of stance-taking. Stance-taking is interactive in nature, meaning that a stance-taker always relates to others when a stance is expressed. In view of this, we take into account the dynamic relationship between the stance-takers, their stance resources and the stance objects towards which a stance is expressed.

Stance-takers: On Flickr, two broad categories of stance-takers can be identified – the photographer and the viewer. There are many kinds of viewer and we see ourselves, the researchers, as a particular type of viewer too. In many cases, it is hardly possible to determine who exactly the **photographer** is due to Flickr's open-endedness or what is referred to as complex footing (Goffman 1981; Thurlow and Jaworski 2011), referring to the different possible participation roles that are made possible on the site. The person who posted the photo may or may not be the one who took it; likewise, the person posing in a photograph may or may not be the photo poster. There may be clues to this elsewhere on the page, for instance in the tags. For the sake of analysis, we focus only on photo pages where the photographer is also the content poster and the site owner. That is one of the reasons why having direct contact with the site owner is crucial in understanding language online. A second type of stance-taker is the **viewer**. Anyone online can view Flickr and they might do so for a wide range of purposes. They can be other Flickr members who express their stance in the form of comments and tags. Note that the photographer may leave comments on his/her own photos too. Thus, a stance-taker may take on multiple roles. A particular type of viewer is the **researcher-analyst** – that is us. We as researchers bring in our own reading paths, world views and all kinds of background know-ledge to serve our specific purposes when interpreting the stance taken by our research participants. It is important that we make our own stance explicit while writing about our observations, so as to acknowledge that our analysis shown here offers only one of the many possible interpretations of the data.

Stance resources: On Flickr, the act of posting something onto Flickr itself is already an act of stance-taking. The image itself can be edited in a way that it indexes a certain kind of position of the stance-taker; for multilingual participants, the languages that they choose to express their stance is a key stance marker. As we discussed in Chapter 5, the decision to include or exclude a language in any situation is certainly an act of positioning and expression of identity.

Stance objects: People on Flickr not only express their views on images and photography. In our study, people also talk about themselves and others, or events related to the content of the photo; some may discuss features on Flickr; and interestingly, many also express their attitudes towards languages. (This will be pursued in Chapter 8.) Stance-takers may also opt to project their sense of self through a particular style of writing, such as taking on an 'expert' voice when talking about photography, or the inclusion of a local slang term when interacting with people who speak the same language. These styles and tones are all available for Flickr users to draw on as stance resources.

With these key elements in the stance-taking process in mind, the analysts can ask themselves questions pertaining to these elements. In Appendix 1, we provide a framework that has guided us through our stance analysis on Flickr. This guideline not only allows us to better understand stance from the perspectives of the photographer, viewer, and researcher, it also goes beyond the immediate context of stance-taking. The basic unit of our stance analysis on Flickr is a photo page. Several sets of questions can be asked in an analysis of stance on a multimodal web page such as a Flickr photo page. These questions aim to facilitate our observation of acts and markers of stance on one photo page from three dimensions: the photographer, the viewer, and the researcher. There is also a 'broadening out' phase which aims to elicit information that may not be readily available in the text in question. For example, we can look for intertextual clues by observing other photos uploaded in the users' photo streams. We can also study their profile pages to find out more about their lives and so on. Note that this framework is not designed exclusively for the study of Flickr; all studies of stance-taking involving multimodal online texts can easily modify this list of questions as a basic framework of analysis.

FLICKR AS A STANCE-RICH ENVIRONMENT

Flickr can be referred to as a 'stance-rich' online environment (Jones *et al.* 2011). The site provides users with a number of optional writing spaces and affordances that encourage opinions and knowledge sharing, through which different types of stance are expressed. To start with, any act of adding something to these writing spaces is an act of stance-taking. One may decide to give their photo a title or leave the space blank, while others may prefer to take full advantage of these writing spaces to *say something* about any stance object. With this broader framework in mind, in our Flickr research project we carried out a case study of the stance-taking of 10 Flickr users' sites. To facilitate this analysis, we deliberately selected users who frequently gave titles, descriptions, and tags to their uploaded content. These 10 users also received comments from others from time to time. Our first task was to identify the common kinds of stance that were often expressed by these Flickr users, as discussed below.

Epistemic stance

Expressing epistemic stance is the stating of facts, knowledge, or beliefs towards certain stance objects. Acts of epistemic stance marking are easy to spot in various writing spaces on Flickr. We have seen people asserting knowledge of what is shown in their photos through providing detailed information about it. The following example, also discussed in Chapter 4, comes from the photo page of *Tinn Tian*, a Chinese participant. Underneath his photo, which displays a famous dish of duck blood curd, *Tinn Tian* writes:

毛血旺

Maoxuewang, a dish of boiled blood curd and other stuff with another name: Duck Blood in Chili Sauce

The main title, which gives just the name of the dish, is written in Chinese only. In English, by contrast, he writes more about the actual ingredients of the dish. Through indicating his insider knowledge with these epistemic utterances, Tinn Tian relates to the global audience on Flickr who may have never come across this dish before. Quite often people gave Wikipedia-like descriptions (and sometimes direct quotes from Wikipedia), such as:

The bridge of Dee was built following a bequest of £20,000 by Bishop William Elphonstone who died in 1514. The bridge was completed by Bishop Gavin Dunbar. It was nearly all rebuilt 1718–23, and in 1841 was widened from 14 to 26 feet under the direction of Aberdeen City Architect John Smith. Until 1832, it was the only access to the city from the south. The bridge still features the original 16th-century piers, coats of arms and passing places.

(meinx)

Some Flickr users, whether they are professionals or have just taken up photography, often position themselves as photographers by way of listing their gear such as cameras and lenses on their profile pages and even tagging the photo with details of the camera used (e.g. *Canon600D, 50mm*); others would see Flickr as a space for learning more about photography (as developed in Chapter 9) and thus they would clearly mark their (lack of) photographic knowledge, often explicitly with 'I know. . .', as shown in the following examples taken from the Flickr sites of *Kristie* and *DG:*

> All I knew was a lot of people took pictures of this, so I did the same thing~
>
> (*Kristie*)

> I know that I still have a lot to learn so I try to absorb the knowledge as much as I can.
>
> (*DG*)

Flickr users' passion for photography is also indexed through other means. Many would include their folk theories or philosophy about photography in their profiles:

> Some people shout. Some people cry. Some people write, fight, drink, do drugs, listen to music, talk to people, crash their cars and so on. For me, shooting photos is my way of dealing with things.
>
> (*EricC*)

> the most important thing of taking photography is your HEART, not what kind of equipment you use
>
> (*Looloo*)

These personal philosophies are asserted at a high degree of certainty of their opinions, using affirmative statements of what is true or not true, which clearly mark their epistemic stance. However, these expressions also carry their feelings and attitudes towards photography, which are markers of their affective stance. Because of their enthusiasm for photography, many users would regard their uploaded content as intellectual property, thus explicitly claiming ownership or authorship of their uploaded content by including a disclaimer type comment, as in *Looloo*'s profile:

> I appreciate all the comments/faves, BUT don't use my photos without my permission, thanks!

The imperative sentence "don't use my photos without my permission" not only allows *Looloo* to claim authorship of her photos, but also implicitly asserts the fact that she takes her hobby seriously. In addition to photo sharing, the high degree of interaction between users makes Flickr a largely social space (see also Barton and Lee 2012). Such social interaction is often manifested through the act of commenting. We have observed that many comments on Flickr do not directly relate to the content of the photo. People may also take the commenting space as a space for interpersonal interaction, so as to make new friends. Because of this, users would claim their identities through various forms of stance marking, such as tagging self-portraits with the pronoun 'me' as a way of positioning the self, thus letting others know who they are and how others should see them. Other signs of self-positioning are more explicitly expressed as comments:

> Yes I am from China. . .Chinese is my mother tongue
>
> (cjPanda)

By telling others where she comes from and what language she speaks, *cjPanda* can position herself within a linguistic and cultural group that is situated in the much broader and global Flickr community. Language is indeed a common stance object on Flickr. From time to time, we find many examples of users' assertion of their knowledge or level of proficiency of English (e.g. 'English is not my first language'), a topic that we will pursue further in Chapter 8.

A number of other stance statements are made to comment on the stance taken by others, which we can refer to as 'meta-stance'. For example:

> I hope my viewers focus on my photos instead of the titles and descriptions.
>
> (sating)

Here, *sating* conveys what she expects of her viewers, that her viewers should relate their stance to her uploaded photos, not the verbal descriptions around them. At the same time, doing so allows her to reposition her viewers' stance, thus guiding their reading path through her photo pages.

Affective stance

Another broad category of stance, affective stance, is concerned with expressions of the stance-taker's personal feelings, attitudes or judgements towards a stance object. Affective stances are often evaluative and other studies may refer to this type of stance as 'assessment' or 'appraisal'. On Flickr, commenters, including the actual content posters, often express their views on a photo uploaded, on photography, and even on their participation in Flickr generally. Many comments by others are marked by affective verbs such as 'I *like* Flickr because. . .' or evaluative adjectives such as '*beautiful* capture' and '*interesting* shot'. Some comments are directed to what is shown in the photo, such as 'This is *ironical* [referring to what is said on a sign]'. Many are more specific remarks on the photographic techniques used: '*Wow*, great composition and *DOF* [depth of field].' Or: 'Excellent lighting and *really superb bokeh*'. [Bokeh is an effect in photography that emphasizes blurry or out-of-focus areas in an image.] Such comments are interesting in that, while praising their stance objects, i.e. the photos, these comments also serve as a way of asserting the commenters' knowledge of photography. These examples are thus also implicitly *epistemic* in nature. According to Du Bois (2007), evaluation is also an act of positioning and alignment, either with the self or others. While assessing specific aspects of the photos, these commenters are also asserting their authority and insider professional knowledge of photography. In fact, many statements that we have come across convey multiple stance types. There is not always a clear-cut boundary between epistemic and affective stances, especially when people talk about themselves:

> I am odd, plus a little crazy
>
> (*Looloo*)

> I live in Taipei and enjoy taking pictures as my favorite hobby.
>
> (*JadeCastle*)

The first example is the description of *Looloo*'s photo where she describes 16 random things about herself. In terms of linguistic form, this is an affirmative statement asserting *Looloo*'s personality. But describing herself as 'odd' and 'crazy' is also a way of expressing her attitudes towards her own personality. Similarly, on *Jadecastle*'s profile page, he states the fact that photography is his hobby, and that it is something that he enjoys doing, thus also expressing his emotion towards this hobby. Epistemic and affective stances co-exist in these utterances.

We have mentioned in the previous section that language is a common stance object in some epistemic stance statements, where the writer asserts their knowledge of a particular language. A point to note is that these statements, although epistemic in form, functionally express an attitude towards people's linguistic preference on Flickr. Let us return to an example that we saw in Chapter 5:

> My English is so . . .. . .poor ! so, I take photos. . .
> 唉中文都一樣不見得是好 ! (sigh. . .my Chinese isn't good either!)
> 都是拍照算了 (I should better take photos.)
>
> (*Tiong*)

Structurally, these few simple statements are just *Tiong*'s own assertion of his 'poor' proficiency level of Chinese and English, and we need to understand both languages to understand what he is saying here. But *why* did he want to write this on his profile page? We can then infer that these statements act as his affective stance-taking towards languages and how one should participate in Flickr. This was supported by an online interview with him, in which he stresses that on Flickr photography should be the main subject matter, not the written word. (See Chapter 8 for a detailed discussion of how people talk about language online.) These examples from Flickr clearly show that the act of stance-taking serves multiple purposes, and that the same statement can express multiple stance types.

Another issue that we have noticed is that commenters on Flickr frequently exercise positive politeness when they convey their attitudes and evaluation towards others. There is often more praise than criticism towards a photo. In our data, we have found many conversational sequences containing the compliment-acceptance adjacency pair (e.g. 'Nice shot!' followed by 'thank you'). While antagonism and hostility in comments are common in many social network sites such as YouTube (see Lange 2007), so far we have not seen any abusive language in our particular Flickr data. (Occasionally there are swear words but they are employed humorously and playfully.) One possible explanation is that, to Flickr users, Flickr is not just a photo sharing site, but also a site to develop interpersonal relationships. Thus, expressing stance towards others and their photos is a way to widen participation and build solidarity with other users. So far we have focused largely on stance-taking by way of the written word. Through case studies of two Flickr pages in the following subsection, we illustrate how words and images can be combined to do the job of positioning the self and others.

TWO CASE STUDIES OF MULTIMODAL STANCE-TAKING ON FLICKR

In Chapter 3, we showed how a photo page on Flickr can be treated as a cohesive piece of text, where words and images work together to make meanings. Here we provide two case studies that illustrate this; the first is an example of how a page is a cohesive piece of text and the second goes into more detail and considers stances from the perspectives of the viewers and the researchers.

Case 1: 'Look at me in the eye'

Figure 7.1 is a photo uploaded to Flickr by *Nadiobolis*, one of the Spanish speakers who participated in our research. We first came across it when analysing her most recent Flickr pages.

David's reading path
When I clicked through to this Flickr page, my reading path started with a quick look at the image. I immediately liked it and wanted to find out more about it. I looked up to the title and down to the description, trying to piece together what it meant. Then I had a quick look at the first comments before looking at the information on the right as to when the photo was taken and down to the tags, which gave more information about where it was taken. I am familiar with using Flickr and I am also used to scanning sites quickly when I am doing my research; sometimes I look mainly at the words and hardly notice the image, but here I returned to the image and scrutinized it carefully.

look at me in the eye...

...and tell me what you think of me
Egyptian sculpture at The Met, NYC

This photo was taken on March 27, 2
PowerShot S70.

44 views   4 comments

This photo belongs to

nadiobolis' photostream (24)

← Oldest photo

Tags

The Met
Metropolitan
museum
museo
The Metropolitan Museum of Art
Egyptian
sculpture

Figure 7.1 Look at me in the eye

Carmen's reading path

I started with the sculpture in the image, which I found eye-catching as the sculpture occupied the centre of the page. Then from the setting shown in the blurry background, I realized that the photo was taken in a museum. From the image, I moved down to read the title 'look at me in the eye. . .'. Out of habit, I scrolled down and browsed through the comments. After that, I moved up again to read the photo description and then the tags to find out where exactly the photo was taken.

The image

The image is a portrait, a common 'three-quarter view' of a head within the genre of portraits. It is a portrait of a sculpture, an image of an image of a person. The staring eyes are central to the composition, with the right eye literally in the centre of the image. They are staring ahead, not quite at the viewer. The image seems carefully composed, with converging lines in the background framing the head. There is more to say about the image itself, but first how is it set in a Flickr page and given meaning by the language around it?

The language

Here, the photographer *Nadiobolis* has provided a title 'look at me in the eye. . .' and a description, which appears as a caption below the photo in a smaller font. It consists of two lines '. . .and tell me what you think of me', which continues the title. The line below is 'Egyptian sculpture at The Met, NYC'. The right-hand vertical panel gives further information. The photo is part of a set named 'nw yrk 2007' containing 58 photos. Below this are the tags she has given to the photo, including 'The Met', 'Metropolitan', 'museum', 'museo'.

Cross-modal coherence
Examining the page for its internal structure, the way it works as a web page, there are several ways in which the layout, image and words make it a coherent, and hence meaningful, multimodal page. First, there is cross-modal cohesion, that is the image and the words are tied in closely to each other. The title mentions 'eye' and draws attention to a central aspect of the image. The words are as if spoken by the sculpture. (This type of persona-taking practice is quite common in online spaces, such as when someone sets up a Facebook account or a blog for a pet and then speaks from its perspective.) Second, the description section describes the sculpture as Egyptian and locates it in the Metropolitan Museum of Art in New York. This information is repeated in the tags and the photo has been placed in a set of New York photos. Further cohesion is provided by the continuing of the title in the description: 'look at me in the eye. . .and tell me what you think of me'.

Intertextual links
The title of the image makes an intertextual link and echoes the title of a song, 'Look me in the eyes', recorded by the Jonas Brothers and others. Song lyrics are commonly used by Flickr users as part of a global music culture. Using the song title, and her other lexical choices, tell us about the particular sort of imagined audience she is constructing, and this is a central part of her stance as a multilingual cosmopolitan Flickr user. Nevertheless understanding does not depend on knowing the intertextual link. What is in the head of the author can be very different from how the viewer interprets it.

Other voices
The page at this point consists of a fairly tight frame provided by Flickr and with content added by the user. It then becomes a space for interaction: other people can add comments below the image, notes on parts of the photo and additional tags. The screen shot as it is displayed on a computer screen shows two comments. Someone added the first comment, saying 'nice perspective with somebody in the back :) '. Then the photographer, *Nadiobolis*, responded 'Thanks Edyta!! Yeah! Those kinds of things make a picture special unexpectedly. . .I thought the same when I saw it :) '. There are then further comments. The first comment made by someone else relates directly to the image and draws attention to a hitherto unmentioned aspect of the photo, a figure in the background. *Nadiobolis* asserts that she too had seen the figure by saying that she had not noticed the figure until she had looked at the photo she had taken.

Further interpretation

The page also provides interpersonal information, about both the participants within the page and the relation between author and viewer, and *Nadiobolis* tells, or reveals, some things about herself and her stance towards the image. She is someone who was in New York in 2007 and she went to the Metropolitan Museum of Art. She uses a familiar name for the museum, the Met, and feels it worth telling us it was an Egyptian sculpture. She knows Spanish and provides tags in English and Spanish. She likes the image, and calls it 'special' and she knows the commenter, as she refers to her as 'Edyta' [a woman's name]. All this information on the page guides the interpretation the viewer makes.

Moving outwards

A further layer of meaning is provided if we dig a little deeper. The page, as a text, is embedded in a larger text, Nadiobolis' whole Flickr photo stream, and as a user she is also part of a larger network of Flickr users from all parts of the world. In fact, it is embedded more broadly in the whole Flickr site and the web itself – there are at least 40 possible click-through links visible on this screen, without including those on drop-down menus. We also know from examination of her site that she is from Latin America. The 'nw yrk' set looks like a vacation trip to New York. The photo looks carefully composed and the eyes of the sculpture must have been striking.

Case 2: 'Handwritting'

For the second case study we present a Flickr page by a Chinese Flickr user, *cjPanda*, showing the ways in which stance-taking is not only a linguistic act, but also a multimodal one. In presenting the case, we shift perspectives from time to time, showing how our researchers' stance leads to our different interpretations of the photo page from each other.

About cjPanda

From her profile and photo stream, we found out that *cjPanda* is a female Chinese Flickr user, currently living in Shanghai. She studied product design at university when she started using Flickr, and now she is a freelance illustrator. Her interests in drawing and design are clearly reflected in the photos she uploads. The majority are photos of her own drawings and doodles. Her passion for art and design is also revealed in the most popular tags on her site – 'drawings' and 'photoshop', as well as in the groups she joins such as 'Moleskine', 'Design Addicts', '5 minute doodle', etc. These activities on Flickr enable us to understand her overall identity positioning – that she wants to tell the world she is interested in art. Many visitors to her site often pay attention not to the quality of her photos, but to the drawings shown in them. In a way, *cjPanda* uses Flickr as a *site of engagement* (Jones 2005) for her and designers in other parts of the world to meet and discuss their works. At a more local level, many of her contacts are also mainland

handwritting

It's not my handwritting...I haven't got the time, It's my friend "Lullaby"s', he hasn't got the time too, he did this when he was 6, I decide to write something in this summer vacation, let's see!

Figure 7.2 cjPanda's photo page 'handwriting'

Chinese people sharing a similar cultural and linguistic background (i.e. using Mandarin as their main language).

Carmen's reading path
My attention was first drawn to the written words around the photo. What actually caught my eye first was the unconventional spelling in the title 'handwriting', and then I moved on to the tags. I noticed that in addition to 'handwritting', there was also a second tag added by another Flickr member, possibly aiming to correct the spelling. I did not view the picture and the handwriting from an aesthetic angle. My reading of the image was guided and constructed by my familiarity with Chinese writing and calligraphy (which I took for granted as something 'ordinary'). My research interest in tagging was one of the reasons why my eyes were drawn to the tags and their spelling. My ability to recognize the Chinese characters shown in the photo also allowed me to search for the original poem on Google. This act took me outside the context of the photo page itself and broadened my understanding of the image.

David's reading path
I noticed that the image was some Chinese writing. Then I looked down at the title noticing that it said handwriting with double t, and wondered if it was deliberate. Looking across to the right, I saw the image was in a set called 'some stuffs called Chinese culture' which is not standard English so assumed *cjPanda* was a second language speaker. I then looked further down and noticed two tags, one with correct spelling and one with the double t. I then moved back to the left-hand side and read the description. I read down through the comments. Then I left the page and clicked through to some of her other photos.

cjPanda's and her viewers' stance

From *cjPanda*'s perspective, the decision and the act of uploading the photo, along with giving the photo a title and a description already indexes her own stance – her intention to offer further information about the Chinese handwriting in the photo. By pointing out that the handwriting is 'not my handwriting', *cjPanda* explicitly acknowledges the work of others, shifting the viewer's attention to another Flickr member, *Lullaby*, who actually wrote these characters when he was six. This also immediately invites the viewers to take account of a third person in the meaning-making process.

The title and description also guide and shape viewers' evaluative stances towards the significance of the main image ('It isn't my handwriting'). The stance initiated by *cjPanda* and her writing around the image also triggered a series of comments from others:

1. *Niniel*: oh god, when he was 6!!!!great :D
2. *girls slayer*: could he writ my name its nice
3. *isolano*: Are you not from China?
4. *cjPanda*: yep Nini, but his English handwritting is. . .ohh sorry I can't talk behind his back,heheh;-)
   isolano: Yes I am from China but nowadays we young Chinese don't like practicing penmanship a lot, I suppose it's a nationwide art, not expert only!=]
5. *cjPanda*: slayer, I think I am able to do this. . .do you have a Chinese name?
6. *Shuke, the Pilot*: sad I can't go back to 6.
7. *woolloomooloo*: beautiful! i love calligraphy. . . ^-^
8. *Rayparnova*: nice texture !
9. *alex.vu*: 这一手字写蛮漂亮的
   (Translation: This is beautiful handwriting!)

Altogether there are nine comments posted by *cjPanda*'s contacts and *cjPanda* herself. Most of the commenters speak a language other than English. For example, *Niniel* from Chile writes in Spanish, and *isolano* is from Portugal. *Shuke* and *alex.vu* are from mainland China and share the same language and writing system with *cjPanda*. *Rayparnova*, from Spain, is multilingual and writes in English, French and Spanish on his site. But here, for this particular photo, almost all of them communicate in English. This already is an act of stance – they write in English to claim their identity as global Flickr members.

To analyse the comments in terms of stance in greater detail, we find a few typical expressions of affective stance on Flickr. Typically, commenters direct their evaluation towards the quality of the photograph, but here we see evaluative stances towards the topics of handwriting, calligraphy and the ability to write this at a young age – but not to the quality of the photograph. So the comments 'Great, beautiful, and nice' are all initiated by and align with *cjPanda*'s title and description, which focus on the handwriting itself.

What is also interesting is people's stance towards Chinese culture and *cjPanda*'s Chinese cultural identity, which are evident in comments 3 and 4:

Comment 3: *isolano*: Are you not from China?
Comment 4 – [. . .] isolano: Yes I am from China but nowadays we young Chinese don't like practicing penmanship a lot I suppose it's a nationwide art, not expert only

cjPanda's response is initially epistemic – both 'I am from China' and 'we young Chinese' are used to align herself with *isolano*'s question. Moreover, the second part of her response is an act of repositioning and aligning herself to the younger generation of Chinese people, who may hold a different attitude towards traditional Chinese culture such as calligraphy. This comment also forms a cohesive tie to one of her photo sets called 'some stuffs called national culture', which seems to be a way of distancing herself from being an insider member of that culture. Later, in response to *girlslayer*'s comment, 'could he write my name', *cjPanda* replies: 'I think I am able to do this' (comment 5). Here, she immediately claims her knowledge of Chinese calligraphy again. This provides a nice example of how Flickr members constantly switch between their local and global selves – *cjPanda*, on the one hand, positions herself as a Chinese person generally; on the other hand, she wants to participate as a global person too. This is achieved by introducing a national culture, which she thinks may be of global interest.

Carmen's researcher's stance
Being Chinese myself, I could read what was written in the image. It did not strike me as a particularly beautiful piece of calligraphy. I was interested in the spelling instead. This can be explained by my role as a Chinese-English bilingual and my own understanding of the learning process of spelling. My own experience of learning English and evaluating others' English have allowed me to develop sensitivity to spelling accuracy, which is the reason why I focused on the spelling first. In short, in my analysis of this multilingual and multimodal page, I positioned myself as a Chinese person, thus aligning with *cjPanda*'s culture. However, being a Chinese person in Hong Kong, I was also aware of our differences (e.g. that we speak different Chinese languages and use different writing systems).

David's researcher's stance
I could not read the Chinese in the image and I felt that I did not understand what the picture was about. The description says it was done when the writer was six years old. I wondered if it was childish writing and whether all Chinese readers would know that it wasn't adult-like. It looked fine to me. Based on what I know about writing systems, I thought about the fact that Chinese writing is more likely to be treated as calligraphy than English writing.

TAKING INTO ACCOUNT THE RESEARCHER'S STANCE

One of the central arguments of this chapter is that, in any study of language online (and indeed any research), the researcher inevitably takes a certain stance or point of view in the process of analysis. The researcher is always standing somewhere, and there is no neutral point to stand from where the phenomenon can be viewed. This is partly based on our background knowledge and our purposes as researchers. In this way the research findings and discussion are influenced by the researchers' stance and how they position and align themselves in relation to the research site and the participants. For instance, when interpreting our Flickr data, we constantly found ourselves alternating between at least three roles. Sometimes we are ordinary viewers or visitors of a Flickr page; at other times, we are highly aware of our role as the researcher-analysts who have made direct contact with some of these participants. We are also active Flickr users who participate in common activities on Flickr just like many of our participants. We see ourselves as insiders who are familiar with ways of participating in Flickr and the affordances in it. Some of our informants have become our Flickr friends. Making these roles explicit not only informs our readers what leads to our current understanding of stance, doing so also guides our readers through their own stance-taking as they interpret our analysis and discussion.

Our sharing of multiple roles in the research does not mean that as the two authors, we share the same stance towards our data. To begin with, we took rather different reading paths when reading *cjPanda*'s photo page. We had different starting points, which were shaped by our prior knowledge of the photographers' images, our knowledge of the languages concerned, etc. David started his reading of the page with the Chinese writing in the image, while Carmen focused first on the spelling of the title. David wondered if the unconventional spelling was deliberate, while Carmen interpreted it against her second language learning background. Carmen's Chinese background also allowed her to interpret the content of the image (the Chinese characters) and what is said in the comments against her insights of Chinese culture. Our reading paths are also guided by the features or affordances of the text. This partially explains our different starting points. What is more crucial in shaping our different ways of interpreting a multimodal Flickr text, however, is our researcher's position and stance, which includes a complex nexus of factors such as our prior knowledge of the site and the language used there that shaped our reading and interpretation of the multimodal data. The important methodological point is that researchers need to make their stance towards the research as explicit as possible.

STANCE-TAKING AS A POWERFUL TOOL FOR ANALYSING LANGUAGE ONLINE

Stance-taking can serve as a powerful analytical tool that cuts across many areas of online research. We now summarize the various ways in which stance-taking can inform language and literacy studies of online texts, some of which can bring new insights into existing concepts and theories of language.

The pragmatics of stance

In our discussion of stance types, we have shown that often there is no clear-cut boundary between epistemic and affective stances. A statement may be epistemic in structure, with explicit stance markers such as 'I think' or 'I believe', but it actually expresses an attitude. How the utterance is used has to be interpreted with respect to its context. As we have seen, the interpretation of stance becomes less straightforward when its social functions such as politeness and people's need to receive positive feedback from their audience are taken into consideration. We have shown many examples from English in this chapter but people from other cultures and language backgrounds are also exercising politeness in language online. In China, for example, Taobao is the biggest online shopping site. Like eBay, sellers are often rated by buyers for their reliability as well as their service. Because of this, sellers have created a specific communication style when interacting with their buyers. For example, they often start a sentence with 親 ('dear') to create a sense of friendliness. This has never been used in everyday conversation in Chinese. The endearment here serves only to attract positive ratings from buyers. Therefore, we suggest that linguistic and structural studies of stance should take into account the pragmatic functions of the stance statements in question, making sense of the inference and implications embodied in the utterance and its immediate, situational, and social contexts. Such a perspective is particularly relevant to studying stance in online communication, where playful and humorous linguistic forms tend to violate traditional beliefs or 'maxims' of conversation. (See, for example, Herring's (2013b) work on the relevance principles in chat rooms; and Yus (2011) also examines language online from the point of view of pragmatics.)

Critical discourse analysis

Throughout this chapter, we have primarily discussed stance-taking online as a multimodal act. There have been studies of stance-taking in new media that take stance-taking as a vehicle for expressing social ideologies (e.g. Walton and Jaffe 2011; Chun and Walters 2011; Thurlow and Jaworski 2011). These studies often start with a particular viewpoint or stance in new media discourse. For example, Chun and Walters' (2011) research on YouTube focuses on the issue of *race*. They look into Orientalism as a particular act of stance-taking. Drawing upon a range of videos featuring the performance of a stand-up comedian Wonho Chung, Chun and Walters critically examine how the performer and responses from his audience (including YouTube comments) collaboratively construct their stances towards Arab Orientalisms. Crucially, the authors also take into account their own 'critical stance' (269) regarding race, acknowledging how their reflection and writing process shape their understanding of the videos. As we have stressed, stances are always inferred. What is said (the form) may not be what the stance-taker actually wants to convey (especially in the case of humour and irony). Such a contextualized, ideological, and critical perspective can be combined with insights from pragmatics, which often aims to reveal not just what is said, but what is *not* said in utterances.

The study of identity performance

In Chapter 6, we discussed how identities are performed linguistically online and how insights from techno-biographies can inform our understanding of identities. Our understanding of stance allows us to make sense of techno-biographies and identities. Techno-biographies are life histories where people talk about their relationships with technology at different points and contexts in their lives. In talking about their relationship with language when going online, the student participants frequently asserted their identities by positioning and repositioning themselves and others. And the repositioning is often achieved by referring to the roles they played in life (e.g. a student, a friend, a family member) and their sense of 'ownership' of a certain language. For example, one student in our Facebook research, majoring in English, often explained his preference for English on Facebook in terms of his major subject ('I am an English major.'). However, when situating himself in a public forum, he would avoid using English because he did not want others to judge his English if he made any mistake in public. This act of repositioning takes into account the perspective of his target readers. On Flickr, there are also many interesting examples of positioning through language choice. For example, in the desciption for the Hispanic photo Group called 'HABLA HISPANA', the content is written in three languages, in the order of Spanish, English, and French. Why is it not written in Spanish only if this is a Hispanic group? There are two possible explanations to this. First, it can be seen as an act of inclusion and exclusion. The orientation or preference for Spanish is already indexed in the order of languages – Spanish first, then English, and finally French. In so doing, the administrator on the one hand clearly conveys the message that 'we are Spanish' and the group is not meant to be a purely English group. Although the group administrator certainly has a local interest at first, s/he does not want to exclude other members on Flickr. This is supported by the group description: 'However, other languages are accepted, anyone is welcome to participate.' This again is an act of positioning the group as a *glocal* community (see Chapter 3) that speaks simultaneously to local and global audiences. All these examples clearly illustrate that stance-taking, i.e. acts of positioning and alignment in relation to others, is useful in understanding linguistic identities online.

The study of folk linguistic attitudes on Web 2.0

Web 2.0 environments such as Facebook and YouTube are stance-rich. On Facebook, there is the key feature of 'status updates' where users write posts that serve a range of discourse functions. According to a study of status updates in Hong Kong by Lee (2011), *opinion and judgement* was the most expressed communicative function. Social network sites give rise to public opinions because of their affordances for self-generated content. The commenting function on many global sites allow stances to be constantly expressed, discussed, negotiated, and contested collaboratively among people from all parts of the world who may not even know each other. While the kinds of opinion expressed by online users are wide-ranging, there is one specific stance object that strikes us as frequently occurring in many new media spaces – attitudes towards linguistic knowledge. In Chapter 8, we discuss the ways in which Web 2.0 offers an unprecedented space for the world to express and discuss their folk attitudes towards the subject matter of language.

8

'MY ENGLISH IS SO POOR'

Talking about language online

- Talking about language in a textually mediated social world
- Types of metalinguistic discourse online
- 'My English is so poor': Self-deprecating metalinguistic discourse on Flickr
- Metadiscursive construction of a supportive social space
- Linguistic reflexivity as powerful digital discourse

TALKING ABOUT LANGUAGE IN A TEXTUALLY MEDIATED SOCIAL WORLD

THEY'RE going THERE with THEIR friends. It's called grammar, use it.!!!

(Facebook)

Some languages are hard, like Chinese. Some are easy, like Spanish. You can learn both, with this group!!

(Flickr)

funny teacher saying foul language

(YouTube)

We do not need to be linguists to have a view about any aspect of language and how we or other people use it. Language has been perceived as a form of cultural capital (Bourdieu 1990) for people to act with in this textually mediated social world. As people become more aware of the social values of the language they use, ideologies or assumptions about standards of language emerge. Language users can easily reflect upon or even assess aspects of language and its use, be it an accent, the grammar and style of someone's speech, or the level of difficulty in learning a language. The quotes at the beginning of this chapter are some web users' views about language, taken from Facebook, Flickr and YouTube. The first one is the title of a Facebook fan page, where Facebook users gather to discuss grammar-related topics in English. The title suggests some easily misspelled homophones in English, which is framed as a 'grammar' issue. The second is part of the description of a group on Flickr called 'Learn a New Language'. The statements evaluate the level of difficulty in learning languages, that Spanish is an 'easy' language while Chinese is 'hard'; while the last one is the title of a YouTube video posted by a secondary schoolgirl in Hong Kong who vlogs about what she sees as incorrect English used by an invigilator at an examination. Utterances that express beliefs and attitudes about language are broadly referred to as *metalanguage*. The term metalanguage is often defined as 'language about language'. Jaworski *et al.* (2004) comment that this notion is too 'literal' and define metalanguage as language 'in the context of linguistic representations and evaluations' (4). When people engage in metalinguistic talk, whether online or offline, they are also engaging in the wider discourse of language ideologies, such as what constitutes standard, good, or correct use of language. It thus also makes sense to call these views about language *metalinguistic discourse*. To date, popular metalinguistic discourses have been largely evaluative and prescriptive. A major source of non-linguists' views of language is mass media, especially news reports. In particular, linguistic features that are publicly recognized as specific to internet communication, such as the use of abbreviations and smileys in texting, have often become a key subject of much metalinguistic discourse in the news. Crispin Thurlow (2007) analysed an extensive corpus of English news articles and identified ways in which young people's use of language in new media is misrepresented. Thurlow found that mass media tend to focus on three themes when constructing young people's online language discursively:

Theme 1: 'the homogenization of youth' – that young people are often portrayed as one single generation and are given labels such as 'Generation text' and 'wired teens'.

Theme 2: 'the de-generation of language' – that young people's new media language practices are threatening standards of language.

Theme 3: 'The exaggeration of difference' – that the newness and difference of internet-specific language is often exaggerated.

These ideas are well illustrated in a classic case when a Scottish schoolgirl submitted an essay written in what was said to be 'text message shorthand'. This is how she began the essay, first cited in the *Daily Telegraph* on 3 March 2003:

My smmr hols wr CWOT. B4, we used 2go2 NY 2C my bro, his GF & thr 3 :- kids FTF. ILNY, it's a gr8 plc.

(Translation: My summer holidays were a complete waste of time. Before, we used to go to New York to see my brother, his girlfriend and their three screaming kids face to face. I love New York. It's a great place.)

Immediately, this piece of national and even international news received a great deal of attention from authorities including teachers and government officials in several different countries. Here is a response from the girl's teacher:

I could not believe what I was seeing. The page was riddled with hieroglyphics, many of which I simply could not translate. When I challenged the pupil, she told me that was how she preferred to write because she found it easier than standard English.

(*Sunday Herald* 2003)

This comment focuses on the peculiarity of texting language as compared to standard language. Concerns are also expressed regarding how the language of texting would negatively affect students' literacy skills. What these reports are clearly missing, as Thurlow (2007) also comments on, is the idea of linguistic creativity and innovation among young people. From the schoolgirl's perspective, as reported by the teacher, writing an essay in text messages was certainly not about her not knowing how to spell – she decided that texting language was more communicative than what she considered to be 'standard English'.

Mass media's (mis-)representations of linguistic practices online certainly have a strong impact on what people think about their own language use as well as language in society more generally. In other words, people's meta-linguistic awareness is always discursively constructed. With the advent of Web 2.0 media, especially publicly available social network sites, meta-linguistic discourses are no longer confined to traditional mass media but can be found in a much wider range of online platforms. With the paradigm shift to more user-generated content on Web 2.0, ordinary web users from all walks of life can talk about language extensively in various writing spaces online, as in the examples cited at the beginning of the chapter. Anyone looking at YouTube comments will observe wide-ranging points of view, from some abusive comments on one's English such as 'HIS ENGLISH SUCKS!' to in-depth discussion of a local dialect, such as 'Le language is called wolof. Its the main dialect back home. There is about 30 different dialectes all together' (which was a comment on a music video of a Wolof song). These new spaces for representing language have important implications for learning, as we will discuss in the next chapter.

This chapter considers what and how people actually talk about language in relation to their online participation. Examples from various web spaces including Flickr, Facebook, and YouTube are used to show the ways in which the web provides a platform for people to publicly reflect upon and discuss language-related topics through self-generated writing, such as personal profiles and comments. It is this emerging aspect of metalinguistic discourse online and the purposes it can serve that this chapter is interested in. The chapter also pays specific attention to how talking about one's knowledge, or lack of knowledge, of a language can serve meaningful social purposes when participating in Web 2.0 spaces, thus becoming an important way of acting online.

TYPES OF METALINGUISTIC DISCOURSE ONLINE

What aspects of language do people represent or discuss in online spaces? Studies of metalinguistic discourses online are emerging but they are mostly reports of individual research studies with a narrow set of data, and a systematic overview of common types of language representations online is missing. This section identifies and discusses five key topics of language that people often talk about in what Squires (2010) refers to as 'sites of metadiscourse' that we have researched or observed.

Linguistic forms and structures

Sociolinguists and dialectologists have long been interested in investigating non-linguists' beliefs, attitudes, and theories of language represented in speech or print media, an area that is termed folk linguistics (Niedzielski and Preston 2000). A major type of folk linguistic view observed online is when people talk about what they think is good or bad of language. Discourses about standards of language and language use also began to emerge in early forms of CMC, including sites that predate Web 2.0. For example, the BBC Voices website has a 'Your Voice' section for ordinary viewers and experts to discuss dialects across the UK. From time to time, a common way for site visitors to represent their language attitudes is through affective utterances, such as this comment on the issue of language change: 'The dissappearance [sic] of the letter "T" drives me mad! I've heard people say words such as letter, better and motorway without pronouncing the "T". It sounds so lazy.' While expressing feelings towards t-dropping ('drives me mad', 'lazy'), this commenter is also aligning to a prescriptive rule of pronunciation, that is, do not drop an intervocalic /t/.

On YouTube, prescriptivism can be reinforced through multimodal means. In the video titled 'funny teacher saying foul language lols' (mentioned in Chapter 4 and discussed in Benson 2010), the vlogger Ruby, a secondary schoolgirl in Hong Kong, criticizes a teacher for mispronouncing simple English words. Ruby starts the video in Cantonese introducing the context to her story – that the invigilator spoke 'primary school level' English at a public examination and she could not stand it. Then, she switches to English in the video because, as she said, she wants the whole world to know some common English errors among Hong Kong people. According to Ruby, the teacher mispronounced 'ask' (as 'ass'), 'zip' (as 'sit'), 'during' (as '*diu2*', a swear word in Cantonese), and 'sheet' (as 'shit'). Ruby, while attempting to correct the teacher, comments several times that the teacher's pronunciation was 'really really funny' and that teachers in general should have a 'higher English level'. The video itself is only one site of metalanguage on this YouTube page. What is more interesting is that the video immediately became a YouTube sensation among local Hong Kong people. Ruby's English pronunciation in the video became a key subject of further metalinguistic discourses in the form of written comments and video responses from others. Many responses criticize Ruby for her poor English (some targeted at her accent) and that she should have taken care of her own English before criticizing others. For example:

brianfan1:	I can't even recognize her accent, is she trying to pretend to be an american? Sorry but her attempt miserably failed.
wtboomer:	1. Did she listen to her accent before you post? Bristish [sic]? Nope. American? Nope. Canadian? Nope. Sounds like a retard to me.
	2. She speaks Chinglish, so why is she making fun of others' Chinglish?

Some commenters even introduce further sets of metalinguistic discourse among themselves. The following example shows how the discussion of Ruby's video has shifted to the grammar of the comment chain and language in new media in general:

yfjameslo:	It's funny how nearly every comment here commits significant grammatical errors as well :P
brianfan1:	sad but true, I think that's partly because of negligence of grammar in SMS nowadays.

What is interesting about this exchange is that, as *yfjameslo* points out how most of Ruby's commenters do not use proper grammar themselves, *brianfan1* immediately frames this within the broader public discourse and moral panics about the negative impact of texting language. This once again demonstrates the discursive construction of new media and how people's ideologies are shaped by media and other public representations of language online.

To different extents, the BBC Voices commenter, Ruby, and her commenters all position themselves as users of correct English, thus having the authority to evaluate and even correct others. A similar phenomenon of self-positioning through metalanguage is also found among German-speaking commenters on YouTube. Androutsopoulos (2013) looks into how German dialects are performed and negotiated in a corpus of videos tagged with German dialects such as Bairisch 'Bavarian' or Berlinerisch (Berlin city dialect). Part of Androutsopoulos' study focuses on viewers' comments on two focal videos – Rinjehaun – 'Berlinerisch fur Anfanger' ('Berlinerisch for beginners'), which is a three-minute dialect lesson, and 'MacBookAir auf Berlinerisch' ('MacBookAir in Berlinerisch'). Although the two videos are quite different in delivery style, the majority of commenters orient their comments to the dialect features in general or how they are delivered by speakers in the videos. Common themes have also been identified, such as taking on an affective stance (e.g. 'I just love that Berlinerisch. Very cool. Weiter machen!' ('Keep it up!')); others may debate the authenticity of the Berlinerisch dialect features used in the video in terms of their own understanding of authentic Berlinerisch:

> Boah ne, sorry, dit is aber ma so ja nich knorke! Da_ hatt er zwar die Vokabeln jepaukt, aber. . . dit klingt so ja nich Original-Berlinerisch. . . keene Stimmmelodie drin, weißte Keule!

> (Translation: 'Oh well, sorry, but this isn't my thing at all! He did learn his lessons, but. . . It doesn't sound like original Berlinerisch, no vocal melody in there, isn't it mate!')

These commenters, through authenticating the video content and showing their insider knowledge of dialects, are also indexing their own linguistic and cultural identities. What is also special about participation in linguistic discussions on YouTube is that, as illustrated by Ruby and the German YouTube participants, metalinguistic discourses and ideologies in new digital media are often initiated by the visual content of YouTube. In other words, they are articulated collaboratively and multimodally.

Internet-specific language

Recognizable linguistic practices online have become a subject of discussion in online spaces too. With computer-mediated discourse gradually gaining public recognition, users of online language have also developed their own linguistic repertoire and conventions for the language they use online. A salient practice is to give labels to what they think of as new varieties of language that they use in online interaction. In a detailed analysis of two comment threads discussing language on the internet, Squires (2010) shows how the commenters often 'enregister' internet language by giving labels such as 'chat lingo', 'IM chat-speak', and 'txt-tlk' to specific forms of language. Commenters' assessments of language online were two-fold – those who considered internet language as a register used only in specific settings tended to be positive about it, while others who juxtaposed their arguments with standard English negatively evaluated language online and its associated features. Clearly, people's thoughts and feelings about online registers are largely shaped by standard language ideologies, which are influenced by mass media representation of language. Squires also identifies *technological determinism* as another broader conception that shapes people's beliefs about new media language. When changes in language emerge at the same time as new technologies, a newer set of reflections about language and its use also emerge as a result. This has important theoretical implications. Metalinguistic discourses are always embedded in the larger context of other discourses in society, i.e. they are situated practices. As social conditions change, ways of thinking and talking about language also change accordingly.

Language teaching and learning

There are instances where web users explicitly take on a language teacher or learner discourse. Many YouTube vloggers, for example, take on new roles as language teachers to offer language lessons for free to their viewers (e.g. 'Learn to Speak French - Vlog - En Français!!! Mon NOUVEAU PROJET POUR VOUS!!'), while others may vlog about 'tips' as to how to learn a language better (e.g. '6 Tips to Learn a Foreign Language - from a Polyglot'). This is more than taking on a teacher discourse. This is also about people transforming their lay knowledge about language into a more authoritative discourse of competent speakers of a certain language. This kind of discourse of teaching and learning is different from the situation where Flickr participants say they act as teachers and learners, as discussed in the next chapter.

Being aware of the diverse linguistic and cultural background of YouTube viewers and with growing multilingual encounters and translingual experiences between vloggers and commenters, there has been evidence showing that people have also become keen language learners and constantly seek language help from one another. The fan-fiction website fanfiction.net, for instance, is a site that exhibits a great deal of discourses of active language learning. The site provides interactive discussion spaces for fan-fiction writers from all parts of the world to share and discuss their works with one another. Users draw upon their school-based and out-of-school linguistic practices when seeking help from and giving feedback to others. Rebecca Black's (2009) study of fanfiction.net presents a good example of how a Chinese-speaking fan-fiction writer, Nanako, learns from other participants of the site in order to improve her works written in English. Her commenters often draw upon their folk linguistic theories, to collaboratively edit her writing, as in the comment: 'there was just a few convention (grammar, spelling, stuff like that.) mistakes, but you had your reasons'. In this way collaborative editing can be achieved on fan-fiction sites.

Translation issues

As shown in Chapters 4 and 5, the web has become increasingly multilingual. Many web developers have also responded to this change and developed online translators or made their sites available in multiple languages.

For example, as of June 2012, Facebook's interface is available in about 70 languages and a 'translations' application was created to enable users to translate content themselves. Issues of translation arise as a result and these sites provide writing spaces for people to discuss such matters. Translation-related metadiscourses are discussed in detail in Lenihan (2011), first introduced in Chapter 5. The study looks into how Irish-language translators engage in the translations application on Facebook. The non-expert translators, who can be any users of Facebook, often draw upon a range of ideas about language endangerment, linguistic purism and verbal hygiene when discussing English-Irish translations. A topic that the Irish translators in Lenihan's study often discuss is 'bearlachas', Irish words that are influenced by English, or what are often referred to as Anglicisms. In the following comment, a translator reveals the ideology of linguistic purism while discussing the term 'Anglicism':

> 'béarlachas' (the modern translation of which is 'Anglicism', while 'bastardisation' (the process of corruption or evolution of the meaning of linguistic terms) would be more accurate.
>
> (cited in Lenihan 2011: 58)

Such talk about translations, as Lenihan argues, illustrates how new web spaces provide the affordances for people to take up possibilities for translingual practices; in addition, metadiscourses about multiple linguistic resources also reveal multilingual web users' attitudes towards their own and others' language choice practices for online participation.

Self-deprecating metalanguage

Globalization of the internet has enabled multicultural and multilingual interaction to take place among users from around the world. A specific type of metalinguistic discourse that seems to be quite pervasive in these multilingual encounters is what we call self-deprecating metalanguage, i.e. utterances where a person downplays their own linguistic abilities. Alongside other languages, English is often at the centre of these self-deprecating comments online. The globalization of internet participants has much to do with this trend. This leads to ordinary web users' strong beliefs about English being the main lingua franca of the web. In the face of global audiences, web users who do not use English as their primary language may either choose to write in a language that marks their local identity or use English to speak to a wider unknown audience, thus participating as a global netizen. Knowledge of English is still seen as an essential linguistic commodity with high communicative value on the web. In Bourdieu's term, being fluent in English is a form of cultural capital. A type of metalinguistic discourse that is strongly represented online is self-deprecating comments about one's knowledge of English.

Returning to Black's case study of a fan-fiction writer, the participant Nanako often plays down her own English writing skills when seeking help from others. In her opening and closing author's notes, she writes: 'Important note: English is my second language and I only spoken it for 2.5 years. So please excuse my grammar and spelling mistakes.' She refers to her 'bad writing. . .' and states 'I am not a good writer. . .'. Identifying herself as weak in English, Nanako in fact creates a supportive environment for her fan-fiction writing where she can elicit constructive feedback from other writers.

As an example of non-English self-deprecating comments on the web, in their study of YouTube comments, Chun and Walters (2011) also note such self-deprecating comments in commenters' feedback on an Asian comedian's Arabic-English bilingual performance in Dubai. Here is a short comment thread where three commenters praise the comedian, Chung, a non-Arab, for his fluent Arabic in the videos. At the same time they play down their own native Arabic competence:

xPsYcHoSys:	SPEAKS BETTER ARABIC THAN ME!!!!! for those of you who dont speak arabic, trust me hes perfectly fluent, no accent either
xx3xotiicxx:	HOLYYY SHITTTTTT. i was not expectin that at ALL he speaks better than my parents :|
L45:	He speaks better arabic than me!

All three comments explicitly compare Chung's Arabic language skills to the commenters' own native knowledge of the language. While the comparative statements all seem to praise Chung and position him as a 'better' speaker of Arabic, the commenters, who are all likely to be Arabic speakers, also take on a native speaker's voice. As Chun and Walters argue, they assert authority and authenticity of a native Arabic speaker that Chung lacks as an outsider. These comments may also be taken as acts of exclusion, marking Chung's otherness as a non-Arab.

As we can observe from the above examples, appearing modest to others and claiming limited knowledge of language can indeed serve multiple social functions. What is interesting here is that making self-deprecating comments is more than just a random choice of utterances. They also become important self-positioning acts where people articulate their language ideologies, create supportive environments, and exercise authority. In our study of multilingual practices on Flickr, such discourses are extremely prevalent. In the following, we provide a detailed analysis of how people talk about English on Flickr and what this salient practice means to social participation online.

'MY ENGLISH IS SO POOR': SELF-DEPRECATING METALINGUISTIC DISCOURSE ON FLICKR

Although the original aim of our study of Flickr was to observe and describe multilingual activities, the participants often revealed their attitudes towards language in various writing spaces and in the interview, often without prompting. These metalinguistic comments about language, collected from people's self-generated content on Flickr and follow-up email interviews, were often centred around their perceived function of English and their knowledge of the language in relation to their online participation. While we have already acknowledged extensive multilingual practices online in Chapter 4, some of our participants expressed in the interviews how they perceived English as the 'universal' language on Flickr (Lee and Barton 2009). As our research progressed and as we observed a wider range of users, we noted that the underlying importance of English is implicitly expressed by way of some participants' self-evaluations of their English proficiency level on their Flickr profile page, photo captions, and comments. This is shown in the following examples by two users from France and Germany respectively:

> Sorry to write in French but my English is too poor to express my feelings
> $\qquad$ (*leyeti*, French)

> My English is limited and not so well as it should be :(
> $\qquad$ (*Batikart*, German)

This initial observation led us to carry out a more detailed case study of these comments. In the next two sections of this chapter, we present a study to explore the ways in which discourses about English are constructed on Flickr. We first show some of the common ways in which people who do not use English as their primary language talk about their knowledge of English on Flickr. We then offer explanations for these acts of self-evaluation of language by drawing upon interview data. In particular, we want to understand how people's perception of their linguistic competence shapes their level of participation and particularly, socialization on Flickr, where photography and image sharing are central.

To understand how Flickr participants construct evaluative comments about their English, a textual database of over 1,600 examples with explicit remarks about one's knowledge and competence in English was first collected from various writing spaces on Flickr, including descriptions, comments, tags, and user profiles. We also focused on utterances where people talk about English. This is because while some Flickr users express their opinions about other languages that they know, such as 'my Japanese is limited' (*[HANDverk]*), our initial observation suggested that English is more frequently mentioned and evaluated than other languages on the site. We started our data collection through looking up five expressions that are commonly used by Flickr members to evaluate their own knowledge of English, using the advanced search function on Google. These search phrases are:

- 'My English is__' (e.g. 'My English is poor.')
- 'I don't know English__' (e.g. 'I'm from brazil, and i don't know english very well..lol.')

- 'I don't speak English __' (e.g. 'i don't speak english, i'm speak french.')
- 'I don't understand English __' (e.g. 'I'm sorry I don't understand English well.')
- 'English is not my __' (e.g. 'English is not my first language.')

An additional search phrase, 'Your English is', was also included in order to elicit other people's response to such self-evaluations.

These six search phrases derived initially from our ongoing active participation in Flickr, as well as our observation from the data in the broader study of multilingual practices on Flickr. We then carried out a basic meaning-based content analysis of the attitudes towards one's own English language proficiency and the stance taken in constructing such discourses, thus allowing us to identify key types of self-evaluation discourse. The immediate linguistic context of these expressions, that is, what the participant said before and after the sentence collected, as well as other texts appearing on their photo pages, were also analysed when necessary. The self-evaluative comments of English collected were first categorized into seven basic types, primarily according to their meaning.

Perceived knowledge of English

These expressions convey writers' affective stance towards their own English with some typical affective adjectives such as 'good', 'bad', 'terrible', 'poor'. Almost all of the expressions aim to play down the writer's linguistic competence:

> My English is poor/terrible /horrible
> My weakest trait is my english ability. . .

Apologetic and forgiveness seeking

In this type, the user asks their target reader to forgive the possible grammatical and spelling errors in their English captions or comments. Some even apologize for not speaking English as their first language:

> my english is not perfect, so excuse my grammar and occasional mistakes in text :)
> (JV image, Czech)

> Well, i'm sorry, my english is so shitty ugh because i'm french so sorry.
> (reddot, French)

Native speaker norm as a model of 'good' English

Self-deprecating comments of this type are often juxtaposed with native speaker norms. Within the corpus, many comments made explicit reference to native speaker English, some of which reveal negative attitudes towards 'not being a native English speaker' or that they are more likely to make mistakes in English as it is not their primary language:

> Sorry for the grammar mistakes, english is not my mother language.
>
> *(Camilo, Spanish)*

> pity that english is not my mother language.. otherwise i'd be glad to give my point of view about the question.
>
> *(wesley)*

External resources

While admitting their limited knowledge of English, some Flickr members explained what was supporting their English writing on Flickr. Some of the sentences collected refer to dictionaries, online translators such as Google Translate, and other people in their lives who can act as literacy brokers in their participation in Flickr:

> My English is Google translator . . . Mi español es el traductor de Google . . .. Mon français est traducteur de Google . . .
>
> *(Angelo, Italian)*

> I don't understand english but I have got translation through this website, this relpy wrote by my daughter, you can type English
>
> *(pklam, Chinese)*

Self-improvement

Although the previous types of metadiscourse seem to represent a rather negative self-image to others, some sentences in the data also express the writer's commitment to learning English and to self-improvement on Flickr:

> I'm really glad I found this site cause apart from sharing my pics I get to practice my English a bit.
>
> *(Gabriel, Polish)*

> my English is poor. Therefore I want to make friends with foreigner, so that I can improve my oral English skill.
>
> *(Kaki Wong, Chinese)*

Self-deprecating humour

A small number of the sentences collected also talk about one's own English in a light-hearted, playful and humorous manner:

> i don't speak english. . .really. . .all i know how to say is. . .i don't speak english.
>
> *(Pam)*

My English is not perfect, so be kind if you're the Shakespeare's kind of person or try to write like this in Spanish.

(*Kris001*, Spanish)

Photography as the lingua franca

To some Flickr members, language is secondary to photography on Flickr. Thus, a small number of sentences in the corpus reflect people's awareness of the central role of photography on Flickr:

I don't understand english very well, but this photo impress me. Sometimes the image is enough.

(*Jean*, Italian)

And here is an example used earlier, in Chapter 5:

My English is so . . .. .. .poor ! so, I take photos. . .
唉中文都一樣不見得是好 ! (sigh. . .my Chinese isn't good either!)
都是拍照算了 (I should better take photos.)

(*Tiong*, Chinese)

Returning to the concept of stance-taking, this initial content analysis of the corpus clearly reveals the participants' stance towards the English they use on Flickr and their perceived affordances of English in their Flickr participation, that is, what sorts of action possibilities that English can offer when writing online. First, the structure of these statements conforms to the two most common types of stance described in Chapter 5, epistemic and affective stances. By expressing their lack of knowledge through cognitive verbs (e.g. 'I don't know English'), and by expressing feelings about their English using common adjectives of evaluation (e.g. 'My English is bad'), the participants position themselves as not-so-proficient English users. In addition, these types of stance are expressed through similar linguistic structure, with extensive use of first-person singular pronouns 'I' and 'my', and words that denote possession such as 'my own English', thus claiming ownership of such 'poor' English.

Why then is it important for the Flickr users to tell others how much English they know or don't know? While it was not our intention to evaluate a particular participant's proficiency level of English, what is striking is that in many instances the participant's English written on Flickr is indeed highly communicative, despite their negative self-evaluations. This is shown in many of the examples above. Another important observation about these utterances is that they are not simply statements about one's knowledge of English. The concerns about English grammar and spelling expressed in the statements are often related to their participation in Flickr, such as how knowledge of English would affect their writing of captions and descriptions, or how participation in Flickr can indeed help improve their English and so on.

To further understand the motivations behind these self-deprecating comments and how they might affect level of participation in Flickr, we interviewed 10 participants via Flickr's private email system. When asked why they wanted to talk about their English knowledge on Flickr, views from the interviewees were quite divided. A number of them explained it in terms of their worries of possible communication breakdown if their readers did not understand their English, such as:

> I scare I write something funny mistakes or peoples don't understood me.
>
> (*digikid*, Finnish)

By the same token, some would take into consideration the self-image that they might project to their target audience if they did not use 'correct' English. Thus, admitting to a low level of English, some expect others to accept the errors in their English. This is illustrated by *Amilia*'s explanation as follows:

> I think by telling people that my English is not good, so they can accept that; 'Oh, his English isn't good enough, that's why there is some grammar error in his photo's description/title.' when there is a grammar error in my photo's description or titles.
>
> (*Amilia*, Malaysian)

A similar idea is reinforced by *Celia*, who pointed out that she could not tolerate errors in her native language:

> Warning people not to know English, because in Portuguese bother me much spelling mistakes and grammatical serious!
>
> (*Celia*, Portuguese)

Both *Amilia* and *Celia* reinforce what Leech (1983) referred to as the Modesty Maxim (which was later renamed just *Modesty* by Leech 2005), i.e. minimizing praise of oneself or maximizing dispraise of oneself in order to achieve certain illocutionary goals. To these Flickr participants, degrading their English proficiency allows them to create a friendly and supportive social space.

To some users, by contrast, telling others how much English they know or do not know is an expression of identity, that English knowledge is part of who they are and who they are to others on Flickr, as *Mika* explains:

> Well, I don't think it's so important to tell people how my english is. [. . .] my poor english level is a part of me. So I thought it was right to notice this point.
>
> (*Mika*, French)

These interview excerpts show that self-deprecations of ones' English skills is more than simply an act of devaluing oneself or just being modest.

As pointed out in Chapter 5, the structure of a stance utterance does not necessarily suggest its pragmatic function. As shown in this chapter, telling others how little English they know does allow these Flickr participants to achieve various meaningful purposes on Flickr. A range of reasons were given by the interview participants. From the limited set of interview data collected, it is at least known that talking about English skills allows participants to build rapport, to ensure mutual intelligibility, and to negotiate identity in the Flickr world. It is also clear that the very act of talking about one's own language skills is an act of opening themselves to the global Flickr world, an act of positioning themselves as active participants.

METADISCURSIVE CONSTRUCTION OF A SUPPORTIVE SOCIAL SPACE

Bringing the examples and analysis of discourses about English in this chapter together, it can be seen that these seemingly negative comments about English abilities are often taken by participants quite positively, and even playfully, as demonstrated earlier under the category 'self-deprecating humour' in the content analysis. For one thing, switching to a different language from their native language is certainly an indication of people's readiness to communicate. Users with limited knowledge of English constantly express keen interest in participating in the internet as global participants who are willing to write in a language that may have little or even no use for them elsewhere in their offline lives.

The strong presence of self-deprecating comments about one's knowledge of English is also evidence of people's strong desire to participate as a competent member on Flickr. Competence broadly refers to expert skills and knowledge one needs in order to become a legitimate member in a given community (Lave and Wenger 1991; see also Chapter 3). To many Flickr users, being competent in English is indeed an important form of cultural capital in their participation. However, at the same time, they are aware that linguistic competence can be constantly negotiated. This is often achieved through the act of self-evaluation such as the data presented in this chapter. Using concepts in stance-taking again, evaluation is an act of alignment and positioning in discourse (Du Bois 2007). By repositioning themselves as not-so-competent English users through self-deprecating comments such as 'My English is so poor', people are at the same time negotiating their identity such that they will be accepted by others as legitimate participants on Flickr. And these negative self-evaluations are a central discourse type for negotiating such membership.

In addition to negotiating membership, a great deal of social networking is also initiated by explicitly declaring one's own English abilities. An example to illustrate this is a photo page that belongs to *CB*, a German speaker, displaying a picture of a Japanese style bento lunch that she had made. Underneath the photo, *CB* wrote her photo title and description in English:

> Bentolunch for tomorrow (Friday)
> Today my new bentobox arrived! It's a pretty bentobox with a little bunny on the top.
> Of course I had to use it, so I prepared my bento for tomorrow quickly ∧.∧
> (Sorry, I know my English is so so bad! I definitly have to learn it better .. T.T

This photo description, though written in quite 'proper' English, contains what we have called 'apologetic' evaluation, written in parentheses: 'Sorry, I know my English is so so bad!'. This, however, brings *CB* a great deal of encouraging and supportive comments from other Flickr users, who even praise her English. Here are some comments posted below the photo caption:

> *pixi125*:   Pretty bento. And I think your English is good!
> *Deebibi*:   Trust me, your English is a lot better than the English of many native
>   speakers. ∧_~
> *CB*:   thank you so much, pixi125.. I learned english for 5 years at school, but I
>   think it isn't good enough for that ><' Hehe, nice to meet you, Deebibi!!
>   Your comment is so nice ∧.∧ [. . .]

All of the comments, including the one written by *CB* herself, point to *CB*'s remark about her English being 'so so bad', instead of the actual content of the image, or the description of the bento lunch underneath. In response to such encouraging comments, *CB*, while expressing her gratitude, stresses again that her English 'isn't good enough.' What seems to be a traditional compliment-giving and compliment response sequence here serves to build solidarity between *CB* and her Flickr friends. Another relevant point about this comment thread is the way the commenters respond to *CB*'s self-evaluation of her English. While praising *CB*'s English, these commenters indeed position themselves as more 'skilled' users of English, which is why they were able to assess *CB*'s English as 'better than native speakers'. *CB*, in this situation, however, does not have this authority to evaluate their English. This interesting power relation echoes Chun and Walters's (2011) analysis of Arabic speakers' comments on the comedian Chung's native-sounding Arabic on YouTube, as discussed earlier in the chapter.

Apart from the standard apologetic type of discourse about her own English, *CB* also expresses commitment to learning English. She says in the photo description: 'I definitly [sic] have to learn it better .. T.T (crying emoticon)'. Her commitment to self-improvement allows her to also reposition herself as an active language learner on Flickr with a positive attitude. It seems that her perceived poor English is actually one of the strongest motivations behind her participation in Flickr. This kind of self-improvement and learning discourse is indeed very prominent in our Flickr data, where users often juxtapose their 'poor English' with their commitment to learning better English through active participation in Flickr.

LINGUISTIC REFLEXIVITY AS POWERFUL DIGITAL DISCOURSE

Reflexivity is a key property of human language. Language users are able to use language to reflect on language and its use in their everyday lives. Metalanguage is a salient dimension of language and talking about language has become a common practice in our increasingly textually mediated social world. New media have also provided new opportunities and spaces for social actors to reflect upon language-related issues, especially in the form of written language. The examples and findings presented in this chapter have clearly shown that web participants often talk about language and the learning of it; people evaluate their own and others' knowledge of language; people are motivated language learners; and people regularly reflect upon their folk linguistic theories. They do not need to be expert users of a certain language to assess it and how it should or should not be used.

Self-deprecating metalinguistic discourse is found to be particularly pervasive in Web 2.0 spaces, as shown in many of our examples. We have discussed a particular example of how people talk about English on Flickr to further illustrate this. The seemingly negative evaluations about one's own English are not simply a result of being modest or self-devaluing; explicitly acknowledging one's limited knowledge of English is indeed a powerful discourse on Flickr as it serves a wide range of social functions, such as social networking and widening participation. The chapter also reveals the ways in which new media sites such as Flickr provide the affordances and writing spaces that enable users to create a collaborative, supportive environment to express their vernacular theories of language through self-generated content.

This chapter also serves to bring together the themes presented in previous chapters about multilingual practices, identity construction and stance-taking. For the particular group of participants in our study, being able to reflect on their language abilities and to show awareness of their language choice is a way of expressing willingness to engage in the increasingly multi-cultural and multilingual online world. In particular, self-deprecating meta-linguistic comments allow users to assert their specific stances or positions towards language in relation to their online participation. In so doing, they are also doing some identity work – they portray themselves as particular kinds of language users, thus asserting who they are to others.

More broadly, metalinguistic discourses are always *situated practices*, a central notion that informs our study of language online. For one thing, these comments are always located on a web page which is in itself part of a complex nexus of other web pages containing other metadiscourses about languages, which in turn are also situated in broader social practices and ideologies, such as public or mass media representation of language in society. As we have seen, participating in metalinguistic discourses also allows web users to co-construct an environment that supports informal, self-directed, and collaborative learning. This also sets the scene for the next chapter about discourses of learning online.

9

EVERYDAY LEARNING ONLINE

- Theories of adult learning
- 365, a deliberate act of learning
- How people learn online
- Language learning in supportive networked spaces

Language and learning are woven into each other in many ways and most learning involves using and extending language. Language provides a powerful medium for learning and for being reflexive. People then have some control over their learning: they articulate their learning, and language provides the discourses, the strategies and theories they operate from. As we have already shown in Chapter 8, in global online spaces such as Flickr, participants often reflect on the learning opportunities they are able to take up, including learning about language. One thing that they are learning is how to use those forms of language appropriately, providing ways to interact with a wider range of people from all parts of the world. New social media have also provided valuable spaces for informal language learning, which we will cover later in this chapter. Within the languages people already know, they are expanding their repertoires and learning new genres and styles. This is true whether the aim is learning to play the guitar, learning to take good photos, learning to be a supportive friend, or learning English. Language can be the aim of learning; it can be a resource for learning, and it can be both. Whatever they are learning, people are participating in new language practices.

This chapter shows how online spaces are important sites of learning of all sorts, especially languages. The chapter examines how online spaces change the ways in which people learn and how these spaces are important in how they support learning. It argues that, with its forms of support and its spaces for reflexivity, the internet can be a particularly good place for learning. The chapter turns first to theories of learning more generally and provides a brief overview of theories relevant to how adults learn in their everyday lives. It then uses examples from the Flickr data, as well as Facebook and IM, to show how key aspects of these theories apply to language online. The chapter points to the role of other people and networks for learning. It then links up with a set of issues around reflexivity, identity and discourses of learning that have been introduced in earlier chapters. The chapter concludes with a focus on language learning showing how informal language learning takes place in various online spaces.

THEORIES OF ADULT LEARNING

So far in this book we have described and worked within a social practice view of language to explore language online. Here we complement that with a social practice view of learning. This approach to language and literacy practices has identified issues such as the importance of interactions with others, of specific forms of participation in different sorts of groups, and of reflexivity. These are key in understanding how language is used. The starting point for this investigation of learning is people in their everyday lives and it is not the more usual starting point of children in schools and other educational settings, where participation is compulsory and learning is relatively controlled by teachers. As explained earlier, understanding people's practices is a prerequisite for examining learning, and learning in everyday contexts is a basis for learning in formal educational settings. In this way, there are educational implications of everyday uses of social media and these are pursued in Chapter 11. While existing research on digital literacies has identified a wide range of learning activities and opportunities in online spaces, a language focus is often missing.

To provide a brief overview of a social practice view of learning, this approach views learning as consisting of active participation in social practices. People are active participants in their learning. They have their own individual aims located within a cultural environment and their learning is purposeful and self-directed. They have their own motivations and make their own meanings and connections to their existing knowledge. People take on different roles and identities within practices and changing the way that they participate in a particular practice can be a form of learning. People are often part of networks of support and communities of practice that support their learning. This approach emphasizes the central role of social interaction and mediational tools, and the importance of appropriate tools as structuring learning environments and supporting learning. Learning is going on all the time, and is often implicit and unnoticed. Nevertheless, people can and do articulate things about their learning and this reflexivity can aid and guide learning. This summary has been adapted from Tusting and Barton (2006), which provides a longer integrated overview of theories of how adults learn. A socio-cultural view of learning where practices are central has been most clearly articulated in the work of Jean Lave on situated learning (Lave 1988) together with Etienne Wenger's work (1998) elaborating ideas of learning within communities of practice. This work stresses the importance of participation and changing forms of participation. These approaches were developed in offline contexts and it is worth examining the extent to which they apply to Web 2.0 activity.

365, A DELIBERATE ACT OF LEARNING

Many of the examples used so far have been taken from the study of multilingualism on Flickr. In this chapter, a new set of Flickr data is being introduced. In the multilingual data, one person was participating in an activity of taking a photo a day for a year. This is referred to as '365' in Flickr discussions, and he belonged to a Flickr group devoted to this. It turned out to be a very common activity that was worth studying in its own right in more detail. 365 is an activity where someone undertakes to take a photo a day for a year and put each one up on Flickr. There are many groups devoted to 365 activities. In some of them the photo can be on any topic; others have specific topics, such as a group where the photos have to be self-portraits. Many Flickr members undertake 365 projects of their own but do not add their photos to group sites. This is a particular photographic practice that was started on Flickr and has spread to other sites, such as Tumblr. It is dependent on a chain of new technologies available for the easy production and circulation of images. This practice was not really feasible in earlier print photography where it would have been expensive and there would have been a time lag between taking the photo and seeing the results. When the 365 groups were set up there was not any particular expectation of feedback or support from others. Nevertheless, it has become a very social activity and, as we will see, there can also be a great deal of self-evaluation in these projects.

Looking across the Flickr sites of photographers who were undertaking a 365 project, it was soon clear that learning was frequently mentioned and so a detailed examination of 365 sites was carried out. Initially, more than 200 sites where people have undertaken a photo a day projects were identified by searching for '365'. From these, 50 sites where people talked about their learning were examined in more detail, again using content analysis to identify key themes. The data from these sites will be referred to as the '365 data' and will be included alongside discussions of learning in the multilingual data. Overall the data consists of analysis of the sites including what people say about learning there, together with online interviews with the multilingual Flickr users. More detailed analysis of this data appears in Barton (2012).

Going back to the multilingualism study, the first point to emphasize is that the people studied were not asked about learning: it was not mentioned in the questions, nor in the interview protocols. They were asked about language choice and multilingual practices. Nevertheless, we found that people frequently mentioned their learning and they spontaneously reflected on how they learned. We had also noticed from further analysis of their Flickr sites, including their profiles, that there were many references to learning. People were drawing on their multilingual resources, developing them and learning to deploy them in new ways. These observations provide the starting point for this examination of learning on Flickr.

Turning to what people were learning, there are different sorts of learning going on side by side in any situation. The Flickr members were learning about a range of topics in a general way and they were learning how to participate in various activities in specific practical ways. People reported they were learning about Flickr. This includes learning about the affordances of the different writing spaces. Initially they have to learn how to use titles and descriptions, tags, commenting and profiles as new spaces. They do this partly through a form of intertextual learning (Lee 2009), drawing on existing practices elsewhere and applying them to new contexts. A simple example of this is that some Flickr users had come across tagging on other sites before they started using Flickr and they drew upon this earlier experience.

At the same time they were learning about photography more generally and that was often their stated aim. More broadly people reported that they were learning about themselves and their lives. They often made comments about this broader perspective. This was sometimes partway through the project or at the end they often looked back and summarized what they had got out of taking a photo a day for a year, as explained by *Jumx*:

> I'm grateful to the 365 project for the many things it has taught me – how to get in front of the camera, for one! . . .I've learned more about portrait photography, lighting, creative use of timers, about myself – my body, my face, my life. Looking back, it's a wonderful chronicle of a year.
>
> *(Jumx)*

These purposes are learned informally as people take up new affordances of Flickr and as they participate actively on the site. To some of the participants, Flickr is a site for learning about photography. To many others, participating in Flickr is a process of discovering new purposes for using Flickr over time. Whether the learning was deliberate or unconscious, participating in Flickr not only provides opportunities for people to learn how to do things on Flickr, it also changes people's writing practices over time as their perceived purposes of Flickr change, a topic which will be discussed later.

HOW PEOPLE LEARN ONLINE

Turning from *what* people learn online to *how* people learn online, we can make several points which are important for any learning: people learn by participation in practices; this involves joining with other people; people reflect upon their online participation; and learning involves taking on new identities.

People learn by participating in practices

Learning can be seen as participation: how people participate in a broader range of practices and the ways in which they change the way they participate. This is active participation in practices and changing forms of engagement. One such change that Lave and Wenger (1991) identified is moving from being on the edge to being central within the practice. They refer to this as 'legitimate peripheral participation'. When applied to online activities, this validates the act of initially observing what other people are doing and lurking as reasonable ways of learning to participate in new activities. In our research, learning by doing can be clearly seen in university students' participation in IM. None of the participants in that study reported that they had ever consulted any documents (such as official websites, online tutorials, the 'help' option in the chat programmes, or guide books) before using IM. When asked how they learnt to use it, many did not see using IM as involving any formal learning:

> I don't need to learn it. . .I just observe
>
> (Erika)

> No I just picked it up!
>
> (JC)

> I don't need to learn anything. . .it's very easy to use!
>
> (Lo)

These comments do not suggest that no learning took place at all. Rather, these views reveal that students' learning-related activities in IM often took place unnoticed and incidentally through participation in informal and routine activities in everyday life. Some students learnt about how to use IM through informal conversations with friends and family. Some acquired knowledge of linguistic resources through everyday experience of using texts. Other cases of learning took place during the actual IM sessions, such as observing how their chat partners use a particular emoticon.

When it comes to more recent Web 2.0 activity, a key feature is that content is user-generated so that learning is embedded in the process of using the internet. In this way the distinction between learning and use begins to break down. As noted earlier, many online participants have had years of experience with different sorts of online communication spaces. Many of their practices in newer sites are indeed carried over from what they have learned in older or existing media. We have noticed, for example, that people learn to write status updates on Facebook not only by participating in Facebook itself, but also by their concurrent participation in IM. To some, status updates on Facebook first reminded them of 'mood messages' on IM, the short messages (usually one-liners) that appear on one's contact list to update friends about current mood or what one is up to. In online spaces, such intertextual learning is a crucial form of learning by participation.

On Flickr, people learn all the time and everywhere. In this way what is happening in Web 2.0 spaces fits well with the earlier work on how people learn. As mentioned earlier, although the multilingual study reported in Chapter 4 was not about learning, the Flickr participants nevertheless often referred to learning when talking about their Flickr activities. Like our observations of learning on IM, the Flickr participants said they just picked up the mechanics of using Flickr without any conscious effort. However, elsewhere they refer to learning about other aspects of life. Some people made explicit references to how they learned, such as deliberately searching for advice about specific problems. They referred to learning more indirectly and explained how others shared their knowledge, referring to other people as teachers or role models. Flickr was seen as a supportive space. Overall people were using Flickr for many purposes and using it in many everyday practices and they took up affordances and opportunities for learning of all sorts.

People draw on others as resources for learning

In the techno-biographies discussed in Chapter 6, we saw that many online participants started their internet experience by learning from their 'technology mentors' such as their parents and school friends. These people not only introduced them to the world of the internet, but also influenced their language choice online in various ways. Similarly, Flickr users are constantly linked in to other users in and beyond the photo-sharing site. They refer to other people when talking about their learning experiences. People talk about experimenting, observing others and taking advice from them. This mixture of activities and the role of others is summarized in the words of another Flickr member, written in his profile in French and repeated in English. He summarizes the different ways he learns:

> I began photography dragged to this passion by a friend. Since then, I love the challenge to try to improve my skills and create beautiful images. I didn't have any specific training, so I had to experiment with different techniques by observing others work and following the advices of my flickr's friends.
>
> (Guianx)

In Chapter 3 we referred to people supporting each other by acting as mediators, mentors and brokers. The examples provided so far of people talking about their activities within Flickr have emphasized the role of others in these ways. One space on Flickr where such networking takes place is commenting, and users have developed a culture of giving positive and encouraging feedback on each other's photos. Positive comments and feedback from others provide a friendly, supportive, and relatively safe environment for informal learning to take place (see also Davies and Merchant 2009; Black 2009). People also talked of the networks of support which they are located in and which they draw upon and the importance of reciprocity. Often they praised Flickr as supporting their learning:

> Flickr has been such a great place to learn and teach, to have a friend or be a friend . . .. to press myself for more or to just seek relief from my busy day.
>
> *(Krix)*

This comment also shows the importance of the software itself and people often discussed and compared different software. Flickr provides a framework of support for learning by the way it is structured. This 'scaffolding' is particularly important when considering online activity. Flickr as a platform can be seen as a sponsor of certain sorts of practices in that it has been deliberately and consciously designed and it is constantly redesigned. Designers want their sites to be easy to use and for people to progress through them in a straightforward way. Online sites are therefore designed to be engaging, and even to be enjoyable.

When discussing this support, it is important not just to identify reading and writing as something which individuals do within networks. Rather, groups of various sorts may use reading and writing in different ways. It is much broader than this and Deborah Brandt (1998, 2001) talks of the role of individuals and institutions acting as 'sponsors' of literacy practices and as supporters and facilitators for people. The idea of sponsors makes it clear that support comes from both individuals and institutions. These sponsors support specific views and provide a framing to act within. Taken together these ideas can help show how people act within the possibilities available to them online, and contribute to that framing. People identify with particular online resources, and in the example here they identify strongly with Flickr and also with others involved in the 365 activity. Participation in 365 can best be seen as participation in an affinity group, a transitory grouping where people join together for a specific purpose, and they may move in and out of such groupings (as discussed in Chapter 3).

These structural supports are complex in online sites. Some structures are from the original makers, the owners (who, with the exception of Wikipedia, are mainly private businesses aiming to make a profit from our use of their products). Around Flickr and many Web 2.0 sites there are also individuals who add tools for everyone to use, and who may or may not be motivated by profit. So Flickr users themselves may use uploading tools, or other tools, for instance to make collages or to edit their pictures, which are made by fellow users. Users may also set up discussion spaces for others to use for teaching and learning, such as the 'Learn a New Language!' group. These can all be seen as sponsoring particular practices. The features of Web 2.0 are ideal for informal learning, given that it is interactive and collaborative, that content is user-generated and that social support and networking are central. On Flickr, learning happens everywhere. Having conflated learning and use, we also accept that there are nexuses of learning, particular places where learning is more likely. The 365 groups and the Flickr blog, for instance, can be seen as particular nexuses of learning. In addition, Flickr can be used as a deliberate educational resource, as we show in Chapter 11.

Reflexivity supports learning

There are spaces for extensive reflection on Flickr and other sites, where a culture of supportive commenting has grown up. Although it is not the primary or the stated purpose of such sites, part of the way in which Flickr and the web in general are providing learning spaces is in the particular spaces where people can self-reflect and talk about themselves, their lives, their hopes and, as we have seen, their learning. Just as educational spaces can provide a safe environment for exploration, the people studied here saw Flickr as a safe environment for learning where they had considerable control and where deliberate acts of learning were supported. These spaces can become transformative ones.

The combination of written language and images is powerful for reflexivity. During the year when people were carrying out 365 they might comment on what they learned from specific photos. In this way, reflexive learning on Flickr is a multimodal act. One man often reported what he had learned from each day's photograph, so for example writing one day:

> Maybe not the most interesting shot for many of you, but for me it's important to not only use the images that I think look the best, but also the ones that I have learnt something through. This whole project has been about learning and the biggest thing I have learned so far is how important light is – in many ways it is the most complex, but valuable tool a photographer has.
>
> (Andx)

He then made similar reflections on other days. Here there was constant learning by him, through reflecting on his self-generated content. In this way, people explore new affordances and create the possibilities for learning.

Reflexivity, that is self-reflection which leads to action, is central to theories of how adults learn. The idea is that people take space and time to reflect on their experiences and it is through such reflection that they turn their experiences into learning. People can 'learn about learning' and become 'autonomous learners' (Benson 2004) in the sense that they are not dependent on formal teachers. While much learning may be incidental and unplanned, learning based on reflexivity can be powerful. Reflection is crucial for transformative learning: that is, certain activities, such as encountering problems, can lead to reflection, enabling people to recognize their experiences and see them in new ways, potentially transforming the personal and the social. This links up with particular approaches to education: transformative learning is an integral part of a social practice pedagogy (Barton *et al.* 2007) and is an essential step in a multiliteracies pedagogy (Cope and Kalantzis 2000: 30–36).

Elsewhere, research on learning in adults' lives has identified the importance of 'imagined futures' as well as pointing to the significance of people's life histories and how these shape current practices and identities (Barton *et al.* 2007). People were seen to make choices about their actions based on a combination of the possible options they perceived in their current circumstances, and the futures they desired or imagined to be possible for themselves. This orientation to the future is an important aspect of reflexivity. Crucially, these imagined futures can change over time – at first people may set out to use Flickr to share their photos with friends and they later join other groups and meet new people when they see the widening possibilities. This is not only relevant for understanding the 365 Flickr activities, but is also true to much of people's online activity, as shown in people's techno-biographies where they talked about changes in practices throughout their technology histories.

What is interesting in terms of learning is that someone's 365 project is often a consciously reflective one. These are deliberate acts of learning. Sometimes people comment on what they are doing as they go along, expressing their hopes at the beginning of the project, then reflecting as they progress with it, and looking back – and forward – when they have finished, or when they give up part way through. Others only reflect on the project when they have finished it. In many cases this involves commenting specifically on their learning from their participation in the 365 project.

In the longest entry in the photo-a-day data, at the end of her 365 project a woman from UAE listed '99 things I learnt from my 365 days project'. In the list she is highly reflexive, in the sense of thinking about and making sense of what she has done and is doing. To give an example of the list:

> 1- I realized how much I adore surreal.
>
> 2- never give up, this project taught me how to handle and stick on my decisions !
>
> 3- concepts first, perspective second, techniques third.
>
> 4- I learnt how to draw/ create my own line in photography.
>
> 5- copying myself or even other people works is boring !
>
> [. . .]
>
> 96- I'm in love with deep or complicated photos who made me think twice.
>
> 97- conceptual type is my thing !
>
> 98- offer the photo what it need so she can offer you great results.
>
> 99- and finally I learnt that good friends who share their true opinions are the ones who love you.
>
> (Anwx)

She combines comments about photography with observations about herself. She then uses this reflexivity to talk about plans and possibilities for the future. This Flickr page has had more than 1,250 views and more than 70 comments from other people complimenting her and discussing the list.

The discussions and comments, such as the ones above, all add up to a particular discourse of learning: that learning is a good thing; it is a challenge; it is fun; it involves other people; and people can be both teachers and learners in their everyday lives. Most work on discourses of learning has been carried out within educational contexts, and has been concerned with identifying dominant discourses which underlie different approaches to teaching (as in Ivanič 2004). Rather than identify dominant discourses, here we are more interested in people's own ways of talking about learning, that is, their vernacular discourses, as in the previous chapter. These will be hybrid, shifting and context-dependent, and will draw on a range of sources (including dominant discourses) but in the data here they sediment into a characteristic way of talking about learning in this space.

There are of course many discourses drawn upon in Flickr, and they can have contradictory characteristics; in Chapter 8 we drew attention to the seemingly more negative discourse where people talk about their lack of knowledge of languages, as in 'my English is so poor'. There is also a limit to the data discussed so far in that it is dealing with comments about learning that were made in passing. However, when asked directly about how they learned, as when they say that they 'just picked it up', learning becomes naturalized and people may not easily reflect upon it.

Learning as taking on new identities

Learning is always about taking on new identities. For the multilingual participants they were often conscious of how using Flickr changed them as they came into contact with new people across the world. In some ways they were developing new ways of becoming multilingual, as discussed in Chapter 5. Often the effects of participation were unexpected. This was apparent with the people taking a photo a day. They sometimes saw participation as life changing, as effectively becoming a different person. We have discussed in Chapter 6 how participants' relationship with technologies are shaped by the different identities and roles they play in both their online and offline lives (such as the example of how Tony shifted between his student and teacher identities on two Facebook sites). In our Flickr data, people reported how unexpected the changes to their lives were:

> I thought it would be fun, challenging, and a great way to document a year in my life. I had NO IDEA at all how much it would change my life.
>
> (kelx)

Some people in the 365 project certainly saw themselves as becoming different people as a result of this learning. The effects that the 365 project had on people's lives were often unexpected, and they expressed surprise at its pervasive influence. This included surprise at the breadth of what they were learning about, even a sense of wonder at their own learning. Some people reported a life-changing year. Often they drew upon the metaphor of learning as a journey, and this could also be realized as a literal journey:

> When I started this project, I was engaged, living in Washington, D.C., had a great job, and had no clue what the hell I was doing with a camera.
>
> During these 365 Days, I have broken off an engagement, quit my job to travel and move to San Francisco, met so many people that I consider my best friends, met a guy that makes me happy, and found my voice through photography.
>
> I never thought when I started this that my life would change so drastically. I never thought that I would meet people through Flickr that I could lean on during one of the roughest years of my life.
>
> *(Dotx)*

LANGUAGE LEARNING IN SUPPORTIVE NETWORKED SPACES

Part of the learning that takes place online is learning to use language. This is both learning about texts and learning about practices, effectively learning the structures of language and also how to use language. James Gee refers to this as 'the internal (design) and external (behaviour) grammars' (Gee 2005: 223). The former refers to the grammar of content while the latter is the grammar of social practices and identities. In Gee's study, where he examined the everyday activity of video gaming, a great deal of the learning consists of the participants learning to extend their language use.

In a large-scale study of the online practices of young people in the United States carried out by Mimi Ito and colleagues, they explore the self-directed learning which takes place on the internet and they show the ways in which the online world lowers barriers to learning (Ito *et al.* 2010). The internet, a space supporting friendship-driven networks, enables young people to learn informally from one another in a stress-free environment. Much of the informal learning in the study took place in what is called 'peer-based interaction' online, such as IM and Facebook. Such learning includes expanding ways of using their first language.

Turning to second language learning, sites such as YouTube allow people to post videos on language learning. Looking through what is offered for learning English, this ranges from the old-fashioned and traditional uses, through zany and parodying videos, to innovative Web 2.0 inspired ones. Similarly, the range of videos for an English speaker to learn Chinese is eclectic. Moving to more informal and often incidental learning, many other global websites create environments where people may interact extensively in more than one language and there is space for the informal learning of second languages. The value of these spaces for language learning is demonstrated in how people talk about languages online as well as in their reflexive accounts in techno-biographic interviews. New media not only offer new platforms for people to reflect upon and articulate their own theories and ideas about learning, as shown throughout this chapter, but these new spaces also give rise to new language learning opportunities, in the context of learning a second or foreign language.

Eva Lam has carried out a series of case studies of the out-of-school second language literacy practices of young Chinese immigrants to the United States. Her work has been concerned with how these young people represent and reconstruct their second language learner identities through participating in online networks. In one study (Lam 2009), she examines in detail how a Cantonese speaking immigrant, Kaiyee, develops her Cantonese and English abilities through instant messaging with three groups – a local network of Chinese immigrants where participants combine Mandarin and Cantonese, a gaming network where African American Vernacular English is used, and finally a transnational network where Kaiyee would mix Mandarin with Shanghainese when chatting with other IM participants. Through drawing upon multiple linguistic resources in these networked groups, Kaiyee and the other young immigrants gradually developed their new multilingual identities alongside their linguistic abilities in English and Cantonese.

There have been many studies of gaming online and the learning that takes place, such as Gee's (2004) study mentioned earlier. A growing body of work looks into the value of video gaming in second language learning. Kuure (2011: 37), for example, shows how Finnish speakers take up opportunities for English language learning offered by online gaming and how these opportunities support social relationships and collaborative problem solving. In Kuure's study, Oskari, a young Finnish man, was frequently exposed to the English language when participating in online gaming and practices around it. He interacted with international gamers in English; and when he was unsure about his English use, he turned to his family who used dictionaries to help him, or to work things out with his peers in chat rooms. To give another example, a major study entitled 'English in a Globalized Finland' interviewed Finnish people of all ages. It found that the internet is a very prominent domain for reading and writing in English. The language is used extensively online for a range of activities, the most common being searching, reading newspapers, participating in discussion forums, ordering goods and services, and playing games (Leppänen et al. 2011).

Another approach is to start out from sites supporting specific practices, so that Benson and Chan (2011), for instance, have examined the practice of subtitling of videos, or fansubbing, which is done largely by young people and is a vernacular practice. This provides a lively space for learning and Benson and Chan found extensive comments that discuss language. People comment on and correct the translations and discuss language issues with each other. In their study, Ito et al. (2010) also mention fansubbing as a space for learning and how the activities young people participate in can include cross-language collaborations, but they do not focus specifically on language learning.

In another study, which is framed in a literacy studies approach, Benson and Chik (2010) explore how university students in Hong Kong take up English learning opportunities online. They specifically examine the learning histories of two university students, CK and Sophie, and discuss how their English improves over time through participating voluntarily in online gaming and fanfiction.net respectively. Both students are actively involved in written communication with native English speakers on these platforms. Sophie, for example, is a keen writer of fan-fiction, texts created by fans of popular novels and other original works, often posted on fan-fiction sites. While posting her work on fanfiction.net, she constantly seeks advice from other English speakers in the network by 'asking and trying', as she puts it. As time goes on, her English knowledge enhances as her fan-fiction texts improve. Such learning activities, as we can observe, are autonomous, self-directed and collaborative. Also focusing on fanfiction.net, Black (2009) offers a close text analysis of the feedback one Chinese teenager receives on her 14-chapter fan-fiction text *Love Letters*. Through drawing upon different discourse strategies, such as self-deprecatory comments on her knowledge of English (see also Chapter 8), Black shows how the fan-fiction authors and commenters co-design a supportive and encouraging English learning environment.

Although these varied studies focus primarily on second language learning of English online, they all point to the important fact that learning in new networked spaces often takes place incidentally and is not controlled by any authority. The learning activities identified are all situated. They often start with a particular purpose, such as to revise and improve on a fan-fiction text; they often involve support from others; they are constantly changing and renegotiated. All these are in line with the social practice view of literacies and learning that we take in this book. These language learning activities also reveal how language learners perceive, take up, and rediscover the affordances of online interaction spaces so as to reassert their cultural and linguistic identities. More broadly, new networked spaces such as Flickr, YouTube, and fan-fiction sites have all proved to be relatively safe and supportive environments for learning of all sorts. There is a shift in the relationship between everyday informal learning and the more formal educational domains, and the spaces between them. The technology breaks down borders between domains of activity. Accepting this shift and taking account of it in designing pedagogies is a major challenge for all fields of learning, including second language learning.

10

LANGUAGE ONLINE AS NEW VERNACULAR PRACTICES

- Vernacular literacies
- Popular photography as a vernacular practice
- Pregnancy as online literacy practices: The case of Peggy
- Redefining the vernacular in a global context

The main research discussed in this book so far, about Facebook, Flickr and Instant Messaging, has started out from these particular online platforms and has gone back and forth between examining the language on the sites and investigating people's language and literacy practices. An alternative starting point, which we are turning to in this chapter, is to step back and to start from social practices in people's everyday lives, their vernacular practices, and to find out how they draw upon new media in carrying out activities in their lives. Specifically, this alternative approach starts from people's lives and examines how they draw upon vernacular language and literacy practices to get things done. We now return to vernacular literacies, which were introduced in Chapter 1. We examine how the practices associated with reading and writing are being transformed by people's participation in online activities and, as a result, how the dynamics of everyday life are changing in profound ways.

This chapter first provides a more detailed overview of the concept of vernacular literacies and examines general changes in literacy practices that have been taking place in the past 20 years. We then revisit the local literacies data collected in the 1990s (Barton and Hamilton 1998). It is worth returning to the social practices documented in that study to see how these have changed as a result of new media. Our starting point is a specific vernacular practice, popular photography, providing a brief history and examining how it has been transformed by new media, specifically Flickr. Drawing on further examples from Facebook and elsewhere, we then return to the characteristics of vernacular literacies and discuss how their meanings are changing in Web 2.0 spaces and how they are now more valued as people participate in more global spaces. The chapter addresses the extent to which the writing practices on Web 2.0 constitute new literacy practices and, more broadly, to what extent the characteristics of vernacular literacies are changing in a global context.

The reason for revisiting the notion of vernacular literacies is that new digital media are changing the ways people can act in their everyday lives. Technologies have been 'domesticated', in that they have moved into having a central role in everyday lives. As we have seen in Chapter 6, everyone has a unique techno-biography. People use computers, the internet and mobile devices in their lives for writing, obviously with email, texting, and instant messaging, but, as we will demonstrate, also in many more ways. Technologies provide ways for people to engage in new activities, ones which they have not engaged in before and which have not been possible before.

VERNACULAR LITERACIES

Vernacular literacy practices are rooted in everyday experiences and serve everyday purposes. Barton and Hamilton's (1998) 'local literacies' study of the role of reading and writing in an English town identified key areas of everyday life where reading and writing had a central role for people. These areas were: *organizing life,* including activities such as checking timetables, writing to-do lists and the records they kept of their finances; *personal communication,* such as the notes, cards and letters people sent to friends and relatives; the practices involved in personal *leisure activities* they participated in including sports and music; the *documenting of life* where people maintained records of their own and their family's lives; the *sense making* people carried out in relation to such things as health issues, legal issues and understanding their children's development; and their *social participation* in a wide range of activities. The vernacular literacies ranged from record keeping and note taking through to extended writing of diaries, fictional writing, life histories and local histories. This framework has been used in other studies, as varied as a study of the practices around Icelandic sagas (Olafsson 2012) and a study of Edwardian postcards (Gillen and Hall 2010). We return to this framework later to show how the ways in which people act in these areas have been transformed by new media and the shifting role of language.

A key feature of vernacular literacies is that they are voluntary and self-generated, rather than being framed and valued by the needs of social institutions. Dominant institutions in fields such as education, law and religion sponsor particular forms of literacy, meaning that they support, structure, and promote particular forms of reading and writing, as described by Deborah Brandt (1998). Brandt refers to everyday literacies as self-sponsored. In dominant institutional literacies, often there are experts and professionals through whom access to knowledge is organized and controlled. Vernacular practices are not particularly approved of by formal domains. They are often downgraded and not valued by schools, especially when associated with popular culture, and there are recurrent moral panics about the deleterious effects of popular culture on young people. These concerns are magnified when combined with moral panics about the effects of social media on young people.

Vernacular texts tend to be circulated locally and not kept for long. As they are relatively unregulated in comparison with dominant literacies and they remain under people's own control, vernacular practices can be a source of creativity and originality, and they can lead to new practices. It was clear from the local literacies study that when people act in their lives, in fact they utilize all the resources available to them and they mix institutional and vernacular practices. People encounter official texts, but what they do with them, their practices, can be vernacular. Vernacular practices can be responses to imposed literacies. Some vernacular responses to official literacy demands disrupt the intentions of those demands, to serve people's own purposes; and sometimes they are intentionally oppositional to and subversive of dominant practices (as in Maybin 2007).

While anyone can participate in vernacular practices by keeping a record of their lives or by doing creative writing, what is also important are the ways in which vernacular activities can provide a voice for groups and individuals who may otherwise not be heard. (See Barton *et al.* 1993; Sheridan *et al.* 2000.) This is particularly true of writing and there is a growing history of studies of the power of everyday writing (such as Camitta 1993; Sinor 2002; Lyons 2007; Blommaert 2008). These have covered monolingual and multilingual studies and have included writing in vernacular languages. We should reiterate the point that when referring to vernacular writing this is not the same use as when the term 'vernacular' is used in reference to vernacular languages, which often refers to local languages. There can be a great deal of overlap but vernacular writing is not necessarily tied to specific languages, especially in a global context such as the internet. Rather, as we have demonstrated in earlier chapters, there is a complex relationship between writing and the specific languages used.

Local Literacies in Lancaster

Lancaster, the site of the original local literacies study, is a city in north-west England. Alongside its physical existence, it has for many years had a 'virtual' existence in, for instance, guide books, maps, and novels. Like elsewhere, Lancaster now has a strong online presence and exists much more strongly as a virtual city. This is based upon the physical infrastructure of fast broadband coverage, along with complete mobile phone coverage, which have all been created within the past 25 years and which did not exist at the time of the original study. The amount of personal technology which people have access to has also changed dramatically. The original study, carried out in the mid 1990s, came across just two computers in the neighbourhood, one in the local community centre and the other in the house of a man who saw himself as a writer. Both computers were used by local people wanting to make simple adverts and print them off. There was no world wide web, no Google, no Facebook and no smartphone apps. Computers and computing were largely restricted to workplaces. Laptops were rare, heavy and expensive. Mobile phones were just beginning to become common and text messaging was just taking off in the late 1990s.

National surveys confirm that most people in Lancaster and in much of the world now have the internet at home and most people have a mobile phone with them throughout the day and practices of meeting and socializing are mediated by their phones. Furthermore, all the main institutions affecting the city have an internet presence. People's vernacular practices around literacy have changed profoundly in a relatively short space of time. To get a gauge of this, Barton and Hamilton (1998) provided an A–Z sample of local groups which existed in the mid 1990s, from the Archaeological Society to the Zen Meditation group. Nearly all of this web of vernacular activity still exists, and these groups now have an online presence. Some groups have locally created sites, like the Lancaster Beekeepers, which lists events, has items for sale, imparts advice, and documents the history of the association. Others are local versions of national sites, such as the local history site. Such sites also link to other spaces, such as Twitter feeds, as well as blogs and Facebook. Like most towns and villages in England, Lancaster has its own Flickr groups used by locals and visitors.

In addition, there are blogs about Lancaster life. As well as individuals' diary-like blogs, there are specific green blogs and conservative blogs. There are satellite images available of Lancaster and anyone can walk the streets of the city virtually with Google Street View. People book restaurants, check movie times and comment on and evaluate hotels, pubs and restaurants. They find out about council services online, and some of these things can only be done online. In these ways online activity is integrated into the everyday practices of people and organizations. People's practices bring together the virtual and the material. So, in a relatively short period of time there has been a dramatic change in people's lives and they have created an online life. This has changed the nature of vernacular practices.

In the data collected 25 years ago, literacy was used by people to make sense of events in their lives and to resolve a variety of problems, such as those related to health, to their jobs, to their children's schooling and to encounters with the law. Often this involved confrontation with professional experts and specialized systems of knowledge, and people often drew on their networks for support and knowledge, thereby becoming expert in a particular domain and becoming a resource for other community members themselves. Literacy was also used for personal change and transformation, both within and outside education-related domains, for accessing information relating to people's interests, for asserting or creating personal identity, and for self-directed learning.

In the six areas of vernacular activity identified earlier, people's practices in the UK have changed significantly in a relatively short period of time. All everyday activities are affected, online and offline. It is not just a question of going online, but of integrating online and offline activities. These changes were beginning to happen in the mid 1990s and are continuing.

1. People now extensively *organize their lives* with appointment diaries and address books on their computers and phones. Arrangements to meet and the micro-coordination of social interaction are mediated by new media. Increasingly, relations with institutions like banks and tax offices are done online, and customers are required in many cases to move away from their previous print-based practices, such as printing transaction histories in a bank passbook, to web-based ones, such as retrieving e-statements online. The local council utilizes digital technology as well as print and face-to-face contact to represent itself and to communicate with citizens about diverse issues such as school entry, recycling and adverse weather. Government policy itself may make new textual demands on people and assume access to up-to-date communication technologies. These findings fit in well with other research that examines how technologies are deployed as people pursue their everyday concerns and interests and how this changes the nature of their literacy practices. Today, while people still reside in physical places, and government institutions still impact on them in those places, people increasingly interact with their virtual, or digital, city intertwining the physical and the virtual.

2. *Personal communication* has been revolutionized by smart phones and social network sites. As a simple example, the holiday postcard now exists alongside the holiday text message or the shared Facebook photographs. Postcards and an extensive variety of greetings cards still exist physically but their meaning and significance are being renegotiated within the greater range of alternative possibilities.

3. What was referred to as *private leisure* in the original study is increasingly done online and, as the boundaries between private and public are renegotiated, much activity is more social and public. In addition, although the online world is strikingly multimodal, it is nevertheless extensively mediated by literacy.

4. Contemporary life is *documented* by the footprints left online through social participation on Facebook and elsewhere. Alongside this, activities like documenting family and local history are supported by easily available online resources.

5. In terms of *sense making*: the internet is a crucial part of researching such things as health issues, and problems with children's development or legal grievances. For many people, to investigate a problem in their everyday lives, their first step is to turn to Google to search the internet. Elsewhere, to find out about particular issues they turn to online discussion groups like Mumsnet, the UK's largest discussion site for parents, or similar sites.

6. Turning to *social participation*, obviously social network sites have a central role. Further, social and political participation is manifested in following and contributing to blogs and Twitter, and other spaces for commenting. And, as pointed out above, nearly all local groups and associations have moved to having an online presence.

POPULAR PHOTOGRAPHY AS A VERNACULAR PRACTICE

We now turn to a particular example of a vernacular practice to see how it has changed. The example provides a way of investigating what has happened to local vernacular practices as they move online. The aim is to examine the extent to which people's online activities constitute vernacular practices, how such practices are located in earlier practices and how the nature of vernacular practices is changing. The example comes from the photo site Flickr. So far in this book we have drawn upon Flickr when investigating the topics of multilingual activity, identity formation, stance-taking, metalinguistic awareness and learning. Here we return to Flickr to examine its use as a vernacular practice or, rather, we examine one vernacular practice that now draws upon Flickr. The brief example is everyday family photography and in particular using photo albums.

Since its early days in the 1840s, photography has been referred to by its proponents as 'the democratic art'. As a vernacular practice it has been relatively cheap, accessible and easy to learn for at least a hundred years. Companies like Kodak from the beginning of the twentieth century were sponsors of these practices, encouraging people to buy simple cameras and to take photos of their everyday life. Photography was an everyday activity and there would often be a camera present on holidays and at celebrations. While it was an everyday activity, the practicalities of taking a photo remained fairly constant throughout the twentieth century. Compared with today, it was also fairly complex and expensive. One would buy a roll of film to take 12, 24 or 36 photos. The camera could only be opened in the dark to load the film or remove it. The film then had to be taken to or sent to a film processor, which would take a few hours or a few days and one would only see one's pictures at the end of the process. Getting copies of photos took further time and money. Photos then might be kept in the envelopes provided by the film processors, or kept in tins, or put in albums.

Creating an album has been a common practice for a long time. Figure 10.1 is an early image showing a family album, dating back to 1864. It is a popular portrait of US President Lincoln sitting with his son Tad (Ostendorf

Figure 10.1 Abraham Lincoln with photo album

1998: 182). This is a well-known photo and is available on Flickr from the Library of Congress photostream, and also on Wikipedia and elsewhere.

This is an interesting example for us here for, although we cannot see the content of the album, we can see people participating in a practice. In this literacy event the father is holding the album and turning the pages. They are close together and they are sharing the text. Their joint attention is on a page of the album. (In fact, there are layers of practices in this particular event. It is a staged event as the photo was taken in a studio and it was then, and still is, common for studios to provide props, like books, to stage formal photos. And, presumably, it was deliberately set up to show the everyday, family side of the president.)

From examination of other representations of albums and their uses, we can say more about practices around such albums. They tend to be shared in small groups, often within families. They are stored in the home, often on bookshelves next to books, and may be passed on across generations. People use them to document their lives. They are part of a range of similar books, such as scrapbooks and postcard albums. Turning to the language within photo albums, the only writing, if any, is usually limited to a name, a place and a date – Who? Where? When? There may be just a name or a date written in the album or on the back of the photo, and one of the frequent frustrations for later generations looking at such albums is the lack of this minimal information. What is written tends to have been written by the original author, although others may later add more information.

In the original local literacies data, there were several occasions when albums were mentioned or shared with the researcher. For instance, after several visits to the house, one woman shared her wedding album with the researcher, going through it in the living room page by page and naming and talking about her relatives. We interpreted this as a strong sign of acceptance. Another informant reported that she had started a 'baby book' of her child with photos, along with details of developing weight and height, but had not kept it up for long.

Writing for a range of purposes

This brief sketch provides a background for returning to Flickr, where the change in photographic practices can be clearly seen. Cameras are now much more ubiquitous and, as part of phones, are carried around everywhere. Many people have more than one camera. Once one has paid for the equipment there are not additional costs in taking a photo. Photos are taken everywhere for particular celebrations such as birthdays and for ordinary events. With digital cameras, it is possible to check the photos on the camera display screen immediately, an action referred to as 'chimping'. Feedback is immediate and if one wants to record a particular scene it is possible to retake photos until a satisfactory version is produced. Often several people take photos of the same event and the immediate sharing then becomes part of the event. Sharing is quick and Flickr is just one of many ways to share photos with friends and strangers alike.

Photography has become digital and people's practices have changed to take advantage of the affordances online. So in our data, a friend bought a new mother a baby journal as a present. It has places to record personal details and changes over time, along with spaces for regular photos as the baby develops. There are equivalent online scrapbooks (e.g. www.baby chapters.com) where all this can be recorded on websites that also provide the option of purchasing high quality physical copies of the scrapbook. In this way, offline and online practices merge seamlessly so that people may still have physical albums and scrapbooks, alongside digital resources.

A person's Flickr photostream can be regarded as an album and often it is broken down into sets that cover specific events, such as weddings and birthdays. In our data, people often first saw Flickr as some sort of album – they were carrying out existing practices of making a photo album in new ways. Often the initial way into Flickr was to use it to share photos such as weddings (one of the most popular tags on Flickr) or birthdays with friends and relatives, especially those who may not live locally, as with this quote from a Scottish photographer:

At first, I intended to use Flickr for sharing photos with friends and family and for storing images only. But I found some of ppl commenting on my work and watching the photo work from other. After that, I keep surfing Flickr daily to keep friendship and to learn/improve my work.

(*andrew*)

Several people in our study reported this progression from sharing with friends and family on to meeting new people. As they participated more, people began to use Flickr for many purposes and different people use it very differently. In terms of the earlier list of vernacular practices, people certainly used it for communicating with others, for leisure, for documenting life and as a form of social participation. This range of purposes can be summarized by what one user said:

To learn about photography; To share my photos; To have fun; To meet people
(*Charleeze*)

These purposes can change and develop over time and are revised as people take up new affordances of Flickr and as they participate in Flickr in different ways. To many, participating in Flickr was a process of discovering new purposes for using the site. For example, some people gradually learned more about themselves and the world. This was often achieved through interacting with other Flickr members:

Sharing images with people – not my photographic skills, but my way of seeing the world . . . and Flickr members are very good at sharing knowledge.

(*Carolink*)

As we have seen in the previous chapter, whether the learning was deliberate or unconscious, participating in Flickr not only provides opportunities to learn how to do things on Flickr, but people also change their writing practices as their perceived purposes for using the site change.

Flickr as a social web space

A very common practice is to use Flickr to socialize. Writing on Flickr is always potentially interactive, as in the comments area. People also compared Flickr with other photo-sharing sites, suggesting the interactive affordance of the site. One of our participants from Hong Kong explained how interactivity on Flickr was different from other sites:

The most interesting characteristic is the interactive nature of the website. Features such as tagging, commenting, favourites, groups, contacts allows me to share my photos with people around the world with the same interests and getting feedback. Whereas most other sites, it is just a one way conversation with you showing the world your photos.

(*HKmPUA*)

Other participants in our study characterized Flickr as a safe and friendly social space:

> I like Flickr because people, especially my own contacts, make friendly and objective comments. Not having any comments may suggest that your photos are not popular; but that doesn't matter. I like the harmonious atmosphere on Flickr, which is very different from other photo sharing sites. On the photo sharing sites I've used before, if you don't receive enough comments, your photos will not be recommended by the administrators. This leads to some people making biased and unsolicited comments about each other's photos (just for the sake of adding up the number of comments). This affects my mood.
>
> (*sating*)

They were very happy to meet strangers through Flickr and chat with them:

> This was the first place I knew to share photos, it started as something I did once a week or so, but then I started to meet people. I guess that's the most interesting feature, the people.
>
> (*ädri*)

Over time other sites have made it easier to load and manage photos and people use photos on different sites for various purposes. In fact, at the time of writing, the use of Flickr is declining (according to figures from www. compete.com in June 2012). There are several possible reasons for this: more sites are offering comparable photo sharing possibilities, like Snapfish, Instagram and Picasa; existing social network sites, like Facebook and Google+, are improving their photo handling properties; and other sites like Twitter and Pinterest offer different niche possibilities for sharing images.

Flickr members also communicate through responding to titles, descriptions and tags given by the photographers. For example, the photo description by a Chinese participant 'i LOVE people-watching. Happy weekend^^', directly addresses the audience by wishing them a good weekend. This immediately initiated a series of comments not only about the content of this photo, 'Mr Doughnut', but also wishing her 'Happy Weekend' in return.

For some people, writing on Flickr helps maintain and extend their physical relationships. Most people reported that they already knew some of their contacts personally when they started using Flickr. When asked what the most interesting feature of Flickr was, 'meeting people' was commonly mentioned:

> This one was the first place I knew to share photos, it started as something I did once a week or so, but then I started to meet people.
>
> (*ädri*)

People also talked of their intended and imagined audiences. We saw this when they shifted from being interested in their existing friends and relatives and began seeing strangers as potential audience. In this way they shifted to participating in a different way and remaking the global flows of language and culture. In various chapters, we have discussed the significance of *audience* in projecting new identities. Taking account of imagined audience is a very salient practice in Flickr and other Web 2.0 spaces and although people also imagine audience in other kinds of writing, this issue seems to have higher significance in Web 2.0. Thus they were interacting with new people, with different people and with people in different places. They were asserting new identities, including complex multilingual global identities that they were projecting to new audiences. In this way they had a sense of themselves as global citizens – or netizens.

PREGNANCY AS ONLINE LITERACY PRACTICES: THE CASE OF PEGGY

In all the cases discussed above the language practices are clearly embedded in people's lived experiences. To give another example of the situated nature of new media, pregnancy is an area of life that has been transformed significantly by new media. Being pregnant used to be mainly a private and personal experience. The advent of new media and social network sites has turned this lived experience into publicly available stories. When our informant, Peggy, found out that she was pregnant, the first thing she did was share the news online, starting with a Facebook status update 'Peggy is pregnant!! =v='. Sharing this news online breaks the traditional Chinese practice that women do not reveal their pregnancy until the end of the first trimester (i.e. after three months). Since then, much of what she posted on both Facebook and her blog was exclusively about her pregnancy. In addition to words, her pregnancy was largely represented through images, including ultrasound X-ray images of her baby, which used to be kept private and rarely shared with others. When Peggy eventually went into labour at the hospital, she made the most of Facebook, starting with the status update '@hospital.' She then kept updating her status every few hours using her mobile phone, such as 'Labour has started'. Just minutes after her long labour, Peggy announced on Facebook, 'After over 20 hours of labor, yatyat was born!' This instantly attracted 25 comments congratulating Peggy and welcoming her new daughter. When Peggy returned home, she resorted to her blog in a post entitled 'A life of three has begun' and adding more details about what had happened in the hospital together with photos of her baby. Since then, she has gone back to blogging and posting summaries of her blog content regularly on Facebook. This small case illustrates how Facebook and other new media were never separable from Peggy's immediate, embodied experiences during her pregnancy. Her extensive use of images alongside her texts shows how digital photography has provided new affordances for the way key moments of life such as giving birth are captured and represented. In fact, the first ever camera photograph taken and shared with friends and family online was a photo of a new born baby, taken by the inventor of the camera phone Philippe Kahn in 1997.

REDEFINING THE VERNACULAR IN A GLOBAL CONTEXT

All aspects of the processes and practices of reading and writing need to be re-examined now that so much reading and writing takes place in new spaces with new affordances. We have provided a detailed example from Flickr. What we have shown about changes in writing practices can also be found in other Web 2.0 sites, including blogs and social network sites, as shown in Peggy's case above. The concept of vernacular literacies can be re-evaluated by pursuing issues raised earlier in the book about the extent to which these are new literacy practices on Web 2.0 and how they are similar to or different from traditional notions of vernacular literacies.

Discovering new affordances for new practices

It is clear that people who are writing in new media spaces are engaging in new vernacular practices. Such newness refers both to doing things that they had not done before and to extending existing practices. (See also Chapter 1 for a discussion on newness.) Based on the interview data, we can see that some existing everyday activities, such as creating a wedding album or sharing family photos, are carried over to these new spaces, that is, participants are carrying out existing practices in new ways. People find that the new media facilitates these practices, in that it is quicker and easier to create such albums and to share them. Their involvement with Flickr often starts out with a desire to carry out existing practices more effectively. They then discover that they can do more with their photos, for example they can easily annotate them and can share a large number of photos with distant relatives. At the same time their photos are being treated differently by others: different people, such as work colleagues, might see the leisure photos and strangers might see and comment on family photos. For the people we studied, they then extended what they did with Flickr into new areas of activity. Their new practices broadened out to include activities such as publicly evaluating other people's photos, classifying their own photos using keywords, making connections between their own and others' photos, and even interacting with international audiences in multiple languages. Tagging is a good example of an activity that participants said was new to them as a way of dealing with their photos. By creating tags, they were organizing and classifying their photos in new ways and making their photos more accessible to others. As we have pointed out earlier, people are not using this writing space just to create their own folksonomies to enable easy searches of their photos, as the designers originally intended. They are not just classifying their photos as a researcher might do. They are also using this writing space to write poems, to make comments and to create idiosyncratic classifications for themselves. Tagging is a vernacular activity where people turn the affordances to their own purposes.

This opened up the possibilities for new uses of their photos. Looking across the data, the ways in which the writing spaces on Flickr are used point to a vibrant area of writing, but at the same time it may challenge existing definitions of writing. Certainly, activities like tagging expand notions of what counts as writing. There are tensions in definitions of reading, writing and literacy online which have already been pointed out (as in Leu *et al.* 2004; Coiro *et al.* 2008) and Brandt (2009) discusses how writing is emphasized on the internet and there are new relationships between reading and writing developing.

These specific activities are part of broader social practices where people are relating to the world in new ways. As a way of examining these broader social practices in which the writing was located, we return to the six areas of life where reading and writing were seen to be of central importance to people, given at the beginning of the chapter: organizing life, personal communication, leisure, documenting life, sense making and social participation. The Flickr users engaged in these areas of vernacular activity in new ways. For example, new forms of social participation developed. They became involved in social networking, for instance in deliberately setting out to get more views for their photos and trying to get a higher chance of being searched for, as in *HKmPUA*'s use of multiscriptual tags where he added tags with the same meaning in English, Cantonese and Mandarin. Like others he wanted to get more comments on his pictures. This data further illustrates how users were also documenting their lives in new ways and how their personal leisure activities, such as their interests in music and in photography, were changing as Flickr took up more and more of their time. On other web spaces, people also discover and take up new affordances. With these new practices in mind, we now turn to the characteristics of vernacular practices discussed earlier and examine how they need to be redefined in the light of activity in new media, with specific focus on Web 2.0 spaces.

Vernacular practices in new media are self-generated

Most Web 2.0 sites provide writing spaces for users to generate content voluntarily. As with other vernacular literacy practices, the new literacy practices described are voluntary and self-generated, as illustrated by people's participation in Flickr. What people do on Flickr has its roots in everyday experience – with the caveat that the framework is provided by a private company driven by commercial concerns. It provides the possibilities and constraints within which people act. Companies such as Yahoo!, the owners of Flickr, can be seen as sponsoring particular practices. Burgess (2007) discusses the Flickr business model and how it sponsors certain practices and Cox (2008) demonstrates how it is designed to satisfy commercial practices. Users are providing data that is of value to the company and it becomes the product which they can sell.

Flickr is also relatively unregulated and largely self-moderated. While there are lively accusations and discussions about censorship more generally on Flickr, this did not come up in our data and the people we studied saw it as providing many possibilities for them to discover new ways of using their photos and to meet people. They appreciated the freedom they had and did not refer to perceived restrictions. Different platforms vary a great deal in this. Elsewhere on the web there are many examples of imposed writing which are highly structured and constrained, as anyone who has ordered goods and services online or has had to fill in an online tax form can affirm. Sites like Amazon have a mixture of obligatory spaces such as filling out an order form and optional open spaces such as book reviews.

Vernacular practices in new media are a source of creativity, invention and originality

On Web 2.0 sites such as Flickr, Wikipedia and YouTube, people are creating, sharing, collaborating and organizing. Users are more active and these sites afford spaces for originality and creativity. This is evident, for instance, in the participants' wide-ranging purposes for writing on Flickr, their creative deployment of language resources, as well as their specific ways of socializing on Flickr. The vernacular writing also led to new practices such as sharing knowledge and supporting each other. This was apparent in the online comments as well as being reported in the interviews. This support was around photography as well as other aspects of life. More generally, creativity can also be seen in the ways in which people are taking different photos from before. The possibility for this arises in part from digital cameras where, once one has the camera, individual photos are effectively free and the results can be immediately seen and evaluated. People can take a large number of different photos and then just delete ones they do not want to keep. In this way, a space for experimentation is opened up where web users can try things out and get instant feedback. In terms of topic it seems that people are taking more photos of the everyday, of the mundane, of the self, exploring one's room, one's body and one's workplace. More people are taking more photographs. (See Van House 2007 on the changing uses of everyday photography, and also Sarvas and Frohlich 2011.) People also undertake systematic investigations such as the 365 projects, described in Chapter 9. In exploring the current possibilities of photography people are increasingly getting ideas from one another, and not primarily from professionals through How-to books and photography magazines. There is a shift in where expertise lies as it moves from being the realm of professionals and becomes more distributed amongst people.

Another central idea to creativity in vernacular practices is 'playability' (Burgess 2007), which refers to the ways in which new digital media afford a space that combines use, play, experimentation, and mashupability. Mashup refers to a process of remixing and reappropriating different modes and resources for meaning making, thus generating new vernacular practices. This is happening on Flickr, which provides spaces for people to combine and play with resources of images and written text to create new content and share it online. Very often, people play with resources on Flickr in this way not only to socialize, but also to learn and support others (see also Davies

2009). Sometimes participants may need technical support from other users, and at other times they may help others with their photography skills. These are all done through visual and verbal means. Creativity and remixing resources are also evident on many other sites that we have discussed in the previous chapters, including IM, YouTube fansubbing, and fan-fiction writing. Although not typically labelled as a Web 2.0 site, IM does share many of the characteristics of Web 2.0 such as self-generated writing and creativity. We have seen in Chapter 4 that college students in Hong Kong play with their linguistic resources of English and Chinese to create new ways of representing meaning. Similarly, YouTube users demonstrate creativity by remixing content from different sources to create a new video that is different from an original piece of work by others.

Vernacular literacies are valued in new media

In many ways the practices seen on Flickr are quite similar to the vernacular practices described in Barton and Hamilton (1998). But in other ways these writing practices on Web 2.0 challenge and extend earlier notions of the nature of vernacular practices. First, vernacular practices have been regarded as being of less value than more dominant practices which are sponsored and supported by education and other external institutions. In the case of Flickr, these local practices are now more valued. What was personal and often private is now put into the public realm. People are making public and giving greater circulation to activities that previously were local and where people could regulate access and use. These activities are no longer confined to the local sphere. People are using these writing spaces consciously and deliberately to tell the world something about their personal experiences or local life. They are knowingly addressing and responding to a global audience to create new identities, in a similar way to the examples presented in Chapter 6. Through making comments on one another's photos, people using Flickr have become reviewers, commentators and evaluators of their own and others' work, drawing on their resources for stance-taking online, as discussed in Chapter 7. The comments they make are often valued by members of Flickr and others, who all draw upon and contribute to expanding global funds of knowledge. At the same time such photos are more valued elsewhere, even within dominant institutions where vernacular practices are generally discouraged: for instance, Flickr is regularly searched by publishers and journalists needing photos of specific topics for books, magazines and newspapers. Teachers and researchers are exploring its use in classrooms, as discussed in Chapter 11, and extensive materials and advice on its educational potential are available on the internet. Returning to our focus on language online, the creative multilingual and multiscriptual practices shown in Chapters 4 and 5 are not always valued in institutional contexts. Moral panics and public discourses about how technologies deteriorate students' literacy skills well illustrate this. However, it is clear from our data that students demonstrate high levels of creativity and dexterity in their digital texts and that hybrid linguistic practices such as code-switching play a crucial role in students' everyday online communication. This tension between students' everyday and institutional text-making practices will be discussed in Chapter 11.

11

LANGUAGE ONLINE AND EDUCATION

- New media in classroom-based teaching and learning of language and literacy
- How understanding online practices can change language teaching and learning

The two previous chapters provide a context for this chapter. Chapter 9 identified some of the vernacular learning that goes on in online spaces and has argued that online spaces can be powerful places to learn. Chapter 10 has shown the growing value of everyday practices. Here we turn to educational contexts, taking account of the everyday. This book does not start with an education agenda, although a growing amount of research in digital literacies offer new meanings of literacy from an education perspective. (See, for example, Buckingham 2007; Davies and Merchant 2009; Alvermann 2011.) Grounded in a social theory of literacy and seeing language online as situated practices, our first step is to examine what people do with online texts in different areas of everyday life. Our language-focused research on new media, however, naturally leads on to the question of how understanding language and literacy practices online can inform educational practices.

This is also a particularly relevant question in the area of language teaching and learning, especially with the rise of moral panics and public discourse about falling standards of language. In this chapter, we address two education-related issues that this book can shed light on. The first starts from existing provision, in that it takes current educational frameworks for granted: how specific digital media can be incorporated into classroom-based teaching and learning, especially in the context of language education. This is about how to do existing practices in new ways and, as suggested earlier, can be the first step in a change in practices. When participants see the new possibilities of technologies and can imagine new futures then they move on to the next step and education has to change. The second section explores how understanding online practices can change language teaching and learning.

NEW MEDIA IN CLASSROOM-BASED TEACHING AND LEARNING OF LANGUAGE AND LITERACY

Computers have played a role in education for a long time. As early as the 1970s, the area of 'computer-assisted teaching and learning' only meant the use of computer software to facilitate classroom instruction and learning. Computer-assisted language learning (CALL) also emerged as an independent field of research (e.g. Warschauer 1996; Levy 1997). The Literacy Studies framework has established the tradition of researching details of everyday and vernacular literacy practices. One primary aim of studying details of people's everyday practices is to influence formal education and policy (as in Hull and Schultz 2002, for instance). The *Literacies for Learning in Further Education* project (Ivanič *et al.* 2009), for example, explores the relationship between college students' everyday and college-based literacy practices, both digital and non-digital. The project has identified characteristics of students' informal literacies such as hybridity, multimodality and collaborative knowledge sharing, which lecturers can draw upon in pedagogy. Although originally the project did not focus primarily on technologies, its findings suggest that new media play a central role in college students' textual practices and meaning making processes.

One of the few large-scale studies of youth digital literacies is Ito *et al.*'s (2010) three-year multi-sited research in the US, as mentioned earlier. This work provides in-depth ethnographic case studies of young people's digital practices and explores how they shape youth's identities and learning experience. Most digital practices are textually mediated. Producing and using texts online occupies much of people's lives. A number of studies highlight the *textual* dimension of digital literacies on various platforms, such as chat rooms (Merchant 2001), instant messaging (Lewis and Fabos 2005; Lee 2007a), video gaming (Gee 2004), and fan-fiction (Black 2009), among others. This body of work, which pays attention to young people's practices, has come to the consensus that digital texts are creative, hybridized and multimodal. For example, Merchant (2001) shows how teenagers display extensive creativity by combining features of spoken conversation and writing in chat rooms. Merchant argues that creativity and hybridity are features of the contemporary social world. In other words, participating in online chat is indeed a way of developing linguistic capital and marketable skills required to participate in the new social order. However, because online chat often takes place in informal and private contexts, they are not valued by formal institutions. Also, focusing on textual practices, Lea and Jones (2011) start with university students rather than teenagers. In making a connection between students' academic textual practices and their everyday, private digital texts, Lea and Jones illustrate that the meaning making process of assessed writing in higher education often involves students drawing upon a wide range of digital and non-digital genres and modes. The importance of researching texts as language online is also highlighted in this chapter and elsewhere in this book.

All of the studies reviewed here are explicitly or implicitly education-oriented. They are either conducted in formal learning contexts, or they discuss implications for formal education. Another key thread of digital literacies research aims to provide practical applications of new technologies to education (as in Haythornthwaite and Andrews 2011). A specific example of this is a study of the value of computer conferencing in university students' writing for assessment, especially in distance learning contexts (Lea 2001; Goodfellow *et al.* 2004). At the same time, there has been a strong tendency to shift to social media or Web 2.0 sites that feature self-generated content, social networking, and collaborative knowledge sharing. More broadly, most of the comparable research on learning online has been concerned with young people in educational settings, such as work reported in Carrington and Robinson (2009) and Sharpe *et al.* (2010). Web 2.0 sites have also been found valuable to support classroom literacy teaching and learning (Braun 2007) and the learning of second and foreign languages (Benson and Chan 2011; Benson and Chik 2010; Lam 2000). In the following, we provide some examples of how popular Web 2.0 platforms have been adopted to facilitate literacy-related teaching and learning activities.

- *Weblogs*: As one of the earliest and most popular examples of what Tim Berners-Lee (2005) refers to as the 'read/write web', weblogs are an ideal space for students to practice reading and writing. Teachers and students around the world have taken up affordances of blogs such as easy self-publishing and continuous updating of multimodal content and turned them into an educational opportunity. A common educational activity involving blogging is that students are asked to choose a topic of their own choice and do bibliographic search on it and then blog about their findings. Not only does blogging provide ample opportunities for authentic writing, it also involves a great deal of reading – for one thing, before students can blog about a topic, they would have to look up and read as well as organize information around their chosen topic. Spaces for commenting can serve as platforms for peer feedback, thus enabling students to become more critical readers. (See Richardson 2006: 40–42 for a comprehensive list of possible classroom uses of blogs; other lists, for blogs and for other platforms, can be found by searching online for sites devoted to teaching.)

- *Wikis*: Like blogging, wikis offer the possibilities for user-generated writing and easy web publishing around a topic, using the form of encyclopaedic entries. The key feature of wikis is however *collaboration* and group-based knowledge creation. Wiki entries are normally written and frequently updated by multiple authors. These affordances encourage collaborative writing and content editing. Through creating wiki entries and editing others' writing, students also get to learn how to work with others and work as a group. Many wikis also include hyperlinks to external sources, which then allow students to think critically about online materials (see also Augar *et al.* 2004 for a review of the pedagogical values of different wikis).

- *Photo sites such as Flickr*: Flickr was used as an example of deliberate vernacular learning in Chapter 9. The educational value of Flickr has been recognized by some literacy scholars (as in Davies 2006; Davies and Merchant 2009). Various features on Flickr may support classroom learning. For example, it provides an extensive database of license-free images (although many photos on the site are copyrighted) for teachers to download as pedagogical resources. The rich array of writing spaces surrounding a photo support different kinds of language teaching and learning activities. The description text box underneath the picture serves as a powerful tool for storytelling around images; tagging allows students to make use of new words they have learned in class to describe an image; Richardson (2006) has found the notes function on Flickr (where one can write annotations on the photos) particularly useful for classrooms and has proposed several ways of using it – for example, a teacher can post a photo and ask students to annotate what they see. The commenting function can encourage participation and discussions among students. And because Flickr connects people from all parts of the world, students who are doing projects on international cultures may use Flickr's keyword search function to look for pictures and information about other countries. With guidance from teachers, students may also get to interact with people from other parts of the world and learn about their languages and cultures.

- *Video sites such as YouTube*: YouTube is another excellent database of multimedia content. The site has been found to promote autonomous language learning, as with the fansubbing example described in Chapter 9. At the level of formal classroom education, more and more teachers are using YouTube as resources for teaching. The multimodal affordances of the site are especially valuable for language learners of all sorts to practice speaking, writing and listening. For example, in class, students may be asked to hold oral discussions around the content of a video on YouTube that they have been asked to watch before class; some teachers may record and host their lessons on YouTube for students to review after class. And because creating and editing videos is relatively cheap and easy, many language teachers would encourage students to make their own videos as an assignment and share them on YouTube. For example, a group of American students present their Spanish project in the form of a short film. The conversation of the characters has been translated into English using YouTube's annotation function. The annotation (by self and others) and commenting functions on YouTube also encourage students to evaluate the content of the videos, thus enhancing interactivity through writing outside the classroom.

- *Virtual worlds such as Second Life*: Second Life is best known amongst educators for its life-like 3D environment, which makes learning activities fun and enjoyable. Teachers and students interact in their virtual worlds as avatars, self-created characters that can take any forms, including humans and animals, who can even fly and teleport within and across worlds. These characteristics allow for an interactive learning environment that mimics face-to-face classroom learning. Compared to text-only online learning spaces, Second Life provides a more personal context for student-student and student-teacher interaction as they feel more involved communicating in a close-to-real-life context. Some students find virtual worlds less intimidating than face-to-face classroom interaction and are more willing to participate. Many universities have created virtual campuses on Second Life (e.g. Ohio University's virtual campus). Second Life is also found valuable for second or foreign language learning (Cooke-Plagwitz 2008). Its multimodal environment supports not only text and images but also voice interaction – which allows language learners to practice speaking skills with avatars from other cultures, thus reinforcing collaborative learning. Other general uses of Second Life in education can be found in Conklin's (2007) list of 101 uses of Second Life in the college classroom. For more on education in virtual worlds, see Peachey *et al.* (2010) and Merchant *et al.* (2012).
- *Microblogging, including Twitter*: Microblogging services such as Twitter have played an increasingly significant role in academic and educational settings over the past few years. For example, Twitter has often been adopted by academics to support backchannel discussion at seminars and conferences (Ross *et al.* 2011) and university lectures (Elavsky *et al.* 2011). Participants are encouraged to post live to Twitter as the presenters are giving their talks. They are usually given a hashtag, a keyword that marks the theme or topic of a tweet, to attach to their posts for easy archiving and searching. The main advantage of doing so is that the live discussion allows outsiders or people who cannot be physically present to follow the event in real time. Twitter has also been found useful in second language learning. Borau *et al.* (2009), for instance, have carried out a case study of using Twitter in an English language class offered to Chinese students. All students were required to post at least seven messages a week and to read other students' posts as a way of practising reading and writing. This not only helps develop a sense of community among students, but also provides opportunities for

learners to 'actively produce language' (Borau *et al.* 2009: 78), including outside the classroom.

- *Social networking sites such as Facebook*: Since its launch in 2004, Facebook has currently become the most popular social network site. Its wide-ranging features and affordances have been adopted by educators and students in various ways. The Group function on Facebook is especially suitable to facilitate both teacher-initiated or student-initiated teaching and learning activities. For one thing, unlike other features of Facebook, Groups are membership-based. The Group administrators can make content private and available to only members who have had approval to join, making it a relatively private and safe course or class-based platform (Lee and Lien 2011; see also the case study below on how it is adopted in an undergraduate linguistics course). Students may also set up private Groups without the teacher's initiative to discuss assignments and organize their projects, as reported in English and Duncan-Howell (2008).

While the *newness* and affordances of these media may be tempting and attractive, exploring how exactly the use of these media can enhance students' learning experience needs to be worked out in each situation. Lewis and Fabos (2005), in their discussion of IM, also remind educators of the possible challenges of introducing students' out-of-school new media practices into classroom teaching:

> The question that should be asked is not how to actually use IM in the classroom but how to apply to school settings the literacy practices we observed young people take up with a great deal of engagement.
>
> (Lewis and Fabos 2005: 496)

Starting from a social practice view, the first step is to understand students' knowledge and their informal uses of new media. As Ivanič *et al.* (2009) make clear, it is not a question of then incorporating the practices into classroom settings. Rather, there will be specific aspects of practices which can be drawn upon. One of the issues to be considered, for example, is that concepts of *time* and *space* in school-based lessons can be very different from those in interpersonal communication among friends. Take IM as an example, private IM activities are often nested and multitasking is taken for granted; whereas in schools classes are organized into individual sessions which do not match with the temporal and spatial flexibility in IM. Researching a different educational setting, Kinzie *et al.* (2005) have explored the potentiality of IM for instructional purposes in university lectures in the US. Their students were assigned a discussion topic in a face-to-face lecture and they were expected to take notes and discuss among themselves while also listening to the lecturer. Although the students were able to multi-task in the lectures, some students found IM distracting in a formal classroom context. Lewis (2007) also reminds us of the issue of need, that is whether or not schools want, and are ready, to acknowledge students' out-of-school and innovative practices in digital literacies.

Facebook group for university courses

To examine how taking into account students' everyday practices can inform educational practice, we provide two examples from our own teaching. We first show a case of how one of us, Carmen, set up a Facebook Group for an undergraduate linguistics course with 33 students. In the spring semester in 2011, a private Facebook Group was created as a platform for course-based communication including sharing of lecture notes and discussion based on shared external content such as web links and videos. The decision to use Facebook instead of other platforms was a result of considering both the teacher's reflection on her experience with educational technologies as well as students' preference as expressed in a course survey. Throughout the 14-week semester, students actively posted in the Group and they made over 350 comments. A strong sense of community was developed outside the classroom context because the Group served to bring together students from different disciplines. The social networking affordance on Facebook also facilitated collaborative learning, with students often sharing newly discovered, course-related information on the web.

While facilitating teaching and learning activities, what was particularly revealing was the ways in which students constantly negotiated and reappropriated their discourse styles and identities according to the changing purposes of the Group. First, the written texts in this Group exhibited a hybridity of languages. Both students and teachers moved beyond the stated medium of instruction, which was English, to mixing linguistic resources, a practice commonly found in informal uses of Facebook. A range of discourse styles were identified, from formal academic announcements by the teacher to more interpersonal and playful posts. The boundary between teacher and students was not always clear. Students sometimes acted as teachers by initiating discussion topics while teachers would also learn something new from these student-initiated posts. These features illustrate that the Group provided what Moje *et al.* (2004) call a 'third space' for teaching and learning. They define a third space as a space that 'brings the texts framed by everyday discourses and knowledges into classrooms in ways that challenge, destabilize, and ultimately, expand the literacy practices that are typically valued in school and in the everyday world' (44). In the case of the course Group, it served as a space where the relatively controlled academic discourse and interpersonal hybrid and informal discourse styles met. Appendix 2 provides further details of this case study.

Exploring students' techno-biographies

Turning from Hong Kong to England, at Lancaster David draws on students' techno-biographies in his courses (taught with Julia Gillen and Uta Papen).

On both the undergraduate language and media course and the MA digital literacies course that he teaches, his starting point with students is to get them to investigate their own practices on and offline. This is also important for getting an idea of what they are using and know about in terms of new technologies (and it inevitably changes from year to year and the course has to adapt to reflect this). Their *techno-biographies* are then data for the course. On the undergraduate course, after investigating their own practices in preparation for the first weekly seminar, the students then have to interview someone different from themselves, like a grandparent or someone from a different culture. This provides a comparative perspective across generations or cultures. The next step is to examine national surveys of internet use to locate their practices in broader quantitative studies which cover the country or the world.

When they get on to projects which they have to carry out for assessment, several of the students include online interviews or surveys. Also they get to see online and offline activities as integrated and not separable. The structure then is a week-by-week moving out from their own experiences, and drawing on different sorts of data. During the course they also explore their online reading paths and they reflect on their changing academic literacy practices. Most of the readings for the course are available online and an early compulsory reading is to watch and take notes on a YouTube video. They also keep a reflective diary of their changing practices since beginning the course and they participate in other online activities.

HOW UNDERSTANDING ONLINE PRACTICES CAN CHANGE LANGUAGE TEACHING AND LEARNING

As a way of showing the significance of the research described in this book for educational practice, we identify several ways in which understanding of online practices can impact on what goes on in the classroom. We keep to our focus on language teaching and learning and are thinking of all levels of education, from pre-school through to college education. We show some ways in which seeing language as a social practice provides theories, methods and data for the language classroom.

1. *Autonomous language learning*: The research reported here has demonstrated that there is a great deal of language learning going on in students' everyday lives which is initiated by them and under their control. It takes place in what for them are *authentic* situations and it provides evidence of *autonomous language learning*. There have been examples of this throughout this book. On Flickr some people deliberately use the site to practice and improve their language. In the IM research, some of the participants, without being prompted, revealed in the interviews how they sometimes stretched the affordances of IM and saw IM as an informal language learning tool. One of the participants, Hang, said IM could serve as a space to practice his Chinese typing and

writing skills. Another person, Wing, recalled that she once wrote to her IM friends in English only in order to prepare for her A-level English examinations. These instances demonstrate students' own approaches to informal learning, such as learning by doing, in their private and everyday lives. These student participants were well aware of what and how to learn in IM. These informal learning activities also allowed students to take charge of their own learning, where they can learn actively, effectively, and enjoyably through a medium of their own choice.

2. *Understanding students' everyday practices*: As we have emphasized throughout the book, our projects have focused on texts and practices online. We always pay close attention to what people do with their texts in their everyday lives instead of just the words on the screen. Understanding details about practices has important implications for education. First of all, while it is important for teachers in the classroom to take advantage of the opportunities offered by new media, it is crucial to draw on activities which reveal what students are doing outside the classroom, including their meaning making resources and their private text-making activities and to understand the nature of online practices. To give one small example, school curricula in many countries have already included email writing, but it is often described as one coherent genre in its own right, and is presented in a rather prescriptive manner (such as rules about how to write an 'effective' email). What the investigation of everyday practices reveals is that email is not a genre, rather it demonstrates the underlying creativity and the superdiverse nature of such platforms. Writing consists of a range of situated activities, and email serves many purposes and can take many forms. Language as social practice provides ways of thinking about and talking about language and literacy, that is, it provides theories of language and literacy, which are of value in the classroom.

3. *Understanding teachers' practices*: Teachers, at all levels, vary in their knowledge and confidence with new technologies. Most teachers in contemporary society are not newbies to technologies but have had years of experience with both educational and informal digital practices. In making decisions about pedagogical uses of everyday technologies, they can be reflexive and constantly reflect upon their own relationships with new media in and outside the classroom context. This may entail a re-negotiation of the relationship between the teacher's knowledge and the students' knowledge along with acceptance of and respect for students' expertise in some areas.

    Understanding teachers' knowledge has been explored, for example, in Graham's (2008) study of how teachers' own experience with technology impacts on their teaching practices. As one example from our own work, the Facebook Group discussed above grew out of the teacher reflecting on her years of experience with both educational and informal technologies. The teacher's multiple identities as a university lecturer, researcher, and an active Facebook user continuously shape her linguistic practices and forms of participation when interacting with students online. This may even extend to becoming a member of her students' online discourse community. In the Group case study mentioned earlier, the teacher was able to adopt a negotiated discourse style that university students often employ in their private online textual practices. Having seen the lecturer adopt their everyday style of online writing, students were happy to take on an informal and even playful voice. This constant negotiation of discourse styles certainly helps create a friendly and pleasant learning environment.

4. *Continuous awareness of students' changing practices*: Digital literacies is a fast-changing area of research as technologies and their use change rapidly. What works one year on a course may be inappropriate the next year and courses need to be in a state of constant flux with spaces for innovation. Teachers and students can research these changing practices. This cannot be achieved by carrying out occasional studies, or reading the results of research carried out a few years ago, but only through ongoing and perhaps longitudinal observations of students' digital practices inside and outside the classroom. Through the methods of techno-biographies described earlier, teachers and students become researchers, and the methods of researching everyday practices can also be used in the classroom. This works at all levels of education and even children under eight years can investigate their own practices in the same way as university undergraduates or teachers on professional development courses can. In this way the relationship between 'out-of-school' and school practices changes.

5. *New pedagogies for new times.* Researchers such as Gunther Kress (1995) have consistently called for a new vision of education to take account of contemporary change. So far, the examples assume that educational provision continues unchanged. However, there is a progression in that at first teachers may be bringing in new technologies to function within existing practices, and then they see further possibilities through the affordances of the media, and start to use the media for new purposes and in the end these are transformed into new practices. The new activities online include the Web 2.0 characteristics identified earlier such as new forms of collaboration, joint production, and knowledge creation rather than learning of just facts.

    Some educators have developed lists of what they refer to as 'twenty-first century skills' (such as the list in Jenkins 2005), many of which are not particularly valued within existing educational practices countries. They are based on these Web 2.0 affordances and emphasize activities such as: playing to experiment; performance adopting identities for improvisations and discovery; multitasking; navigation across media; and drawing on and contributing to collective intelligence. While we would prefer not to isolate them as separable skills, and would locate them within practices, it is worth examining how these practices bring different aspects of language to the fore. Coming from a different direction it is also important to see how Gee's lists of principles of learning (2003) impact on language practices. These approaches challenge contemporary education to change. For classroom-based courses, there is a need to develop a pedagogy where the online is central and it is not brought in just to boost existing practices. What goes on in the classroom is intimately bound up in what goes on outside it. Ultimately the dislocation of time and space online can fundamentally change the nature of education.

6. *Informing language policies in the classroom*: As shown in Chapters 4 and 5, multilingual literacy practices have gradually become a crucial way of participating in the globalized online world. This also has important implications for policies related to medium of instructions in multilingual communities like Hong Kong that have focused largely on using one language at a time in academic settings. The level of dexterity and creativity that students demonstrate in online communication is an important indicator of their preference for a more linguistically diverse learning environment. Our findings of multilingual practices in IM and Facebook among students in Hong Kong have provided empirical evidence, both in the form of authentic texts and students' insider knowledge, that there are mismatches between discourse styles in different contexts. Different combinations of languages and scripts, alongside other text-making resources, are evident in online writing by multilingual people around the world (Danet and Herring 2007). Very often, it is the affordances (including constraints) of the media that open up new meaning making possibilities that are not normally available in offline settings, classrooms included. The language education policy in Hong Kong, for example, is one that fosters linguistic purity (see detailed discussion in Evans 2002). Classroom instructions and written assignments are expected to be in either English or Chinese but not mixed-code. As with other vernacular literacy practices, hybrid linguistic practices online are not always valued in institutional practices. However, code-switching online often demonstrates students' abilities to creatively remix their existing text-making resources to respond to constraints of the media, so as to achieve different communicative purposes.

12

RESEARCHING LANGUAGE ONLINE

- Texts and practices: The question of starting point
- A mixed-method approach
- Online methods and being responsive to participants' lives
- The researcher's stance

This chapter has a focus on methodology. As well as providing an overview of major methods of researching online texts in existing studies, it includes approaches adopted in our own research projects on new media language and literacies. We first raise the issues of the starting point of studies researching language online. We then discuss both traditional methods (including observation and interview) and newer methods (such as auto-ethnography and techno-biography) adopted in the research on IM, Flickr, and Facebook, which have been covered in the previous chapters. Other topics discussed include: the importance of combining both texts and practices; developing a responsive methodology; the researcher's stance; and challenges of carrying out research on the internet.

TEXTS AND PRACTICES: THE QUESTION OF STARTING POINT

There are many possible starting points for examining language online and a recurring issue for researchers who are interested in both language as text and language as practice is where to begin. If we have decided to research a particular website or platform, should we start by observing the written word shown on the screen? Or should we start by understanding practices, through, for example, interviewing text producers or users?

The answer to these questions is closely tied to the aims of the research. Several key methodological approaches have been identified within linguistic studies of computer-mediated communication, which were overviewed in Chapter 1. Much early research on language online took a variationist approach, i.e. aiming to describe what was seen as a new variety of language that is used exclusively for online communication. Such studies tended to focus on characteristics of potentially 'new' structural features that were considered to be specific to the internet. Under this approach, online language data were collected without considering specific social contexts of use. Generalizations about linguistic features of the internet were then made through observations of such decontextualized data. Some examples of this trend include Ferrara *et al.*'s (1991) 'Interactive written discourse', Shortis' (2001) *The Language of ICT*, and Crystal's (2006) notion of 'Netspeak'. With a similar starting point, other studies were carried out by drawing on methods from discourse analysis and sociolinguistics.

A large body of work adopts quantitative methods. Much of this work involves collecting a large corpus of texts in order to make generalizations based on statistical results, such as Herring and Paolillo (2006) on blog genres and Baron (2010) on IM. Such linguistic descriptions are important in understanding the extent to which the web has introduced new varieties of language that are specific to different types of CMC. However, feature counting does not address the situated nature of language in use. That is why other studies began to complement text analysis with user surveys and interviews (e.g. Cherny 1999; Nardi *et al.* 2000). As an example of this trend, one of us carried out a study that looked into linguistic practices of email and IM among young people in Hong Kong (Lee 2002). In this study, two sets of texts were collected, from email and from ICQ (an IM program), with the aim of generating descriptive statistics of the frequency of occurrences of features such as emoticons and abbreviations in each set of data. These findings were complemented by a questionnaire survey and interviews. The primary focus of the above studies is CMC as *text* and as *language*.

Understanding language online within a social practice theory of language and literacy makes it possible to rethink the meanings of text in our data, and to also consider how texts are produced in authentic contexts of use, and most importantly, why people employ different linguistic strategies in different contexts of use. Certainly, linguistic descriptions alone cannot deal with these issues. It also follows that starting the research with just observing the words in texts on particular platforms is not enough to inform an understanding of what writing online means in people's lives. In view of this, research on digital literacies emerged to look into details of everyday digital practices (e.g. Ito *et al.* 2010). This work has *practices* as a basic unit of analysis. The researchers also consider how pedagogy can take into account students' everyday digital practices. Following a social practice theory of literacies, digital literacies scholars also adopt more ethnographic-style methods in researching details of people's everyday digital practices. Davies and Merchant (2007), for example, analyse academic blogging as a social practice. They adopt an *auto-ethnographic* approach in their research on the literacy practices of their own blogging activities. (See Anderson 2006 for an explanation of this approach in social science research, and it was also used in Barton 2011b.) Such an approach also allows them to highlight the advantages of conducting insider research. In particular, their first-hand knowledge of blogging not only allowed them to collect rich data about what actually happens in blogging; it also raised issues about ethnography as a method for online research, such as the benefits of carrying out auto-ethnographic research online and the researchers' relationship to the digital culture being researched.

As described in Chapter 1, our research on language online focuses on text-making practices, 'the ways in which people choose and transform resources for representing meanings in the form of texts for different purposes' (Lee 2007c: 289). Understanding online text-making practices involves not just analysing structural features of language, but also observing particular ways of creating and using texts, moving towards investigating the how and the why of text-making through observing details of participants' lives. People's perceptions, feelings, and values are also taken into consideration within this theoretical construct. In short, the essence of text-making practices is to study texts in terms of what people do with their texts. As a different starting point, a practice-based approach can also begin with people's everyday lives outside the screen. This serves as a way of looking at how technologies have transformed these already existing practices.

With these conceptual framings in mind, we argue that texts and practices are inseparable in researching language online. However, as we have stressed throughout the book, we do not see language as simply a set of structural features, nor is it just a mode alongside other modes of representing digital discourse. Language online is also situated social practice. Different ways of using language serve a range of discourse functions in different social contexts, leading to different intended illocutionary meanings of what is said. Ways of deploying linguistic resources are shaped by various factors situated in people's everyday lived experiences of language use and beyond. In this regard, neither language nor practice should be seen as the sole point of departure. Instead, these methods go back and forth between data of language and data of people's practices. When observing the words on a website, we frequently get to learn something about the life of the text producers such as where they are from, what they do for a living, their interests and hobbies, their linguistic repertoire in online and offline situations, and so on. With Flickr, for instance, looking at people's profiles, and their language used in various writing spaces, can reveal a great deal about the user's linguistic and cultural identities they are presenting. This combination of analysing online discourse as well as people's practices is also captured in Androutsopoulos' (2008) discourse-centred online ethnography.

A MIXED-METHOD APPROACH

Throughout the book, various studies conducted by us have been cited as examples to illustrate issues related to language online. In this section, we provide detailed descriptions of the methods of data collection adopted in three of the research projects involving different forms of new media online. The three studies in question are the study of IM text-making practices, the research on multilingual practices on Flickr, and the study of Web 2.0 writing activities.

The overall methodological assumption in our research is that understanding writing in web-based environments involves connecting texts and practices, both of which are crucial in understanding the production and use of language online. Without looking closely at the texts, we would not be able to understand the actual linguistic products of activities online; and without observing users' lives and beliefs about what they do with their online writing, we would not be able to see the dynamics of language online. Through the lens of text-making practices, we are also able to understand language online from the user's perspective. Connecting traditions of linguistic analysis with practice-based research requires new methodological design and the reshaping of traditional methods in response to the changing affordances of new media. A mixed-method approach is preferred, as no one single method can be employed to address all research questions pertaining to both the texts and the practices surrounding them. Sometimes we need to combine quantitative and qualitative methods; at other times, we move back and forth between face-to-face methods and online methods. It is important to be explicit about research methods and instruments so as to present and discuss issues and challenges involved in doing online research more generally.

The IM study

The overall aim of the IM project was to understand how young people in Hong Kong deployed their multilingual, multiscriptual, and multimodal resources when participating in IM. Because the overall objective of the study was to understand the situated nature of language deployment on IM, it generally took a qualitative and multiple case study approach. Data were collected from a group of 19 young people in Hong Kong, aged between 20 and 28. It should be noted that the data were collected between 2006 and 2007 and the methods adopted drew upon what was available at that point in time. Looking for informants for this study was not an easy task, given the amount of personal and private communication involved in IM. New informants emerged at different points in time. Some started participating at a very early stage while some were identified later by way of existing informants, an approach referred to as 'snowballing'.

Two points are worth noting regarding the research design of the IM study. First, not all participants were researched with the same research procedure. Rather, it was a 'responsive' methodology, as discussed below. Second, the same participant might have been involved in the study through different pathways of data collection. Some participants were studied through the first pathway below, which involved a mixture of traditional ethnography and online methods, including the following stages:

(i) *Initial observation*: This involved the researcher going to the participants' home or student residence and sitting behind them to take field notes as they were sitting at their computer and chatting with their friends online. This way, the researcher had access to the participants' private spaces of communication. This close observation of messaging also revealed other online practices such as multi-tasking – some participants often switched to other applications such as using MS Word for homework, with IM in the background at the same time. (See Appendix 3 for a list of what was covered in this observation session.)

(ii) *Collection of chat logs*: The participant was asked to print out the chat history from phase (i). This ensured the authenticity of the textual data.

(iii) *Face-to-face interview*: Based on the researcher's field notes, a face-to-face interview was then conducted with the participant on the spot.

(iv) *Initial analysis*: Then the researcher went away and analysed all the data collected from (i)–(iii). This phase started with a discourse analysis of the chat texts. Linguistic features identified in texts then became themes for follow-up interviews.

(v) *Follow-up*: Based on the themes emerging from (iv), follow-up interviews were conducted either face-to-face or online, depending on how accessible the participants were. Keeping in touch with the informants helped track changes in their IM usage. For example, towards the end of a semester, some participants began to use IM for project discussion with classmates instead of just for social and interpersonal chat.

As the research progressed, an alternative procedure was developed in response to the participants' everyday digital lives. In this second pathway, the participants were studied primarily through online methods.

(i) *Electronic logbook*: Each participant was asked to keep a seven-day word-processed diary or logbook, in which the participant described their daily IM and online activities. They were also asked to copy and paste their chat logs onto this logbook, which was then emailed to the researcher. (See Appendix 4 for guidance notes for the logbook writers.)

(ii) *Initial analysis*: The logbooks were analysed and coded for content. Interview topics were identified from this analysis.

(iii) *Online interview*: Follow-up interviews were mostly done through IM. This interview method was particularly suitable for researching students who the researcher did not know well or had only met electronically, or those who were not able to meet with the researcher face-to-face.

While a close observation of the IM messages was important in understanding textual features, insights from qualitative data such as interviews and logbook allowed the researcher to delve into the participants' lives and how their IM text-making might have been mediated by other online practices. For each participant, a profile was created according to information obtained from field notes and the various stages of data collection. Across-case analysis was also conducted, with an aim to look for emerging themes and patterns.

The Flickr research on multilingual practices

The original research aim of the Flickr study was to understand how people deployed their linguistic resources when interacting with an international audience. We began the study by eliciting data about the level of linguistic diversity and the overall distribution of languages on Flickr. To do so, the first step was to conduct an exploratory observation of 100 Flickr sites. These sites were selected from one of the largest interest groups on Flickr, called FlickrCentral, where users with a wide range of linguistic and geographical backgrounds can be identified. As joining groups is an optional activity, this was also an effective way of identifying active users, which was our main target group. We observed the first 100 users we came across on FlickrCentral, considering only those who had actively contributed written content, including giving titles, descriptions and tags to many of their photos. From these 100 sites, we obtained descriptive statistics about the presence and distribution of English and other languages in major writing spaces, including profiles, titles and descriptions of photos, tags and comments. As much as possible, we also noted languages used by the users and their locations. Despite this being set up as an English medium site, we noted the presence of many other languages and half of the sites in the initial analysis included languages other than English, as reported in Lee and Barton (2011). Having familiarized ourselves with the technological possibilities and general trend of multilingualism on Flickr, we then collected multilingual texts on the site and contacted the producers of these texts. Our starting point, or our primary unit of analysis, was a selection of Flickr sites, that is, the individual web spaces where users can upload their photos. We also focused largely on Flickr activities that involve user-generated writing. We collected mixed-language texts from four distinct writing spaces provided on Flickr: profiles, titles and descriptions, tags and comments.

Having obtained a snapshot of the multilingual situation on Flickr, the next step was to take a closer look at individual users' multilingual practices in these different writing spaces on Flickr. Separate from the 100 sites described above, we identified a set of sites where English and other languages co-exist. We were able to select 30 active users, 18 Chinese speakers and 12 Spanish speakers. By 'active' users, we are referring to people who regularly uploaded photos and contributed writing to the site, for example, in the form of photo captions and comments. These 30 focal participants came from various geographical areas where Chinese or Spanish were the main languages, but apart from this criterion, we studied the first active users we came across. They were first invited to complete an online survey questionnaire about their general Flickr practices. The survey covered questions about what they used Flickr for, and what languages they would use in different areas on the site and why. There was a 50 per cent response rate to our initial request, which we considered as high for an online request to strangers. The reason for this high response rate may well be that all participants were first approached through Flickr's private email system called FlickrMail, which is only available to members; in that initial email, we identified ourselves as fellow Flickr users as well as academic researchers; the survey was posted on a free online survey site which was easily accessible to the respondents.

The survey was then followed up by a series of email interviews, so as to identify different ways of participating in Flickr and ways in which these people deployed their linguistic resources on their own sites. (See Appendix 5 for an example of an email sent to one of the interviewees). As we started to develop a closer relationship with the participants, we sometimes switched to our personal email accounts, according to their preference. Our informants all had a large number of photos and one recurrent issue in online research is how to sample from what can potentially be too much data. To narrow down the scope, for each participant in the research, we examined the 100 most recent photos they had uploaded. In the interviews, our questions then focused on specific areas of these Flickr sites as well as the answers to the initial survey questionnaire. In so doing, we were able to pay close attention to details about actual situations of Flickr use. The interview data were then coded and categorized according to emerging themes from the transcripts. Our research interest in Flickr also grew out of our personal participation in this site. We thus also carried out auto-ethnographies of our own activities on Flickr, which we cover in greater detail below when discussing researcher's stance.

This core study of Flickr then acted as a starting point for additional studies of language online. For example, the additional study of people undertaking the project of taking a photo a day began from observing that one of the participants in the main Flickr study was involved in this and was a member of a 365 group. Initially, more than 200 sites where people had undertaken a-photo-a-day projects were identified by searching for '365'. These sites were looked at broadly and from them, 50 sites where people talked about their learning were examined in more detail, using content analysis to identify key themes.

The Web 2.0 writing research: techno-biographies

The third key study we have drawn upon in this book is a study of Web 2.0 writing activities among young people in Hong Kong. In addition to identifying major Web 2.0 activities, the research specifically looks into the ways in which a group of bilingual undergraduate students in Hong Kong deploy their multiple linguistic resources on Web 2.0 sites, and how that relates to their identity performance online. This study was carried out from 2010 to 2011. Two phases of data collection were involved and multiple methods were adopted: the first phase of data collection aimed to elicit demographic information about the students and to identify case participants through an initial online questionnaire survey sent to all undergraduates at a university in Hong Kong. Over 170 undergraduate students responded. This was followed by 'persistent observation' (a term used in Herring 2004) of selected participants' most frequented Web 2.0 sites, the links to which were provided by the participants in the questionnaire. Similar to the Flickr research, the survey questionnaire for this study also covered questions about the participants' linguistic practices in different online and offline domains, such as the language(s) they said they would use when writing an email to a professor, or when they looked up information for their homework on the web, and so on. This first phase of the study then served as a basis for designing the interview protocol in phase two of the study.

The core data came from detailed techno-biographic-style interviews with 20 participants, all of whom indicated in the survey that they agreed to further participate in the research as case participants. These student participants also shared a similar set of linguistic resources. That is, they speak Cantonese as their primary language in everyday life, while having knowledge of standard written Chinese, a standard written variety taught in school and used in institutional contexts; written Cantonese, a non-standard local variety of writing, may also be used for informal purposes. English is one of the official languages in Hong Kong and is taught as a second language in Hong Kong. Mixing Chinese and English in utterances then becomes a prevalent linguistic practice among these young participants.

Each techno-biographic interview started with a screen-recording session, where a student participant was asked to go online for about 30 minutes with their screen activities recorded using the screen-recording software Camtasia. This was then followed by a face-to-face interview lasting between 30 and 50 minutes, in which the screen recording was played back and the participant went through and discussed the recorded online activities with the researcher. The questions in the interview revolved around their linguistic practices in online and offline contexts in different phases and domains of the participant's life, as well as new topics that emerged during the conversation. Follow-up interviews were carried out via the private message function on Facebook (as all participants reported to be active Facebook users). See Appendix 6 for the key areas and questions that were covered in the techno-biographic interviews.

Both within-case and across-case analyses were carried out. For each participant, a profile was first created according to the information obtained from field notes and the various stages of data collection described above. All of the transcripts were coded using the qualitative data analysis software ATLAS.ti to examine emerging patterns across participants. In addition to the interview data, what the participants wrote on Facebook, their blogs, and IM was also analysed as data of techno-biographies. These new media provide new affordances and ways for online users to write about themselves, thus allowing them to create and constantly update their own auto-biographies in real time. The meaning of technobiography has also been extended to include online profiles, status updating, and visual representation of the self through images.

ONLINE METHODS AND BEING RESPONSIVE TO PARTICIPANTS' LIVES

The research projects on new media outlined above have made extensive use of online methods. These methods range from conducting surveys on the internet through to observing participants' lives on the web unannounced and interviewing participants via email or real-time chat. At the same time the internet can be used as a research tool for providing various methods of qualitative data collection such as interviews and participant observation. Using these approaches we examine what people do online and the sense they make of the online world. These methods can be seen as part of ethnographic approaches, which highlight people's perspectives and locate their activities in broader cultural contexts. In an extensive discussion of virtual methods, Hine (2000) emphasizes the importance of seeing the internet as culture and the key role of ethnographic approaches:

> Naturalistic studies overall, and ethnography in particular, have posed a challenge to the limited view of CMC provided by experimental studies. In highlighting the rich and complex social interactions that CMC can provide, researchers have established CMC as a cultural context. In doing so, researchers have drawn upon frameworks that focus on the construction of reality through discourse and practice. A style of ethnography that involves real-time engagement with the field site and multiple ways of interacting with informants has proved key in highlighting the processes which online interaction comes to be socially meaningful to participants. In claiming a new field site for ethnography and focussing on the construction of bounded social space the proponents of online culture have, however, overplayed the separateness of the offline and the online.
>
> (2000: 27)

Hine's approach fits in well with a literacy studies' focus on practices. Using a new literacies framework, Leander reviews Hine's study along with other virtual ethnographies as 'connective ethnographies' (Leander 2009). We would emphasize that often these are 'ethnographic approaches', drawing upon a useful distinction from Bloome and Green (1992) who differentiate between the full immersion in a culture involved in 'doing an ethnography' and the narrower and more focused aim of 'drawing on ethnographic approaches' (as also discussed in Barton 2011a). Often online research is doing the latter.

A recurrent method that we have adopted is online interviewing. It is a useful instrument that complements online surveys. Surveys on their own have sometimes been criticized as a data collection tool because of their lack of selection criteria when choosing focal participants (Dillman 2007). This is why in our various projects we complement online surveys with interviewing carefully selected participants. Online interviewing has proved particularly useful for researching data that involves personal and private communication that the participants would not have been comfortable to discuss with the researchers elsewhere. Crucially, the physical presence of the researcher is not required in an online interview. This can also create a relaxed research atmosphere and avoid any possible embarrassment that might exist in a face-to-face context. For example, in the IM research, most interviews were conducted via IM, which was at the same time the main research site of the study. With this method, the IM participants who were relatively quiet in face-to-face interviews turned out to be very articulate in the online context. As one participant explicitly reflected, without being prompted, towards the end of an IM interview session:

I like it this way [doing an ICQ interview] because I feel less nervous. I can have a clear mind when I write my messages.

The relatively relaxed interviewing atmosphere created by IM is also noted by Voida et al. (2004). They argue that through IM, both the interviewer and the interviewee can communicate interactively without feeling obliged to engage themselves in intense listening and note-taking activities. In addition, the time lag between messages, i.e. when we were waiting for each other to type our reply, allowed time for both the participant and the researcher to organize and reflect upon their thoughts. Although drawbacks of online interviews have been acknowledged (for example by James and Busher 2006), data collected from our online interviews often yielded much richer information about the participants' perceptions and ideologies than face-to-face interviews would have done.

In deciding what then makes the most appropriate online interviewing tool O'Conner et al. (2008) outline the pros and cons of using asynchronous or synchronous tools. Because of its delayed mode of communication, asynchronous tools such as email allow the participants to take their time to think before they respond; whereas synchronous platforms such as IM resemble the level of interaction in face-to-face talk, which email lacks. Indeed, any form of CMC can become an interviewing tool. We have realized that the most effective online interviewing platform is one that is readily available on the site that we are researching, or something that the participants are already familiar with and use actively in their everyday life. In our research, we have always been able to identify an interviewing tool from the actual research site (using IM, FlickrMail, and private messaging on Facebook for carrying out the interviews).

We also realized the importance of identifying useful research tools and methods based on the participants' existing situated online experiences. At the time of carrying out the IM research, both using IM and processing Word documents on a computer were integral in university students' lives in Hong Kong. These are the activities with which students identified and felt most comfortable. Understanding students' existing online practices allowed the researcher to develop a *responsive methodology* (Stringer 1999; Barton *et al.* 2007) that revolved around these two electronic tools – interviewing via IM and writing diary entries on MS Word. Fitting data collection activities into participants' everyday practices, together with the flexibility of time and space provided by these electronic methods, can greatly enhance student participants' interests and motivation when taking part in the process of data collection, especially one that involves multiple data collection stages over a long period of time.

Issues of ethics and privacy

Virtual ethnography shares many principles of traditional ethnography and in many ways it also has its concerns of ethics. However, online research also brings up new issues. Ethics, especially in relation to issues of privacy and ownership, has been a major topic of debate amongst online researchers (e.g. Elgesem 1996; Herring 2002). The Association of Internet Researchers (AoIR) has published a comprehensive *Ethics Guide* online (Ess and AoIR 2012) providing worked examples of informed consent forms and outlining key ethical concerns when carrying out research on the internet. The *Guide* is not a recipe, however, and may not be applicable to all contexts of internet research. There are certainly unsolved problems when it comes to researching multimodal content, and using screen shots, images and public comments.

Major questions that online researchers are still addressing are:

- What kind of public space is the online world and who owns and has rights over the use of publicly available texts online?
- When and to what extent should anonymity be assured? When should screen-names of participants be preserved as they appear online? When do faces need to be censored?
- When is it ethical to *lurk* unannounced or observe without participating in publicly available sites?
- In what situations can freely available online content be used for research purpose without seeking permission?
- If permission is needed, what kind of permission is needed and whose permission should be sought?
- In what way can researchers seek consent from strangers online?

While informed consent has been widely adopted in research involving people, internet researchers have noted that privacy can only be protected to a limited extent in online research (Elgesem 1996; Herring 2002). For example, in the IM research, new IM chat sessions often occurred unplanned and spontaneously while observing the participants. While chatting with one person, new messages from other chat partners might also arrive simultaneously and unpredictably. It was, therefore, not possible for the researcher to contact all participants prior to the observation sessions and consent from the participants' chat partners was sought only if the logs were cited in publications. Elgesem (1996) points out that since the internet is an open and public space, participating in online communication already assumes some risk of making information publicly known. Thus, there are limits to which one's online privacy can be claimed. There are also likely to be different answers to these questions depending on the sensitivity of the data and the vulnerability of the participants.

Herring (2002) also points out that informed consent might seriously affect the quality of CMC research, especially research that involves studying group identities in public CMC such as IM and chat rooms. She explains that signing an informed consent form could imply an additional identity, i.e. the research subject. This extra identity imposed on the chat users may have a strong impact on the naturalness of interaction as participants may be consciously aware of their role as research participants. These concerns and issues are also taken account of in our research projects. In a context where the data is not sensitive and the participants are not vulnerable, we believe we are able to preserve the authenticity of our data and fulfil our aim of studying people and their lives. For example, in our initial invitation letter to our Flickr participants (via private FlickrMail), we always positioned ourselves as active Flickr users showing interest in their photographs and their language use on the site, while also suggesting their potential in being research participants in our project. We made it clear to the participants that their content was used strictly for research purposes, and that they could withdraw from the study at any point. In cases where we wished to publish their self-produced content and even their faces, we wrote to the participants concerned again to seek their written permission. In short, while there still remain uncertainties regarding online research ethics, we adopt a flexible approach and try to protect our participants as far as possible, while still being able to capture the naturalistic and authentic aspects of our research sites.

THE RESEARCHER'S STANCE

Finally, we highlight our roles and our stance as researchers of language online. Just as good qualitative research makes other aspects of its methodology explicit (Barton 2011a), we believe it is essential for researchers themselves to make their relationship to the research, that is, their stance, explicit in their analyses and writing. As data collection and analysis proceeded, we became aware of the multiple roles we played at different stages of our studies. First of all, our interests in researching new media, be it IM, Flickr, or Facebook, all grew out of our own personal participation on these sites. As well as studying the sites and users, we constantly reflected upon our own participation, thus carrying out our own auto-ethnographies, or to be precise, our auto-netnographies, 'autobiographical personal reflection on online community membership' (Kozinets 2010: 188).

Take the Flickr research as an example. Both of us have been active users of Flickr for more than six years. As discussed earlier, we regularly upload photos to our photostreams; we provide tags and write about our photos; and we make contact with other Flickr users and comment on their photos. In addition to our familiarity with Flickr, we both know an additional language besides English – one of us is a Chinese-English bilingual and the other has knowledge of Spanish, coincidentally the two most used languages on Flickr after English. Our multilingual experiences on Flickr inform our understanding of the relationship between English and other languages online, offering some insider perspectives to our research. In other words, our position as a researcher of Flickr was partly enabled by our role as an insider and active user of Flickr. To our research participants, we were sometimes their Flickr contacts or friends; at other times, we were their site visitors and researchers. Some of these roles were consciously and immediately reflected upon as we interacted with our informants, while some were revealed as we analysed the data. Davies and Merchant (2007: 173) have usefully summarized the ways in which new media researchers position themselves:

- 'Researcher as identifier of new tropes' (i.e. discovering the 'newness' of technologies);
- 'Researcher as insider' (i.e. an active user of the technology examining other users of the technology in question);
- 'Researcher as analyst' (i.e. analysing texts and practices);
- 'Researcher as both subject and object' (i.e. doing auto-ethnographies);
- 'Researcher as activist' (i.e. studying the social impact of new technologies).

The boundaries between these roles can be fuzzy and very often they overlap. From our experience, simultaneously being both an insider and an analyst has benefited our research immensely. Just like doing ethnographic research on any site, online researchers need to familiarize themselves with what goes on in their research sites before they can study them. This means more than just signing up for an account and lurking – in our cases, we constantly participated as active and experienced users. We already possessed insider knowledge prior to the studies. In the IM research, for instance, the researcher's familiarity with IM-specific language features in Hong Kong (such as code-switching and a range of Asian emoticons) allowed her to compare her own experience and knowledge with the informants' practices, thus discovering the diversity in text-making practices surrounding IM. As 'insider' analysts, understanding our informants' online practices through reflecting upon our own allowed us to understand both the texts and text-making practices in greater depth.

In short, we see online methodology as an additional way of under-standing participants' lives online, instead of something that competes with or challenges traditional methods. It also does not mean that the researcher has to shift their research site entirely to an online context – the online and the offline work closely with each other in our approach. A language-focused approach to digital literacies research, together with a multitude of tradi-tional and online research methods, provide a rich array of data for us to understand better the relationship between online and offline lives, or more precisely, how the online is embedded in participants' everyday lives, which is crucial in understanding participants' text-making as situated literacies. When applied to linguistics or discourse-based research, virtual ethnography has also proved extremely useful in understanding the social functions of computer-mediated discourse.

13

FLOWS OF LANGUAGE
ONLINE AND OFFLINE

- Offline presence of internet language
- Public enregisterment of internet language
- Commodification and indexicality of internet language
- Where we are now

OFFLINE PRESENCE OF INTERNET LANGUAGE

We have called this book *Language Online*. Our primary interest has been texts and practices in the context of internet writing spaces. At the same time, throughout the book, we have presented cases and examples demonstrating the everydayness of language online and how it travels across online and offline domains of life. It is the domestication of technologies that blurs the boundary between the so-called online and offline worlds, which is also changing traditional conceptualizations of community and networking. Wellman's argument cited in Chapter 1 that '[t]he cyberspace-physical space comparison is a false dichotomy' (2001: 18) is not an exaggeration. Many of people's online activities have their roots in offline ones, as shown in Chapter 10. The demolishing of the online-offline dichotomy is also evident in everyday linguistic practices, in that people carry out their lives weaving together online and offline resources. This final chapter offers a linguistic angle to the relationship between online and offline contexts, moving on to understand the increasingly diversified nature of language, life, and the global world.

This book has provided many examples of how people's writing activities online are embedded in everyday social practices. We have seen in several chapters that college students deploy specific meaning making resources online to project different identities, including the roles they already play in their offline lives as students, friends, family, and teachers, as in Chapter 6; interacting with people through language and image on Flickr is turned into important learning opportunities, ranging from learning to take better photos to learning to become a better person, as discussed in Chapter 9; pregnancy becomes a major online literacy event, as shown in Peggy's case in Chapter 10, where she travelled seamlessly between Facebook and her blog before and after she gave birth to her daughter. These episodes of language online clearly demonstrate that writing activities on the internet are not separable from people's lived experiences off the screen.

The situated nature of language online is also evident at a more micro-linguistic level. Linguistic features that are commonly considered to be specific to 'online' communication have made their way to our everyday off-screen contexts. Public spaces are gradually infiltrated with texts with traces of what public discourse would refer to as 'textese' or Netspeak. This seems to be happening all around the world. Here are a few examples:

- A London convenience store is called '4 UR Convenience' (Figure 13.1);
- An English academic department in Hong Kong has 'English @ CUHK' as their department logo;
- A sign on the wine shelf in a supermarket in New Zealand warns customers to 'THNK B4 U DRNK';
- '@' indicates a public computer area in a hotel in Spain.

There are many more examples of this that we cannot cover here.[1] What we can observe immediately though is that many of these public texts contain features identified in the first generation of CMC research that focused on linguistic description of a CMC genre containing features such as word reductions, acronyms, and letter and number homophones. (For the sake of convenience, we use 'internet language' in this chapter to refer to these features.) The @ sign, though originally used in other contexts that predate the internet, has been popularized by its use in email addresses and more recently on Twitter. Honeycutt and Herring (2009) have identified 12 functions of the @ sign on Twitter and show how these uses facilitate interactional coherence within the complex network of tweets. An important function of @ on Twitter is to address another user in a tweet (e.g. @CarmenLee). The @ sign is now widely used in public places to represent the locational preposition

---

[1] Interested readers may refer to our set of data posted on Flickr: http://www.flickr.com/photos/onofflineproject/

Figure 13.1 '4 UR Convenience', a convenience store in London

'at' (e.g. 'Only @ Watsons'). The Facebook 'Like' has made its way to the offline world as a key element in print-based advertising. Other features include playful punctuation and emoticons in public signs.

The examples given above are based on English only. What is even more interesting is how some of these English-based expressions are inserted into texts in other languages, as shown in Figure 13.2. This poster is an advertisement for a fitness centre in Hong Kong. As a common marketing strategy nowadays, the ad asks potential customers to become a fan of the fitness centre by 'liking' its fan page on Facebook in exchange for a gift. The Facebook 'Like' button here is not only an additional marketing strategy in the poster, but is indeed part of the syntax of the slogan '– Like 即賞' ('Like us and you will be rewarded'). The act of liking posts on Facebook has introduced new meanings to the verb 'like'. In the case of the slogan here, 'Like' is not taken literally but should be interpreted as the act of clicking the 'Like' button on Facebook. Although the Chinese equivalent to 'Like' is available on Facebook, the poster designer decided to use a mixed-code message to speak to the local Hong Kong customers who are used to code-switching in speech.

PUBLIC ENREGISTERMENT OF INTERNET LANGUAGE

The growing presence of specific forms of language in public places is a clear sign of public enregisterment of language. Enregisterment refers to the process through which 'a linguistic repertoire becomes differentiable within

Figure 13.2 Fitness centre in Hong Kong

a language as a socially recognized register of forms' (Agha 2003: 231). As access to the internet and communication over networked spaces becomes commonplace, public discourses and metalinguistic descriptions about the influence of the internet also grow. It is easy for people to talk about their language use online and its possible influences. Metalinguistic labels like 'chatspeak', 'textese', and 'textspeak' have been used by the mass media and in public discussions, and even linguists in early CMC research, to refer to specific features of language that seem to be exclusive to the internet. The existence of these labels is evidence of a recognizable and emerging 'variety' of language that is quite different from other forms that are already in use. In this case, internet language use often contrasts with existing 'standard' language. While internet language is often misrepresented by mass media and other public discourses (see Chapter 1), our data shown in the previous section suggest that people are at the same time gradually accepting such features of language as 'normal'. Internet language is no longer just a set of innovative codes used by a small group of people. Some frequently used abbreviated forms such as LOL ('laugh out loud') and BFF ('best friends forever') have been codified in the *Oxford English Dictionary*, which suggests that these linguistic forms have become part of people's everyday language practices, whether online or offline.

COMMODIFICATION AND INDEXICALITY OF INTERNET LANGUAGE

Language is always indexical. Sociolinguists have discussed how language and its forms, such as an accent, can convey specific social meanings and identities. The growing presence of internet language in offline contexts also serves to index and position particular social identities such as people of a certain age group and lifestyle. Crystal (2005) once argued that SMS abbreviations are designed to accommodate the technological limits of texting, and that they have no place in other contexts where such limits do not exist. The growing presence of online linguistic features in broad domains of offline life clearly shows that such linguistic features do have their values in offline contexts.

Abbreviations used in texting are no longer just a way of responding to the word limit on mobile phone texting systems. With easier and cheaper mobile technologies with no word limit imposed on texting, abbreviations and initialisms have still survived. One of the reasons is the commodification of internet language, in that language online is given marketable and economic values. That is why the examples we have shown are mostly present in commercial domains. We have seen OMG printed on bags and shirts, emoticons in print-based advertisements, and the @ sign is found in many shopping centres in big cities. The indexical values of these features have to be interpreted in their immediate contexts of use. In contemporary society, internet language has become an important form of cultural capital that indexes 'coolness' (boyd 2006), being modern, having an urban lifestyle, and perhaps youthfulness. And in societies where English is not used as a primary language, these social meanings are further reinforced because of the use of English-based internet language in local public texts. All these also provide further evidence that vernacular linguistic practices are valued in new media linguistic landscapes. As part of the development of a super-diverse society, Blommaert suggests that language features used in text messages have developed into a 'supervernacular', 'a particular and new type of sociolinguistic object: semiotic forms that circulate in networks driven, largely, by new technologies' (2013, 3). The examples we have seen in the previous sections are, however, no longer text messages when moved to offline contexts. Mobile texting codes are not just one supervernacular. They have been reshaped and refashioned into further varieties to suit different purposes. This also fits in with the situated approach to written language that is taken in this book.

WHERE WE ARE NOW

Propositions about literacy practices made two decades ago already made it clear that literacy is historically situated and that literacy practices change (Barton 1994b). These two characteristics of literacy practices also apply to linguistic practices online. Language online is historically situated where changes take place constantly according to human decision-making. People draw upon and often reappropriate familiar practices from their previous experience with technology whenever they come across a newer medium. With this in mind, what is commonly conceived of as internet language is hardly new – abbreviating or shortening a word has been a common word formation process through history; and the @ sign and Facebook 'Like' are amongst the many examples of pre-existing semiotic forms being given new pragmatic meanings when they move between contexts, whether online or offline. Thus, it is not language but what people do with it that has become different and changes. As a way of summarizing what we have discovered about changing linguistic practices brought about by new media, the following list characterizes some of the things people do with language online. When engaging in writing activity online, people:

- participate in new multilingual encounters, use and develop minority languages, are more tolerant of language varieties and more informality;
- project new identities, explore multiple identities and different senses of the self;
- position themselves and others through multimodal means, combine semiotic resources in new ways, invent new relations between language and images;
- respond to new affordances and deal with constant change, participate in highly textually mediated activities;
- are more reflexive; reflect on their learning, undertake intentional projects, learn in different ways, and new ways;
- reshape vernacular practices, make vernacular practices public;
- sort, classify, categorize in different ways, collaborate in new ways, participate in digital scholarship, contribute to knowledge;
- do more reading and, especially, more writing, are changing the relation between writing and reading.

The issues raised in this chapter both return us to the beginning of the book and hint at possible further directions. Topics such as the changing materiality of language and the shifting commercial control of language are all perennial issues. New media are constantly being developed at any moment and so are their related language and literacy practices. Research on new media, like any subject areas, is ongoing and dynamic. The above list is likely to be dated soon as technologies change and what people do with them change. For instance, spoken language may have increasing importance online and there may be shifts in what is paid for and what is available free, along with conflicts over who can say what online. Returning again to our discussion of newness in Chapter 1, practices online are deictic. Concepts, descriptions, and theories of language online thus need constant updating. Nonetheless, language is fluid and keeps moving and changing across domains, time, and spaces. Language flows and changes with people, their social practices, identities, and purposes.

APPENDICES

APPENDIX 1: TWO FRAMEWORKS FOR ANALYSING LANGUAGE ONLINE

1.1 SOME LINGUISTIC PHENOMENA TO ATTEND TO WHEN ANALYSING LANGUAGE AND IMAGE GENERALLY

This is a short list of topics. The specific areas vary according the purpose of the analysis and the nature of the data:

- *Participants:* how they position themselves and others, how they address others
  - I, me, you, we
  - Sentence types, questions and imperatives
  - Hiding the self, passives, nominalizations
- *Intertextuality* and voices of others
- *Metalinguistics* and talk about talk
- *Modal verbs, hedges,* etc. . ...
- *Conversational devices:* Well, I mean
- *Digital devices* such as !!!!! :)
- *Beginning and endings,* Given and new: such as 'I think that. . ..' and '. . ..:)'
- *Warrants,* how people back up what they say, through:
  - Assertion of beliefs
  - Experience
  - Deduction
  - Reference to other people

1.2 A FRAMEWORK FOR ANALYSING MULTIMODAL AND MULTILINGUAL STANCE-TAKING ON FLICKR

This shows the step-by-step stages used to analyse stance.

The photographer's stance (in different writing spaces)

- How does the photographer use the title and description to express what s/he knows about the image?
- How does the photographer use the title and description to express her feelings and attitudes about the image? (e.g. Does he/she explicitly evaluate the image? Does the description focus on a particular part of the image?)
- How does the photographer use a particular language/image to tell others who s/he is?
- How does the photographer use a particular language/image to relate to his/her viewers (e.g. contacts, commenters, strangers)?

The viewer(s)' stance (mostly via *comments*)

Generally, this is about how the comments tie intertextually and cohesively to the image, the title, the description, the tags, etc. on the page.

- How do the commenters express knowledge/belief/opinion/feeling towards (a particular part of) the image?
- How do the commenters express knowledge/belief/opinion/feeling towards the title and/or description?
- How do the commenters refer to a previous comment?
- What languages do the commenters use to make their comments?
- How do they relate to other commenters?
- How do they relate to the photographer? (e.g. through a common language)

The researcher-viewer's stance (the analyst's gaze)

- What is your reading path, e.g. what draws your attention first? What do you look for next?
- How does your role as a researcher and your research agenda shape your reading path?
- How does your prior knowledge of the content of the image and/or the language(s) used shape the way you analyse the photo page?

The researcher-viewer as a Flickr user

- How does your knowledge about Flickr and its affordances shape your reading path and the way you study the photo page?

- How does your own experience in using Flickr shape your reading path and the way you study the photo page?
- How do your attitudes towards Flickr shape your reading path and the way you study the photo page?

BROADENING OUT

Go back and forth iteratively between the image and the researcher's stance to inform the stance analysis.

Observe further:

- Other photos in the photo stream;
- Other information about the photographer (e.g. the profile page);
- Any other external links to make more sense of this all (e.g. the user's blog).

APPENDIX 2: USING FACEBOOK GROUP IN AN UNDERGRADUATE LINGUISTICS COURSE

Reflections on Facebook group in an undergraduate linguistic course
(by Carmen Lee)

In my own teaching, I have explored different tools to facilitate out-of-classroom interaction with my students in Hong Kong, from learning platforms like WebCT to social network sites such as Twitter and Facebook. WebCT was selected in my first year of teaching because it was a tool that I had used when I was a student. In my own courses, however, students did not log in as often as I wished and sometimes even missed important information that I posted. After two years, I added Twitter with the hope that students would participate in backchannel discussion during my lectures and back home they would receive updated information about the course. To my surprise, however, very few students signed up for a Twitter account. What I have learned from these years of combining technologies with face-to-face classroom interaction is that we do not simply select a platform that we teachers think can improve students' learning; what is more important is to consider a tool that is situated in students' everyday lived experiences (see also Ivanič et al. 2009 on how college students learn outside of school). That is why at the end of my courses, I often ask students to assess their online learning experience. One year, a student suggested "Start a Facebook group because we use FB every day!" And so I did it!

In the spring semester in 2011, I formed a Facebook Group for my senior undergraduate course Language, Literacy and Technology, which 33 students were taking. While sharing most features on Facebook, a 'Group' on Facebook is a membership-based area that gathers people with shared interests and purposes. A Group may be public or private (called a Closed Group). My course Group was a closed one meaning that only course members were allowed to join the Group and read the posts there. In this Group, all members were encouraged to take the initiative to write posts. Students and teachers interacted through multimodal means, from text-based posts and comments to images from other sites and videos from YouTube. A feature that is exclusive to the Group area on Facebook is 'Docs', which allows members to compose and share text-based documents – that is also where I share my lecture notes with the students. Participation in the group was voluntary and no contribution in the Group was formally assessed. All students joined the Group as they interpreted their Facebook participation as part of their general participation grade, which counted towards 10 per cent of their overall coursework. At the end of the course, a questionnaire survey of students' experience of using Facebook in the course revealed that 92 per cent of them preferred the Facebook Group to other course platforms that they had used. This positive feedback was partly due to the fact that all students were already avid Facebook users. A course-based platform on Facebook would not have created extra work for them. Whenever they logged in to Facebook, the latest course information was there. In terms of level of participation, although most original posts were still teacher-initiated, over 350 comments (together with many 'Likes') were made by students throughout the 14-week semester. It was also apparent that a strong sense of community was developed outside the classroom context (e.g. offering opportunities for students from different faculties and majors to interact outside class). The social networking affordance on Facebook also facilitated collaborative learning, with students often sharing newly discovered, course-related information on the web, thus taking on the role of a teacher at the same time.

A strong sense of community was developed both inside and outside the classroom through adopting a hybridity of discourse practices by the course participants. Although the Group was academic in nature and was initiated by the teacher, course members drew upon a mixture of conventional and unconventional language practices that did not seem to exist in the physical classroom context. The following extract shows an original post by a student Carrie, who shares her view on an internet-specific word ('geilivable') that she found on the Yahoo Dictionary website (Hong Kong version), followed by a comment from me, the course lecturer.

Carrie Chan: This page really shocks me today! I haven't thought of having this as proper vocabulary in English! BTW using 很牛 to explain 給力 is still too vague to those non-Chinese netizens. . .
(NB: In the original post, Carrie shares a web link to the word geilivable Yahoo Hong Kong Dictionary. Geilivable is a blending of the Chinese internet jargon geili, meaning to give force, and the English suffix -able.)

Carmen Lee: thanks for sharing, carrie! and here are more examples:
http://news.xinhuanet.com/english2010/china/2010-12/25/c_13663775.htm

In this post, Carrie adopts a hybrid discourse style that does not normally exist in formal academic interaction. First of all, the post employs code-switching, which is commonly found in students' informal digital communication (as shown in the IM example in Chapter 3). Second, internet-specific discourse features such as 'BTW' and trailing dots (. . .) are incorporated into the post. Third, the hyperlinks embedded in Carrie's post and my response also demonstrate *intertextuality*, a major characteristic of young people's textual practices (Ivanič *et al.* 2009; van Meter and Firetto 2008). This student-initiated post also provides a nice example of how Facebook affords collaborative learning. It shows how Carrie exercised agency (Satchwell, Barton and Hamilton, forthcoming) and shared her views on this newly discovered information with the rest of the class, including the course lecturer. Thus, the roles of teacher and student are not always clearly defined and are constantly renegotiated in this space.

Course participants had different opinions about the relationship between how they wrote in this Facebook Group and how they wrote elsewhere on the internet, as two students reflected:

> sometimes it's more formal when i write in facebook group as it is like an academic platform. but it also depends on the nature and formality of that message. if it is not related to academic field, i would rather switch to some chinglish as it looks more friendly and funny.
>
> > (*Big C*, online interview)

> I used English only in the group, and I seldom do that elsewhere on facebook. I do think this is an academic group, so I feel uncomfortable about using loose grammar, having typos and using excessive Netspeak features. However, I use emoticons all the time as in other online platforms.
>
> > (*Tony*, online interview)

These two students were well aware of the text-making resources available to them for meaning making in this teacher-initiated space. While seeing the Group as an academic discussion platform, they also brought in their everyday, private, vernacular online text-making practices to the Group interaction. Even though Tony pointed out he was not entirely comfortable to adopt a non-standard linguistic style in the Group, emoticons could be tolerated, which turned out to be Tony's negotiated form of online academic discourse.

As the lecturer, I also found myself constantly negotiating between my university teacher identity and my active Facebook user identity through reappropriating my language use in this Group. For example, I once shared a YouTube video that introduces a new book written entirely in PowerPoint style. This is how I described the video in my post:

> *Carmen Lee*:   hmmm writing a novel in PowerPoint format sounds fun! More thoughts for the notion of 'affordances'. hmmmmm..I wonder if that makes writing easier or more challenging.. :-)

In this post, while attempting to remind students of course-related concepts (affordances), I frame my message in a relatively informal, interpersonal discourse style that is typically found in youth online writing, such as the insertion of emoticon :-), trailing dots (..) and hedges (hmmm) to indicate that I was thinking and I welcomed ideas from the class. This also allowed me to play down my lecturer identity in the course so as to build rapport with my students.

APPENDIX 3: OBSERVING ELEMENTS OF IM ACTIVITIES

Observing elements of IM activities

(i) *Participants*: How many people is the informant chatting with? Who is s/he chatting with? Are they using nicknames? Does the informant always appear to be online in IM? Are there other people in the physical setting (apart from the researcher)?

(ii) *Texts*: Apart from texts in the chat window, are there other texts on the screen? Are there other texts in the off-screen setting? If so, are the texts related to the chat? How are alert systems and text boxes, menus, icons, and toolbars being used by the informant?

(iii) *Tasks*: Does the informant use IM for chatting only? Does the informant do other things in his/her physical environment while using IM (e.g. reading, writing short notes, talking on the phone)? Are there other types of reading and writing activities? Does the informant talk about the chat content with other people? What else is done on the screen (e.g. checking email, surfing the web, using search engines, other computer-based activities such as typing assignments, listening to music files)? Do texts determine what actions the informant is going to take in IM? How does the informant read, write, and send messages?

(iv) *Resources*: What IM programme is the informant using? Does the informant use any technological tools to facilitate IM, e.g. does s/he use Chinese inputting systems? Does s/he use other inputting devices in addition to the keyboard?

(v) *Modes/Media of Interaction*: Is the interaction only based on typing? Does the interaction take place in words only? What does the text look like (languages, scripts, and other semiotic symbols)? Is there any talking in the off-screen setting?

(vi) *Time*: When does the informant start logging on/off IM? When does the chat session begin? When does it end? How long does it take? How many chat sessions are performed within this time frame? Is it a continuous session or does the informant stop chatting for a while to attend to other activities?

(vii) *Places and Settings*: Where is the computer situated? Is it a shared computer? To what extent is the setting private or public?

APPENDIX 4: NOTES GIVEN TO LOGBOOK KEEPERS IN THE IM STUDY

Notes given to logbook keepers

A logbook of online chatting activities
Please keep a record of how you use online chat in the next seven days.
Note the following points in particular:

- Don't forget to activate the 'save history' function.
- When do you start communicating online? Until when? How many times have you used chat programmes on a particular day?
- Where do you chat online? E.g. at home in your room, in a computer lab, etc.
- Why do you chat? This refers to the purpose(s) e.g. private chat, discuss homework, etc.
- With whom? E.g. friends, classmates, family, etc. You may include their names.
- Do you use more than one chat programme at the same time?
- What else do you do when you chat?
    - On-screen activities: e.g. using Word or PowerPoint to do your homework, listening to music, checking email, browsing websites. . .
    - Off-the-screen activities, e.g. scribbling notes on paper, talking on phone, watching TV, talking to people around you. Also try to note down any media available in your surroundings.
    - What else do you do while you're looking at the screen? Do you read aloud your messages? How do you use your mouse?
- Please copy and paste your chat history – you may omit anything that you don't feel like disclosing. You are not obliged to give me everything.
- You may make use of the following template for keeping your records. You may use any language and format of your own choice. There is no limit on length. Choose a method that you feel most comfortable with, e.g. you can write as if you're writing a diary.
- You may add extra pages if necessary
- If you are unable to keep your record on a specific day, you can skip that day and continue the following day.
- Method of submitting the logbook: you can email the document to me or print it out and give it to me in person.

DAY 1

Start-time of ICQ/MSN:

End-time of ICQ/MSN:

Record of chat-related activities

Please paste your chat history (all or selected) in the space below.

APPENDIX 5: SAMPLE EMAIL FROM INTERVIEWER IN FLICKR RESEARCH

This is an example of an email that the researcher sent to the participants after they had answered the online questionnaire. The questions were individually designed for each person.

Dear XXX,

Thank you so much for responding to the questionnaire so quickly. We are very interested in some of the things you've said in the questionnaire.

Could you please take your time and answer the following open-ended questions as detailed as possible. You may write your answers in English or Chinese or mixed code. Please let us know if you want us to clarify any of the questions.

First of all, we are interested in particular times when you use English and Chinese:

1. Is there any reason why you give this photo a Chinese and English name but the description is only written in English? (link to photo page)
2. Why did you name and describe this photo in English only? (link to photo page)
3. Recently you seldom tag your photos. Why?
4. Why is your profile page written in both Chinese and English?
5. Who do you see as the audience for your photos? Who are you trying to reach? (E.g. any particular community, or people who speak a particular language, or people who share some of your background and interest, etc.)
6. Before using Flickr, did you do anything like tagging of your photos or commenting on other people's photos? And did you communicate with other people around the world before Flickr and blogging?
7. In the questionnaire, you said it is more polite to use English if the others do not understand Chinese. How do you know whether your viewers understand Chinese?
8. What is the role of English in your life? Do you need to use English in other aspects of your life apart from Flickr?

If it is easier for you, you can write to us at: (researcher's personal email)

Thank you very much for your time. We look forward to hearing from you as we are very interested in what you have to say.

Best Regards,

David and Carmen

APPENDIX 6: TOPICS COVERED IN THE TECHNO-BIOGRAPHIC INTERVIEWS

Other than using techno-biographic interviews as a research instrument, these questions and topics can serve as a basis for classroom discussion.

Current practices

- What are the sites you use most often, and what are the ones you have contributed to?
- Do you visit different sites in different places (home computer, school computer, mobile devices)?

Ways of participation

- How much reading and writing do you do on these sites?
- What are the different functions of these sites?
- Do you make cross reference (i.e. similar content posted on different sites, though may be written in different ways)?
- Do you enjoy posting on these sites? Why?
- Do you use different languages/scripts on different sites? Why?
- How often do you post pictures/videos on these sites?
- Do you write things about your photos? What do you write?
- Any interesting experience in posting status updates on Facebook/ blogging, etc.?

A day in the life

- Think of yesterday, what technologies did you first deal with when you woke up, how did it continue during the day?
- Can you imagine a day without the internet? What difference would this make to your life?

Technology-related life history

- When and how did you start using the computer?
- What did you use the computer for at that time?
- When and how did you start using the internet?
- When and how did you send your first text message? Write your first blog? Search Wikipedia? Start using Facebook? Etc.

Transitions

- Have you noticed any changes in your computer/mobile phone use over the years? What are they (e.g. different phases like secondary school life vs. uni life)?

Domains of life

- Do you use different technologies in different areas of your everyday life, e.g. at home, at school, at work? Other domains, such as religion, sports, politics, music, etc.

Cross-generational comparisons

- Do you notice differences between the technologies used by your parents and yourself? How about your grandparents? Are there younger children in your family who are exposed to technologies? How are their online activities different from yours?
- Do you notice any differences in technology use between your own and your friends from other countries? How about gender differences?

Imagined future

- What does the internet mean to you now and what do you think your internet use will be like in 10 years' time?

BIBLIOGRAPHY

Agha, A. (2003) 'The social life of cultural value', *Language and Communication*, 23: 231–274.

Alim, S. and Pennycook, A. (2009) 'Glocal linguistic flows: hip-hop culture(s), identities, and the politics of language education', *Journal of Language, Identity and Education*, 6(2): 89–100.

Alvermann, D. E. (ed.) (2011) *Adolescents and Literacies in a Digital World*, 3rd edn. New York: Peter Lang.

America Online (2005) 'AOL's third annual instant messenger trends survey'. Online. Available HTTP: <http://www.aim.com/survey/> (accessed 1 May 2012).

Anderson, L. (2006) 'Analytical autoethnography', *Journal of Contemporary Ethnography* 35(4): 273–295.

Androutsopoulos, J. (2006) 'Multilingualism, diaspora, and the Internet: codes and identities on German-based diaspora websites', *Journal of Sociolinguistics*, 10(4): 520-47.

Androutsopoulos, J. (2007) 'Language choice and code-switching in German-based diasporic web forums', in B. Danet and S. C. Herring (eds) *The Multilingual Internet: Language, Culture, and Communication Online*, New York and Oxford: Cambridge University Press.

Androutsopoulos, J. (2008) 'Potentials and limitations of discourse-centered online ethnography', *Language@Internet*, 5, article 8. Online. Available HTTP: <http://www.languageatinternet. de/articles/2008> (accessed 1 May 2012).

Androutsopoulos, J. (2009) 'Language and the three spheres of hip-hop', in H. Samy Alim, A. Ibrahim and A. Pennycook (eds) *Global Linguistic Flows: Hip-hop Cultures, Youth Identities, and the Politics of Language*, New York/London: Routledge.

Androutsopoulos, J. (2013) 'Participatory culture and metalinguistic discourse: performing and negotiating German dialects on YouTube', in D. Tannen and A. M. Trester, *Discourse 2.0: Language and New Media*, Washington DC: Georgetown University Press.

Augar, N., Raitman, R. and Zhou, W. (2004) 'Teaching and learning online with wikis', in R. Atkinson, C. McBeath, D. Jonas-Dwyer and R. Phillips (eds) *Beyond the Comfort Zone: Proceedings of the 21st ASCILITE Conference*, Perth, 5–8 December. Online. Available HTTP: <http://www. ascilite.org.au/conferences/perth04/procs/augar.html> (accessed 1 May 2012).

Baron, N. (2003) 'Why email looks like speech: proofreading, pedagogy, and public face', in J. Aitchison and D. Lewis (eds) *New Media Language*, London: Routledge.

Baron, N. (2010) 'Discourse structures in instant messaging: the case of utterance breaks', *Language@Internet*, 7. Online. Available HTTP: <http://www.languageatinternet.org/ articles/2010/2651/?searchterm=naomi%20baron> (accessed 30 August 2012).

Barton, D. (1994a) 'Globalisation and diversification: two opposing influences on local literacies', in D. Barton (ed.) *Sustaining Local Literacies*, Clevedon: Multilingual Matters; and also in *Language and Education*, 8(1–2): 3–7.

Barton, D. (1994b) *Literacy: An Introduction to the Ecology of Written Language*, 1st edn, Oxford: Blackwell.

Barton, D. (2001) 'Directions for literacy research: analyzing language and social practices in a textually mediated world', *Language and Education*, 15(2–3): 92–104.

Barton, D. (2007) *Literacy: An Introduction to the Ecology of Written Language*, 2nd edn, Oxford: Blackwell.

Barton, D. (2009) 'Understanding textual practices in a changing world', in M. Baynham and M. Prinsloo (eds) *The Future of Literacy Studies*, Basingstoke/New York: Palgrave Macmillan.

Barton, D. (2011a) 'Ethnographic approaches to literacy research', in *Encyclopedia of Applied Linguistics*, Chichester: Wiley-Blackwell.

Barton, D. (2011b) 'People and technologies as resources in times of uncertainty', *Mobilities*, 6(1): 57–65.

Barton, D. (2012) 'Participation, deliberate learning and discourses of learning online', *Language and Education*, 26(2): 139–150.

Barton, D. and Hamilton, M. (1998) *Local Literacies*, London: Routledge.

Barton, D. and Hamilton, M. (2005) 'Literacy, reification and the dynamics of social interaction', in D. Barton and K. Tusting (eds) *Beyond Communities of Practice: Language, Power and Social Context*, Cambridge: Cambridge University Press.

Barton, D. and Hamilton, M. (2012) *Local Literacies*, London: Routledge.

Barton, D., Bloome, D., Sheridan, D. and Street, B. (1993) 'Ordinary people writing: the Lancaster and Sussex writing research projects', *Lancaster University: Centre for Language in Social Life Papers*, 51.

Barton, D., Ivanič, R., Appleby, Y., Hodge, R. and Tusting, K. (2007) *Literacy, Lives and Learning*, London: Routledge.

Barton, D. and Lee, C. (2012) 'Redefining vernacular literacies in the age of web 2.0', *Applied Linguistics*, 33(3): 282–298.

Baym, N. K. (2010) *Personal Connections in the Digital Age*, Cambridge, UK/Malden, MA: Polity.

Baynham, M. and Prinsloo, M. (eds) (2009) *The Future of Literacy Studies*, Basingstoke/New York: Palgrave Macmillan.

Bechar-Israeli H. (1995) 'From <Bonehead> to <cLonehEad>: nicknames, play and identity on Internet Relay Chat', *J. Computer-Mediated Communication*, 1(2). Online. Available HTTP: <http://jcmc.indiana.edu/vol1/issue2/bechar.html> (accessed 1 May 2012).

Bennett, S., Maton, K. and Kervin, L. (2008) 'The "digital natives" debate: a critical review of the evidence', *British Journal of Educational Technology*, 39(5): 775–786.

Benson, P. (2004) 'Autonomy and information technology in the educational discourse of the information age', in C. Davison (ed.) *Information Technology and Innovation in Language Education*, Hong Kong: Hong Kong University Press.

Benson, P. (2010) 'Funny teacher saying foul language: new literacies in a second language', paper presented at the 17th International Conference on Learning, Hong Kong Institute of Education, 6–9 July 2010.

Benson, P. and Chan, N. (2011) 'TESOL after YouTube: fansubbing and informal language learning', *Taiwan Journal of TESOL*, 7(2): 1–23.

Benson, P. and Chik, A. (2010) 'New literacies and autonomy in foreign language learning', in M. J. Luzón, M. N. Ruiz and M. L. Villanueva (eds) *Digital Genres, New Literacies, and Autonomy in Language Learning*, Newcastle upon Tyne: Cambridge Scholars Publishing.

Berker, T., Hartmann, M., Punie, Y. and Ward, K. (eds) (2005) *Domestication of Media and Technologies*, Maidenhead: Open University Press.

Berners-Lee, T. (2005) 'Berners-Lee on the read/write web'. Available HTTP: <http://news.bbc.co.uk/2/hi/technology/4132752.stm> (accessed 3 August 2012).

Black, R. (2009) 'English language learners, fan communities, and twenty-first century skills', *Journal of Adolescent and Adult Literacy*, 52(8): 688–697.

Blackledge, A. and Creese, A. (2009) *Multilingualism: A critical perspective*, London: Continuum.

Block, D. (2004) 'Globalization, transnational communication and the Internet', *International Journal on Multicultural Societies*, 6(1): 13–28.

Block, D. and Cameron, D. (eds) (2002) *Globalization and Language Teaching*, London/New York: Routledge.

Blommaert, J. (ed.) (1999) *Language Ideological Debates*, Berlin: Walter de Gruyter.

Blommaert, J. (2008) *Grassroots Literacy*, London: Routledge.

Blommaert, J. (2010) *The Sociolinguistics of Globalization*, Cambridge: Cambridge University Press.

Blommaert, J. (2011) 'Supervernaculars and their dialects', *Working Papers in Urban Language & Literacies*, paper 81. Online. Available HTTP: <http://www.kcl.ac.uk/innovation/groups/ldc/publications/workingpapers/WP81.pdf> (accessed 1 May 2012).

Blommaert, J. and Rampton, B. (2011) 'Language and superdiversity: a position paper', *Working Papers in Urban Languages and Literacies*, paper 70. Online. Available HTTP: <http://www.kcl.ac.uk/projects/ldc/LDCPublications/workingpapers/70.pdf> (accessed 1 May 2012).

Bloome, D. and Green, J. L. (1992) 'Educational contexts of literacy', *Annual Review of Applied Linguistics*, 12: 49–70.

Borau, K., Ullrich, C., Feng, J. and Shen, R. (2009) 'Microblogging for language learning: using twitter to train communicative and cultural competence', in M. Spaniol *et al.* (eds) *ICWL '009 Proceedings of the 8th International Conference on Advances in Web Based Learning*, Heidelberg: Springer-Verlag Berlin. Online. Available HTTP: <http://www.carstenullrich.net/pubs/Borau09Microblogging.pdf> (accessed 1 May 2012).

Bourdieu, P. (1990) *The Logic of Practice*, Cambridge: Polity.

boyd, d. (2006) 'A blogger's blog: exploring the definition of a medium', *Reconstruction*, 6(4). Online. Available HTTP: <http://www.danah.org/papers/ABloggersBlog.pdf> (accessed 28 July 2012).

boyd, d. (2007) 'Why youth (heart) social network sites: the role of networked publics in teenage social life', in D. Buckingham (ed.) *Youth, Identity, and Digital Media*, Cambridge, MA: MIT Press.

Brandt, D. (1998) 'Sponsors of literacy', *College Composition and Communication*, 49: 165–185.

Brandt, D. (2001) *Literacy in American Lives*, New York: Cambridge University Press.

Brandt, D. (2009) *Literacy and Learning: Reflections on Writing, Reading, and Society*, San Francisco, CA: Jossey-Bass.

Braun, L. W. (2007) *Teens, Technology, and Literacy; or, Why Bad Grammar Isn't Always Bad*, Westport, CT: Libraries Unlimited.

Bucholtz, M. and Hall, K. (2005) 'Identity and interaction: a sociocultural linguistic approach', *Discourse Studies*, 7(4–5): 585–614.

Buckingham, D. (2007) 'Digital media literacies: rethinking media education in the age of the internet', *Research in Comparative and International Education*, 2(1): 43–55.

Burbary, K. (2011) 'Facebook demographics revisited – 2011 statistics'. Online. Available HTTP: <http://www.kenburbary.com/2011/03/facebook-demographics-revisited-2011-statistics-2/> (accessed 1 May 2012).

Burgess, J. (2007) *Vernacular Creativity and New Media*, Unpublished Ph.D. Dissertation, Queensland University of Technology, Brisbane, Australia, Online. Available HTTP: <http://eprints.qut.edu.au/archive/00010076/01/Burgess_PhD_FINAL.pdf> (accessed 12 September 2012).

Burgess, J. and Green, J. (2009) *YouTube: Online Video and Participatory Culture*, Malden, MA: Polity.

Busch, B., Aziza J. and Angelika T. (2006) *Language Biographies for Multilingual Learning*, Cape Town: PREAESA Occasional Papers 24.

Camitta, M. (1993) 'Vernacular writing: varieties of writing among Philadelphia high school students', in B. Street (ed.) *Cross-cultural Approaches to Literacy*, Cambridge, UK: Cambridge University Press.

Canagarajah, A. S. (2007) 'The ecology of global English', *International Multilingual Research Journal*, 1(2): 89–100.

Carr, N. (2010) *The Shallows: What the Internet Is Doing to Our Brains*, New York: W. W. Norton.

Carrington, V. and Robinson, M. (eds) (2009) *Digital Literacies*, London: Sage.

Cherny, L. (1999) *Conversation and Community: Chat in a Virtual World*, Stanford, CA: CSLI Publications.

Ching, C. C. and Vigdor, L. (2005) 'Technobiographies: perspectives from education and the arts', paper presented at the First International Congress of Qualitative Inquiry, Champaign, IL.

Chun, E. and Walters, K. (2011) 'Orienting to Arab Orientalisms: language, race, and humor in a YouTube video', in C. Thurlow and K. Mroczek (eds) *Digital Discourse: Language in the New Media*, New York/London: Oxford University Press.

Coiro, J., Knobel, M., Lankshear, C. and Leu, D. J. (eds) (2008) *Handbook of Research on New Literacies*, New York: Lawrence Erlbaum.

comScore (2009) 'Hong Kong internet users spend twice as much time on instant messengers as counterparts in Asia-Pacific region', online. Available HTTP: <http://www.comscore.com/Press_Events/Press_Releases/2009/10/Hong_Kong_Internet_Users_Spend_Twice_as_Much_Time_on_Instant_Messengers> (accessed 6 September 2012).

Conklin, M. (2007) '101 uses for Second Life in the college classroom', online. Available HTTP: <http://facstaff.elon.edu/mconklin/pubs/glshandout.pdf> (accessed 5 September 2012).

Cooke-Plagwitz, J. (2008) 'New directions in CALL: an objective introduction to Second Life', *CALICO Journal*, 25(3): 547–557.

Cope, B. and Kalantzis, M. (2000) 'Designs for social futures', in B. Cope and M. Kalantzis (eds) *Multiliteracies*, London/New York: Routledge.

Cox, A. (2008) 'Flickr: a case study of web 2.0', *Aslib Proceedings*, 60(5): 493–516.

Crandall, J. (2007) 'Showing'. Online. Available HTTP: <http://jordancrandall.com/showing/index.html> (accessed 1 May 2012).

Crystal, D. (1997) *English as a Global Language*, Cambridge: Cambridge University Press.

Crystal, D. (2005) 'The scope of internet linguistics'. Online. Available HTTP: <http://www.davidcrystal.com/DC_articles/Internet2.pdf>.

Crystal, D. (2006) *Language and the Internet*, 2nd edn, Cambridge: Cambridge University Press.

Crystal, D. (2011) *Internet Linguistics: A Student Guide*, London: Routledge.

Danet, B. (1998) 'Text as mask: gender, play, and performance on the net', in S. G. Jones (ed.) *Cyberspace 2.0: Revisiting Computer-Mediated Communication and Community*, Thousand Oaks, CA: Sage Publications.

Danet, B. and Herring, S. C. (eds) (2007) *The Multilingual Internet: Language, Culture, and Communication Online*, New York/Oxford: Oxford University Press.

Davies, J. (2006) 'Affinities and beyond! Developing ways of seeing in online spaces', *e-learning-Special Issue: Digital Interfaces*, 3(2): 217–234.

Davies, J. (2007) 'Display, identity and the everyday: self-presentation through online image sharing', *Discourse*, 28(4): 549–564.

Davies, J. (2009) 'A space for play: Crossing boundaries and learning online', in V. Carrington and M. Robinson (eds) *Digital Literacies: Social Learning and Classroom Practices*, London: Sage.

Davies, J. and Merchant, G. (2007) 'Looking from the inside out: academic blogging as new literacy', in M. Knobel and C. Lankshear (eds) *A New Literacies Sampler*, New York: Peter Lang.

Davies, J. and Merchant, G. (2009) *Web 2.0 for Schools*, New York: Peter Lang.

Dillman, D. A. (2007) *Mail and Internet Surveys: The Tailored Design Method*, Hoboken, NJ: Wiley & Sons.

Dor, D. (2004) 'From Englishization to imposed multilingualism: globalization, the Internet, and the political economy of the linguistic code', *Public Culture*, 16(1): 97–118.

Du Bois, J. W. (2007) 'The stance triangle', in R. Englebretson (ed.) *Stancetaking in Discourse: Subjectivity, Evaluation, Interaction*, Amsterdam: John Benjamins.

Eckert, P. (1999) *Linguistic Variation as Social Practice*, Oxford: Blackwell.

Economic Times (2010) 'Twitter snags over 100 million users, eyes money-making'. Online. Available HTTP: <http://www.reuters.com/article/2010/04/15/us-twitter-idUSTRE63D46P20100415> (accessed 30 August 2012).

Elavsky, C., Mislan, C. and Elavsky, S. (2011) 'When talking less is more: exploring outcomes of "Twitter" usage in the large-lecture hall', *Learning, Media and Technology*, 36(3): 215–233.

Elgesem, D. (1996) 'Privacy, respect for persons and risk', in C. Ess (ed.) *Philosophical Perspectives on Computer-Mediated Communication*, Albany: State University of New York Press.

English, R. M. and Duncan-Howell, J. A. (2008) 'Facebook goes to college: using social networking tools to support students undertaking teaching practicum', *Journal of Online Learning and Teaching*, 4(4): 596–601.

Ess, C. and the AoIR Ethics Working Committee. (2002) 'Ethical decision-making and Internet research: recommendations from the AoIR Ethics Working Committee. Association of Internet Researchers (AoIR)'. Online. Available HTTP: <http://www.aoir.org/reports/ethics.pdf> (accessed 6 September 2012).

Evans, S. (2002). 'The medium of instruction in Hong Kong: policy and practice in the new English and Chinese streams'. *Research Papers in Education*, 17: 97–120.

Facebook (2012) 'Like'. Online. Available HTTP <http://www.facebook.com/help/like> (accessed 6 September 2012).

Ferrara, K., Brunner, H. and Whittemore, G. (1991) 'Interactive written discourse as an emergent register', *Written Communication*, 8(1): 8–34.

Fishman, J. (1998) 'The new linguistic order', *Foreign Policy*, 113: 26–40.

Flickr. http://www.flickr.com.

Flickr Blog (2011) '6,000,000,000'. Online. Available HTTP: <http://blog.flickr.net/en/2011/08/04/6000000000/> (accessed 6 September 2012).

Gee, J. P. (2003) *What Video Games Have to Teach Us about Learning and Literacy*, New York: Palgrave Macmillan.

Gee, J. P. (2004) *Situated Language and Learning*, London: Routledge.

Gee, J. P. (2005) 'Semiotic social spaces and affinity spaces: from *The Age of Mythology* to today's schools', in D. Barton and K. Tusting (eds) *Beyond Communities of Practice: Language, Power and Social Context*, Cambridge: Cambridge University Press.

Gee, J. P. and Hayes, E. (2011) *Language and Learning in the Digital Age*, London/New York: Routledge.

Gershon, I. (2010) *The Breakup 2.0: Disconnecting Over New Media*. Ithaca, NY: Cornell University Press.

Gibson, J. J. (1977) 'The theory of affordances', in R. E. Shaw and J. Brandsford (eds) *Perceiving, Acting, and Knowing*, Hillsdale, NJ: LEA.

Gibson, J. J. (1986) *The Ecological Approach to Visual Perception*, Hillsdale, NJ: LEA.

Gillen, J. and D. Barton (2010) *Digital Literacies: A Research Briefing*. London: ESRC Teaching and Learning Research Programme – Technology Enhanced Learning.

Gillen, J. and Hall, N. (2010) 'Edwardian postcards: illuminating ordinary writing', in D. Barton and U. Papen (eds) *The Anthropology of Writing*, London: Continuum.

Giltrow, J. and Stein, D. (eds) (2009) *Genres in the Internet: Issues in the Theory of Genre*, Amsterdam: John Benjamins.

Goffman, E. (1959) *The Presentation of Self in Everyday Life*. New York: Doubleday.

Goffman, E. (1981) *Forms of Talk*. Philadelphia: University of Pennsylvania Press.

Goodfellow, R., Morgan, M., Lea, M. and Pettit, J. (2004) 'Students' writing in the virtual university: an investigation into the relation between online discussion and writing for assessment on two masters courses', in: I. Snyder and C. Beavis (eds) *Doing Literacy Online: Teaching, Learning and Playing in an Electronic World*. Cresskill: Hampton Press.

Graham, L. (2008) 'Teachers are digikids too: the digital histories and digital lives of young teachers in English primary schools', *Literacy*, 42(1): 10–18.

Grinter, R. E. and Palen, L. (2002) 'Instant messaging in teen life', in *Proc. ACM Conf. Computer-Supported Cooperative Work CSCW'02* (New Orleans, LA), 4(3): 21–30.

Hachman, M. (2012) 'Facebook now totals 901 million users, profits slip'. Online. Available HTTP: <http://www.pcmag.com/article2/0,2817,2403410,00.asp> (accessed 1 May 2012).

Hargittai, E. (2010) 'Digital na(t)ives? Variation in Internet skills and uses among members of the "Net Generation"', *Sociological Enquiry*, 80: 92–113.

Haythornthwaite, C. and Andrews, R. (2011). *E-learning Theory and Practice*. Los Angeles: Sage.

Heath, S. B. (1982) 'Protean shapes in literacy events: ever-shifting oral and literate traditions' in D. Tannen (ed.) *Spoken and Written Language: Exploring Orality and Literacy*, Norwood, NJ: Ablex.

Held, D. and McGrew, A. (2001) 'Globalization', in J. Krieger (ed.) *Oxford Companion to the Politics of the World*, Oxford: Oxford University Press.

Herring, S. C. (1994) 'Politeness in computer culture: why women thank and men flame', *Cultural Performances: Proceedings of the Third Berkeley Women and Language Conference*. Berkeley

Women and Language Group. Online. Available HTTP: <http://ella.slis.indiana.edu/~herring/politeness.1994.pdf> (accessed 6 September 2012).

Herring, S. C. (1996) 'Two variants of an electronic message schema', in S. C. Herring (ed.) *Computer-Mediated Communication: Linguistic, Social and Cross-Cultural Perspectives*, Amsterdam: John Benjamins. Online. Available HTTP: <http://ella.slis.indiana.edu/~herring/2variants.1996.pdf> (accessed 1 May 2012).

Herring, S. C. (2001) 'Computer-mediated discourse', in D. Schiffrin, D. Tannen and H. Hamilton (eds) *The Handbook of Discourse Analysis*, Oxford: Blackwell.

Herring, S. C. (2002) 'Computer-mediated communication on the Internet', *Annual Review of Information Science and Technology*, 36: 109–168.

Herring, S. C. (2004) 'Slouching toward the ordinary: current trends in computer-mediated communication', *New Media and Society*, 6(1): 26–36.

Herring, S. C. (2013a) 'Discourse in web 2.0: familiar, reconfigured, and emergent', in D. Tannen and A. M. Tester (eds) *Discourse 2.0: Language and New Media*, Washington, DC: Georgetown University Press.

Herring, S. C. (2013b) Relevance in computer-mediated conversation, in S. C. Herring, D. Stein and T. Virtanen (Eds.), *Handbook of Pragmatics of Computer-Mediated Communication* (pp. 245–268). Berlin: Mouton.

Herring, S. C. and Paolillo, J. C. (2006) 'Gender and genre variation in weblogs', *Journal of Sociolinguistics*, 10(4): 439–459. Online. Available HTTP: <http://ella.slis.indiana.edu/~herring/jslx.pdf> (accessed 1 May 2012).

Hine, C. (2000) *Virtual Ethnography*, London: Sage.

Honeycutt, C. and Herring, S. C. (2009) 'Beyond microblogging: conversation and collaboration via Twitter', paper presented at the 42nd Hawaii International Conference on System Sciences, Waikoloa, Big Island, Hawaii, January.

Horner, K. and Krummes, C. (2011) 'Small languages in globalized spaces: conflicting representations of Luxembourgish on YouTube'. Paper presented at the Language in the Media Conference, Limerick, June 6–8.

Hull, G. and Schultz, K. (2002) 'Connecting schools with out-of-school worlds', in G. Hull and K. Schultz (eds) *School's Out!*, New York: Teachers College Press.

Hyland, K. (2002) 'Genre: language, context, and literacy', *Annual Review of Applied Linguistics*, 22: 113–135.

Hymes, D. (1962) 'The ethnography of speaking'. In T. Gladwin, W. Sturte-vant (eds) *Anthropology and Human Behavior*, Washington, DC: Anthropol. Soc. Wash.

Internet World Stats (2010) 'Top ten languages used in the web', *Internet World Stats*. Online. Available HTTP: <http://www.internetworldstats.com/stats7.htm> (accessed 5 November 2010).

Ito, M., Baumer, S., Bittanti, M., Boyd, D., Cody, R., Herr, B. *et al.* (2010) *Hanging Out, Messing Around, Geeking Out: Living and Learning with New Media*, Cambridge, MA: MIT Press.

Ivanič, R. (2004) 'Discourses of writing and learning to write', *Language and Education*, 18(3): 220–245.

Ivanič, R., Edwards, R., Barton, D., Martin-Jones, M., Fowler, Z., Hughes, B., Mannion, G., Miller, K., Satchwell, C. and Smith, J. (2009) *Improving Learning in College: Rethinking Literacies across the Curriculum*, London: Routledge.

Jaffe, A. (2009) *Stance: Sociolinguistic Perspectives*, Oxford: Oxford University Press.

James, N. and Busher, J. (2006) 'Credibility, authenticity and voice: dilemmas in online interviewing', *Qualitative Research*, 6(3): 403–420.

Jaworska, S. (2011) 'Language, migration, and the new media: negotiating linguistic identities in German and Polish virtual diasporic space in the UK'. Paper presented at the Language in the Media Conference, Limerick, June 6–8.

Jaworski, A., Coupland, N. and Galasiñski, D. (eds) (2004) *Metalanguage: Social and Ideological Perspectives*, Berlin: Mouton de Gruyter.

Jenkins, H. (2005) *Confronting the Challenges of Participatory Culture: Media Education for the 21st Century*, Chicago, IL: MacArthur Foundation.

Johnson, S. and Ensslin, A. (eds) (2007) 'Language in the media: theory and practice', in S. Johnson and A. Ensslin (eds) *Language in the Media*, London: Continuum.

Jones, G., Schieffelin, B. B. and Smith, R. E. (2011) 'When friends who talk together stalk together: online gossip as metacommunication', in C. Thurlow and K. Mroczek (eds) *Digital Discourse: Language in the New Media*, New York/London: Oxford University Press.

Jones, R. (2004) 'The problem of context in computer mediated communication', in P. Levine and R. Scollon (eds) *Discourse and Technology: Multimodal Discourse Analysis*, Washington, DC: Georgetown University Press.

Jones, R. (2005) 'Sites of engagement', in S. Norris and R. Jones (eds) *Discourse in Action*, London: Routledge.

Jones, R. and Hafner, C. (2012) *Understanding Digital Literacies*. London: Routledge.

Kennedy, H. (2003) 'Technobiography: researching lives, online and off', *Biography*, 26(1): 120–139.

Kinzie, M. B., Whitaker, S. D. and Hofer M. J. (2005) 'Instructional uses of Instant Messaging (IM) during classroom lectures', *Educational Technology and Society*, 8(2): 150–160.

Knobel, M. and Lankshear, C. (2007) *A New Literacies Sampler*. New York: Peter Lang.

Ko, Kwang-Kyu (1996) 'Structural characteristics of computer-mediated language: A comparative analysis of InterChange discourse', *Electronic Journal of Communication/La revue électronique de communication* 6(3). Online. Available HTTP: <http://www.cios.org/www/ejc/v6n3g6. htm> (accessed 6 September 2012).

Koutsogiannis, D. and Mitsikopoulou, B. (2007) 'Greeklish and greekness: trends and discourses of "glocalness"', in B. Danet and S. C. Herring (eds) *The Multilingual Internet: Language, Culture, and Communication Online*, New York/Oxford: Cambridge University Press.

Kozinets, R. V. (2010) *Netnography*. London: Sage

Kress, G. (1995) *Writing the Future: English and the Making of a Culture of Innovation*, Sheffield: National Association for the Teaching of English.

Kress, G. (2003) *Literacy in the New Media Age*, London/New York: Routledge.

Kress, G. (2004) 'Reading images: multimodality, representation and new media', paper for the Expert Forum for Knowledge Presentation: Preparing for the Future of Knowledge Presentation. Online. Available HTTP: <http//www.knowledgepresentation.org/BuildingThe Future/Kress2/Kress2.html> (accessed 1 May 2012).

Kuure, L. (2011) 'Places for learning: technology-mediated language learning practices beyond the classroom', in P. Benson and H. Reinders (eds) *Beyond the Language Classroom*, Basingstoke: Palgrave Macmillan.

Lam, W. S. E. (2000) 'L2 literacy and the design of the self: a case study of a teenager writing on the Internet', *TESOL Quarterly*, 34(3): 457–482.

Lam, W. S. E. (2009) 'Multiliteracies on instant messaging in negotiating local, translocal, and transnational affiliations: a case of an adolescent immigrant', *Reading Research Quarterly*, 44(4): 377–397.

Lange, P. (2007) 'Publicly private and privately public: social networking on YouTube', *Journal of Computer-Mediated Communication*, 13(1). Online. Available HTTP: <http://www.cs. uwaterloo.ca/~apidduck/CS432/Assignments/YouTube.pdf> (accessed 1 May 2012).

Lankshear, C. and Knobel, M. (2007) 'Sampling "the new" in new literacies', in M. Knobel and C. Lankshear (eds) *A New Literacy Studies Sampler*, New York: Peter Lang.

Lankshear, C. and Knobel, M. (2011) *New Literacies: Changing Knowledge and Classroom Learning*, 3rd edn, Buckingham: Open University Press.

Lave, J. (1988) *Cognition in Practice*. Cambridge: Cambridge University Press.

Lave, J. and Wenger, E. (1991) *Situated Learning: Legitimate Peripheral Participation*, Cambridge: Cambridge University Press.

Lea, M. (2001) 'Computer conferencing and assessment: new ways of writing in higher education', *Studies in Higher Education*, 26(2): 163–181.

Lea, M. and Jones, S. (2011). 'Digital literacies in higher education: exploring textual and technological practice'. *Studies in Higher Education*, 36(4): 377–393.

Leander, K. M. (2009) 'Towards a connective ethnography of online/offline literacy networks', in J. Coiro, M. Knobel, C. Lankshear and D. J. Leu (eds) *Handbook of Research on New Literacies*, New York: Lawrence Erlbaum.

Lee, C. (2002) 'Literacy practices of computer-mediated communication in Hong Kong', *Reading Matrix*, 2(2) Special Issue: *Literacy and the Web*. Online. Available HTTP: <http://www. readingmatrix.com/articles/lee/article.pdf> (accessed 1 May 2012).

Lee, C. (2007a) 'Affordances and text-making practices in online instant messaging', *Written Communication*, 24(3): 223–249.

Lee, C. (2007b) 'Linguistic features of email and ICQ instant messaging in Hong Kong', in B. Danet and S. C. Herring (eds) *The Multilingual Internet: Language, Culture, and Communication Online*, New York/Oxford: Oxford University Press.

Lee, C. (2007c) 'Text-making practices beyond the classroom context: private instant messaging in Hong Kong', *Computers and Composition*, 24(3): 285–301.

Lee, C. (2009) 'Learning "new" text-making practices online: from instant messaging to Facebooking', *The International Journal of Learning*, 16.

Lee, C. (2011) 'Texts and practices of micro-blogging: status updates on Facebook', in C. Thurlow and K. Mroczek (eds) *Digital Discourse: Language in the New Media*, New York/London: Oxford University Press.

Lee, C. and Barton, D. (2009) 'English and glocal identities on web2.0: the case of Flickr.com', in K. K. Tam (ed.) *Englishization in Asia*, Hong Kong: The Open University of Hong Kong Press.

Lee, C. and Barton, D. (2011) 'Constructing glocal identities through multilingual writing practices on Flickr.com', *International Multilingual Research Journal*, 5: 1–21.

Lee, C. and Lien, P. (2011) 'Facebook group as a third space for teaching and learning'. Paper presented at The Second International Conference Popular Culture and Education, Hong Kong Institute of Education, Dec 7–10.

Leech, G. (1983) *Principles of Pragmatics*. London: Longman.

Leech, G. (2005) 'Politeness: is there an East-West divide?', *Journal of Foreign Languages* 6: 1–30.

Lenihan, A. (2011) '"Join Our Community of Translators": language ideologies and Facebook', in C. Thurlow and K. Mroczek (eds) *Digital Discourse: Language in the New Media*, New York/London: Oxford University Press.

Leppänen, S., Pitkänen-Huhta, A., Nikula, T., Kytölä, S., Törmäkangas, T., Nissinen, K., *et al.* (2011) 'National survey on the English language in Finland: uses, meanings and attitudes', *Studies in Variation, Contacts and Change in English*, 5.

Leu, D. J., Kinzer, C., Coiro, J. and Cammack, D. (2004) 'Toward a theory of new literacies emerging from the Internet and other information and communication technologies', in R. Ruddell and N. Unrau (eds) *Theoretical Models and Processes of Reading*, 5th edn, International Reading Association.

Levy, M. (1997) *CALL: Context and Conceptualization*, Oxford: Clarendon Press.

Lewis, C. (2007) 'New literacies', in M. Knobel and K. Lankshear (eds) *A New Literacies Sampler*, New York: Peter Lang.

Lewis, C. and Fabos, B. (2005) 'Instant messaging, literacies, and social identities', *Reading Research Quarterly*, 40(4): 470–501.

Lexander, K. V. (2012) 'Analyzing multilingual texting in Senegal: an approach for the study of mixed language SMS', in M. Sebba, S. Mahootian, and C. Jonsson (eds) *Language Mixing and Code-switching in Writing*, London: Routledge.

Lien, F. P. (2012) 'Communicative acts and identity construction on YouTube first-person vlogs: the case of English-speaking teenagers', unpublished M.Phil. Thesis. The Chinese University of Hong Kong.

Lyons, M. (ed.) (2007) *Ordinary Writings, Personal Narratives*, Oxford: Peter Lang.

McClure, E. (2001) 'Oral and written Assyrian codeswitching', in R. Jacobson (ed.) *Codeswitching Worldwide II*, Berlin: Mouton de Gruyter.

McLuhan, M. (1967) *The Medium is the Massage*, Harmondsworth: Penguin Books.

Maybin, J. (2007) 'Literacy under and over the desk', *Language and Education*, 21(6): 515–530.

Mendelson, A. L. and Papacharissi, Z. (2011) 'Look at us: collective narcissism in college student Facebook photo galleries', in Z. Papacharissi (ed.) *A Networked Self: Identity, Community, and Culture on Social Network Sites*, London: Routledge.

Mendoza-Denton, N. (2008) *Homegirls: Language and Cultural Practice among Latina Youth Gangs*, Malden, MA: Blackwell.

Merchant, G. (2001) 'Teenager in cyberspace: an investigation of language use and language change in internet chatrooms', *Journal of Research in Reading*, 24(3): 293–306.

Merchant, G., Gillen, J., Marsh, J. and Davies, J. (eds) (2012) *Virtual Literacies: Interactive Spaces for Children and Young People*, London: Routledge.

Mills, K. A. (2010) 'A review of the "digital turn" in the new literacy studies', *Review of Educational Research*, 80(2): 246–271.

Moje, E. B., Ciechanowski, K. M., Kramer, K., Ellis, L., Carrillo, R. and Collazo, T. (2004) 'Working toward third space in content area literacy: an examination of everyday funds of knowledge and discourse', *Reading Research Quarterly* 39(1): 40–70.

Moor, P. J., Heuvelman, A. and Verleur, R. (2010) 'Flaming on YouTube', *Computers in Human Behavior*, 26: 1536–1546.

Myers, G. (2010a) *Discourse of Blogs and Wikis*, London/New York: Continuum.

Myers, G. (2010b) 'Stance-taking and public discussion in blogs', *Critical Discourse Studies*, 7(4): 263–275.

Nakamura, L. (2002) *Cybertypes: Race, Ethnicity, and Identity on the Internet*, New York: Routledge.

Nardi, B. A., Whittaker, S. and Bradner, E. (2000) 'Interaction and outeraction: instant messaging in action', in *Proceedings of Conference on Computer Supported Cooperative Work*, New York: ACM Press.

Niedzielski, N. A. and Preston, D. R. (2000) *Folk Linguistics*, Berlin: Mouton de Gruyter.

Och, F. (2005) 'The machines do the translating', *Google Blog*. Online. Available HTTP: <http://googleblog.blogspot.hk/2005/08/machines-do-translating.html> (accessed 6 September 2012).

O'Connor, H., Madge, C., Shaw, R. and Wellens, J. (2008) 'Internet-based interviewing', in N. Fielding (ed.) *The Sage Handbook of Online Research Methods*, London: Sage.

Olafsson, D. (2012) 'Vernacular literacy practices in nineteenth-century Icelandic scribal culture', in A. Edlund, *Att läsa och att skriva: Två vågor av vardagligt skriftbruk i Norden 1800–2000*. Umeå: Umeå universitet & Kungl. Skytteanska Samfundet.

Ostendorf, L. (1998) *Lincoln's Photographs: A Complete Album*, Dayton, OH: Rockywood Press.

Page, R. (2011) *Stories and Social Media*, London: Routledge.

Paolillo, J. C. (2007) 'How much multilingualism? Language diversity on the Internet', in B. Danet and S. C. Herring (eds) *The Multilingual Internet: Language, Culture, and Communication Online*, New York/Oxford: Oxford University Press.

Pavlenko, A. (2007) 'Autobiographic narratives as data in applied linguistics', *Applied Linguistics*, 28(2): 163–188.

Peachey, A., Gillen, J., Livingstone, D. and Smith-Robbins, S. (eds) (2010) *Researching Learning in Virtual Worlds*, London: Springer.

Pennycook, A. (2008) 'Translingual English', *Australian Review of Applied Linguistics*, 31(3): 30.1–30.9.

Petrie, H. (1999) 'Writing in cyberspace: a study of the uses, style and content of email.' Unpublished Paper sponsored by MSN Microsoft.

Phillipson, R. (1992) *Linguistic Imperialism*. Oxford: Oxford University Press.

Phillipson, R. (2004) 'English in globalization: three approaches', *Journal of Language, Identity and Education*, 3(1): 73–84.

Plester, B. and Wood, C. (2009) 'Exploring relationships between traditional and new media literacies: British preteen texters at school', *Journal of Computer Mediated Communication*, 14(4): 1108–1129.

Prensky, M. (2001) 'Digital natives, digital immigrants'. *On the Horizon* 9(1): 1–6.

Raine, L. and Wellman, B. (2012) *Networked: The New Social Operating System*, Cambridge, MA: MIT Press.

Reckwitz, A. (2002) 'Toward a theory of social practices: a development in culturalist theorizing', *European Journal of Social Theory*, 5(2): 243–263.

Richardson, W. (2006) *Blogs, Wikis, Podcasts, and Other Powerful Web Tools for Classrooms*, Thousand Oaks, CA: Corwin Press.

Ross, C., Terras, M., Warwick, C. and Welsh, A. (2011) 'Enabled backchannel: conference Twitter use by digital humanists', *Journal of Documentation*, 67(2): 214–237.

Sarvas, R. and Frohlich, D. M. (2011) *From Snapshots to Social Media: The Changing Picture of Domestic Photography*, New York: Springer.

Satchwell, C., Barton, D. and Hamilton, M. (forthcoming) 'Crossing boundaries: digital and non-digital literacy practices in formal and informal contexts in further and higher education', in Goodfellow, R. and Lea, M. (eds) *Literacy in the Digital University*. London: Routledge.

Schatzki, T. (2012) 'A primer on practices: theory and research', in J. Higgs *et al.* (eds) *Practice-based Education: Perspectives and Strategies*, Rotterdam: Sense Publishers.

Scollon, R. (2001) *Mediated Discourse: The Nexus of Practice*, London/New York: Routledge.

Sebba, M. (2007) 'Identity and language construction in an online community: the case of "Ali G"', in P. Auer (ed.) *Social identity and Communicative Styles: An Alternative Approach to Linguistic Variability*, Berlin: Mouton de Gruyter.

Sebba, M. (2012) 'Researching and theorising multilingual texts', in M. Sebba, S. Mahootian and C. Jonsson (eds) *Language Mixing and Code-Switching in Writing*, London: Routledge.

Sebba, M., Mahootian, S. and Jonsson C. (eds) (2012) *Language Mixing and Code-Switching in Writing*, London: Routledge.

Selfe, C. and Hawisher, G. (2004) *Literate Lives in the Information Age: Narratives of Literacy from the United States*, Manwah, NJ: Lawrence Erlbaum.

Sellen, A. J. and Harper, R. H. (2003) *The Myth of the Paperless Office*, Cambridge, MA: MIT Press.

Semiocast (2010) 'Half of messages on Twitter are not in English: Japanese is the second most 188 used language'. Online. Available HTTP: <http://semiocast.com/downloads/Semiocast_Half_of_messages_on_Twitter_are_not_in_English_20100224.pdf> (accessed 26 June 2010).

Sharpe, R., Beetham, H. and de Freitas, H. (eds) (2010) *Rethinking Learning for a Digital Age: How Learners Are Shaping Their Own Experiences*, London/New York: Routledge.

Sheridan, D., Street, B. and Bloome, D. (2000) *Writing Ourselves: Mass-Observation and Literacy Practices*, Cresskill, NJ: Hampton Press.

Shohamy, E. and Gorter, D. (eds) (2009) *Linguistic Landscape: Expanding the Scenery*, London: Routledge.

Shohamy, E., Ben-Rafael, E. and Barni, M. (eds) (2010) *Linguistic Landscape in the City*, Bristol: Multilingual Matters.

Shortis, T. (2001) *The Language of ICT*, London: Routledge.

Silverstone, R. and Haddon, L. (1996) 'Design and the domestication of information and communication technologies: technical change and everyday life', in R. Mansell and R. Silverstone (eds) *Communication by Design: The Politics of Information and Communication Technologies*, New York: Oxford University Press.

Sinor, J. (2002) *The Extraordinary Work of Ordinary Writing*, Iowa City: University of Iowa Press.

Snyder, I. (ed.) (1998) *Page to Screen: Taking Literacy into the Electronic Era*, London and New York: Routledge.

Snyder, I. (2001) 'A new communication order: researching literacy practices in the network society', *Language and Education*, 15(2&3): 117–131.

Specter, M. (1996) 'World, wide, web: 3 English words', *The New York Times*, 14 April, 4–5.

Squires, L. (2010) 'Enregistering internet language', *Language in Society*, 39: 457–492.

Stringer, E. T. (1999) *Action Research*, London: Sage.

Sunday Herald (2003) 'Teachers call for urgent action as pupils write essays in text-speak'. Online. Available HTTP: <http://www.umtsworld.com/lastword/lw0129.htm> (accessed 6 September 2012).

Swales, J. (1998) *Other Floors, Other Voices: A Textography of a Small University Building*, Mahwah, NJ: Erlbaum.

Tagg, C. (2012) *Discourse of Text Messaging*, London: Continuum.

Thurlow, C. (2007) 'Fabricating youth: new media discourse and the technologization of young people', in S. Johnson and A. Ensslin (eds) *Language in the Media*, London: Continuum.

Thurlow, C. and Jaworski, A. (2011) 'Banal globalization? Embodied actions and mediated practices in tourists' online photo sharing', in C. Thurlow and K. Mroczek (eds) *Digital Discourse: Language in the New Media*, New York/London: Oxford University Press.

Turkle, S. (1995) *Life on the Screen: Identity in the Age of the Internet*, London: Simon and Schuster.

Tusting, K. and Barton, D. (2006) *Models of Adult Learning: A Literature Review*, Leicester: NIACE.

Urry, J. (2003) *Global Complexity*, Cambridge: Polity.

Urry, J. (2007) *Mobilities*, Cambridge: Polity.

Van House, N. A. (2007) 'Flickr and public image-sharing: distant closeness and photo exhibition', paper presented at Computer/Human Interaction Conference, San Jose, CA, April–May 2007.

Van Meter, P. N. and Firetto, C. (2008) 'Intertextuality and the study of new literacies: research critique and recommendations', in J. Coiro, M. Knobel, C. Lankshear and D. J. Leu, *Handbook of Research on New Literacies*, New York: Lawrence Erlbaum.

Vertovec, S. (2007) 'Super-diversity and its implications', *Ethnic and Racial Studies*, 30(6): 1024–1054.

Vertovec, S. (2010) 'Towards post-multiculturalism? Changing communities, conditions and contexts of diversity', *International Social Science Journal*, 61: 83–95.

Voida, A., Mynatt, E. D., Erickson, T. and Kellogg, W. A. (2004) 'Interviewing over instant messaging', in *Proceedings of CHI Conference 2004*, 1344–1347.

W3techs (2012) 'Usage of content languages for websites'. Online. Available HTTP: <http://w3 techs.com/technologies/overview/content_language/all> (accessed 6 September 2012).

Walton, S. and Jaffe, A. (2011) '"Stuff white people like": Stance, class, race, and internet commentary', in C. Thurlow and K. Mroczek (eds) *Digital Discourse: Language in the New Media*, New York/London: Oxford University Press.

Warschauer, M. (1996) 'Computer-assisted language learning: an introduction', in S. Fotos (ed.) *Multimedia Language Teaching*, Tokyo: Logos International.

Warschauer, M. (2002) 'Languages.com: the Internet and linguistic pluralism', in I. Snyder (ed.) *Silicon Literacies: Communication, Innovation and Education in the Electronic Age*, London: Routledge.

Warschauer, M., El Said, G. R. and Zohry, A. A. (2007) 'Language choice online: globalization and identity in Egypt', in B. Danet and S. C. Herring (eds) *The Multilingual Internet: Language, Culture, and Communication Online*, New York/Oxford: Oxford University Press.

Wellman, B. (2001) 'Physical place and cyberplace: rise of personalized networking', *International Journal of Urban and Regional Research*, 25(2): 227–252.

Wenger, E. (1998) *Communities of Practice: Learning, Meaning and Identity*, Cambridge: Cambridge University Press.

West, L. and Trester, A. M. (forthcoming, 2013) 'Facework on Facebook: conversations on social media', in D. Tannen and A. M. Trester, *Discourse 2.0: Language and New Media*, Washington, DC: Georgetown University Press.

Wikimedia. 'Language proposal policy'. Online. Available HTTP: <http://meta.wikimedia.org/wiki/Language_proposal_policy> (accessed 6 September 2012).

Wodak, R. and Meyer, M. (2009) *Methods of Critical Discourse Analysis*, 2nd edn, London: Sage.

Wright, S. (2004) 'Introduction', *International Journal on Multicultural Societies*, 6(1): 13–28.

YouTube (2012) 'Statistics'. Online. Available HTTP: <http://www.youtube.com/t/press_statistics> (accessed 6 September 2012).

Yus, F. (2011) *Cyberpragmatics: Internet Mediated Communication in Context*, Amsterdam: John Benjamins.

INDEX

@ sign (use of) 179–80, 183

abbreviations 38, 118, 165, 181–83
actor network theory 35
adult learning 20, 125–26
affinity groups 32, 47, 130
affordances 17, 19, 27–29, 39, 55–56, 183;
    Flickr 59; IM 59
ALL CAPS 88
Androutsopoulos, J. 14
Arabic 43, 64
Association of Internet Researchers 174
Assyrian 64, 65
Asturian 65
asynchronous communication 53
audience 17, 21, 56–57, 82, 147
authorship 17, 44, 93
autonomous learning 131, 136, 156, 160–1

Barton, D. 13, 159
Basque 65
Berners-Lee, T. 155
bilingual text corpora 63
bilingual writing 57
Black, R. 113, 114–15
blogging 6, 155–56
blogs 9, 87, 155–56
Brandt, D. 130, 139

cameras 93, 144
Cantonese 43, 49–50, 74

Catalan 44, 65
Chinese 44, 45, 47, 50, 58, 63, 74, 80, 83, 104,
    171
Ching, C. C. 71
cloud translation 63
code switching 46, 48–51, 53, 54, 58, 64, 66, 80
commenting systems 10
communities of practice 32–33, 125
competence 121
computer assisted language learning (CALL)
    154
computer-mediated communication (CMC)
    4–5, 43, 53, 68, 165, 175, 179; and gender
    research 69; discourse features of 5
computer-mediated discourse (CMD) 4, 5–6, 8
computer-mediated discourse analysis
    (CMDA) 5
convergence culture 39
corpus analysis 21, 87
critical discourse analysis 14, 104–105
Crystal, D. 8, 11, 42, 44, 70, 165, 182
cultural capital 68, 108, 121, 182
cultural ecology 71

deictic 8, 183
design 27–9, 38, 53, 130
diasaporic websites 65–66
diasporic communities 65
digital discourse 44, 166
digital divide 10
digital literacies 4, 13, 125, 154, 165–66

digital natives 10, 85
discourse analysis 6 ,14, 16, 21
Discourse centred online ethnography
    (DCOE) 14
discourse communities 32
domains of activity/life 12, 24
domestication of technologies 2, 70, 138–39,
    178
Dor, D. 43
Dropbox 70

eBay 104
educational practices, change in 160–63; use
    of microblogging 157–58; use of photo sites
    156; use of social networking 158; use of
    video sites 156–57; use of virtual worlds 157;
    use of wikis 156; weblogs 155–56; with new
    media 153–160
Egyptian Arabic 64
email 53, 165
emoticons 5, 30, 38, 165, 176, 180, 182
English language 11, 43, 45, 50, 58, 60, 80, 83,
    101, 114, 116, 121, 171
English-Caribbean 66
enregisterment 180

face 88
Facebook 28, 38–39, 40, 52, 69, 146;
    collaborative translation 63; 'Like' 88–89,
    180; linguistic diversity 52–53; online
    translation 62; profile 72; status update 38,
    52–53, 73; translation issuses 114; use in
    educational practices 158, 159
facework 80
fan-fiction 113, 124–25, 136, 151, 154
fansubbing 135, 151,
Fishman, J 42, 43
flaming 88
Flickr 30, 31, 36–38, 40, 45, 58, 59, 65, 73, 83–84,
    111, 149, 150; 365 126–27, 132–3, 170; as a
    vernacular practice 142–47; comments/
    commenting 38, 94, 130; decline 146; in
    educational practices 156; linguistic diversity
    45; photography 119–21; profiles 37, 46, 72;
    screennames 45, 69; self-deprecation on
    115–21; socializing 145–46; stance taking
    90–102; tags/tagging 37, 46–47, 94, 148–49;
    titles and descriptions 46; translating
    content 61; writing spaces 148–49
folk linguistic theories 93, 106, 110, 123
folksonomies 37, 148

gaming 33, 79, , 134, 135, 136, 154
Gee, J. 33, 134, 163
gender 69

German 65, 112
global citizenship 48, 82
globalization 13, 21, 34–36, 64, 83, 114; and
    language 34
glocalization 34, 83–84
Google 26, 116
Google Scholar 70
Google Street View 140
Google Translate 63
Google+ 146
Graham, L. 71
grammar 17, 108, 111
Greek 44, 66

Hakka 77
Hawisher, G. 71
Heath, S. B. 12
Herring, S. 9
Hong Kong 49, 74, 163, 170
humour 89, 90
Hymes, D 12

ICQ 77
identity 6, 18, 31, 64, 67–68, 81, 133–34, 147,
    183; and language choice 68–70;
    construction online 82–83; management
    68; markers 46, 57; national 75, 81;
    performance 82, 84, 105
informal learning 20, 131
Instagram 146
instant messaging (IM) 8, 40, 48, 58, 128, 151,
    154, 158, 160–61, 167–69, 173; code
    switching 48–51
internet language: commodification and
    indexicality) 182; in public use 180–81;
    offline presence 178–80
Internet Relay Chat (IRC) 68
intertextuality 17
Ito, M. 134, 154

Jones, R 14

Kahn, P 147
Kennedy, H 71
knowledge creation 21
Kress, G. 2

Lam, E 135
Lancaster 139–40
language 2–3, 21
language acquisition 73
language as situated practice 3
language biographies 73
language choice 17, 60, 62; posts 58; use of
    medium 59; users 56; viewers 56–57

language ideologies 6, 108
language learning 61
language online 4, 107–10
Lave, J. 32, 126
learning online 19–20, 124–36, 155, 183;
    deliberate learning 126–7, 132, 156, 159;
    FlickR 365 126–27; identity 133–34; language
    learning 134–36; participation 128–29;
    reflexivity 131–33; resources 129–31
Lee, C. 49, 159
lingua franca 83, 114
linguistic ideologies 64
linguistic imperialism 43, 55
linguistic landscape 18
linguistic negotiation 57
linguistic output 8
linguistic pluralism 55
linguistic resources (in IM use) 49
LinkedIn 69
literacies 8
literacies studies 13
literacy events 12
literacy practices 12, 24, 70, 84, 85; sponsors
    130; text-making practices 40, 49, 161,
    166–7
literacy skills (and moral panic) 11
literacy studies 8, 11–14, 24–25, 28, 33, 35
local literacies 138–40, 144
Lunfardo 58, 65
Luxembourgish 64

Mandarin Chinese 49
Maori 63
mashupability 150
mass media 6, 11, 109, 181
McLuhan, M 1–2
media studies 17, 21
metalanguage 6, 108
metalinguistic discourses 82, 108
metalinguistic discourses, internet specific
    language 112–13; linguistic reflexivity 123;
    self-deprecation 114–21, 123; supportive
    social spaces 121–22; teacher/learner
    discourse 113–14; translation issues 113–14;
    prescritivism 110
micro-blogging 38, 51
Microsoft Bing 63
migration 35
minority languages 64–65, 183
mixed methods approach, Flickr research
    169–70; IM study 167–69; techno-
    biographies research 171–72
mobile phones 27–28
mobilities 65
modesty 120

Moodle 70
moral panics 7, 10–11, 19, 81, 111, 139, 151
morphology 17
MS Word 70
MSN Messenger 49
multilingual encounters 48, 60, 183
multilingual practices 44, 57, 82
multilingualism 17, 21, 35, 44
multimodality 18–19, 29–30
Myers, G. 87–88

netiquette 88
netizenship 84
netspeak 11, 70, 165, 179
networked individualism 84
new literacies 13
new media, role in teaching and learning
    154–60
new media discourse 104, 111
new technologies, and social change 2–3;
    impact on academia 2
newness 7,9, 108, 148, 158, 176, 183
newspapers 26

Och, F. 63
online, definition 7
online translators 60, 62
online/offine differences 7, 21, 34, 64, 84, 178
online/offline identity 80, 179
Orientalism 104
Oxford English Dictionary 181

paperless office 28
Persian 44, 65–66
persona-taking practice 98
photo albums 143–44
photo sharing 39, 144–45, 147
photography 2, 73, 93, 142–44; creativity in 150;
    digital 67–68, 144
Picasa 146
Pinterest 146
politeness/negative politeness 88, 96, 104
pragmatics 6
Prensky, M. 10
presentational culture 68
publicly private/privately public 68

reading path 27, 30, 91, 94, 96–7, 100, 103,
    160, 185
reflexivity 19, 123, 125, 131–33, 183
research methodology 11, 21, 29, 164–74;
    ecological approach 13, 28, 56, 71, 85; ethics
    and privacy 174–75; ethnography, auto-
    ethnography, virtual ethnography 13, 2–22,
    166, 172, 174, 176, 177; IM study 167–69;

mixed-method approach 167–72; quantitative 165; responsive methodology 22, 164, 174; situated approach 55; texts and practices 164–67; variationist approach 165
research methods, IM 173; informed consent 175; lurking 174; online interviewing 173; online methods 172–74; online survey 173; virtual methods 172
researcher stance 99, 102–03, 175–77
Romanized Cantonese 50

scaffolding 130
Scollon, R. 14
screen names/nicknames 45–46, 69
second language education 54
Second Life 157
self-presentation 85
Selfe, C. 71
site of engagement 99
situated practices 51, 123
Skype 40
SMS texting 4, 6, 8, 11, 70, 108, 109, 111
Snapfish 146
social network sites 6, 9, 28, 51, 63, 106
social networking 7, 9, 40, 73, 121
social practice theory 25, 166
social practices 7, 11, 13, 24–25, 71, 137
sociolinguistics 3, 6, 73
Spanish 44, 45, 65, 83, 111
speech communities 32, 60
stance 19, 31–32, 81, 87–90; affective 87, 93, 94–96; analysis of 91; epistemic 87, 92–94, 93, 104; evaluative 94, 101; Flickr 92–94; pragmatics of 104
stance marking 88
stance objects 91, 95
stance resources 91
stance takers 90–91
stance taking, multimodal 89
superdiversity 7, 35
supermobility 7, 35
supervernacular 182

Tagg, C. 70
tagging 37, 100
Taobao 104
techno-biographic approach 70–82, 85; interviews 72
techno-biography 10, 71, 111, 132; continuous status updating 73; in educational practice 159–60; online profile 72–73; visual representation 73
techno-linguistic biography 18, 73, 78; attitudes 81–82; home-school experience 79–80; key phases of technology use 78–79;

online/offline linguistic resources 80
technological determinism 5, 13, 19, 53, 113
technology mentors 78, 129
technology-related life 70
teenagers 71
text 3, 11–12, 14, 16–17; multimodal 30; online 26
textually mediated, self 84–85; social world 13, 15–16, 25–27, 107, 123
Thurlow, C. 108
transformative learning 131–32
translating content online 61–62
translation 18
translingual interaction 60–61
translingual practices 11, 18, 39, 54, 60–61
transliteration 49
Twitter 9, 26, 38, 52–3, 146, 157–58, 179, 186; linguistic diversity 52

Urry, J. 84
user profiles 72

vernacular literacies 138–39; pregnancy 147; value 151
vernacular practices 20, 45, 89, 137–38, 183; changes in 141–42; creativity in 150–51; new affordances 148; photography 142–44; user generated content 149–50
Vertovec, S. 35
Vigdor, L. 71
visual images 73
vlogs 39, 89, 113
VOIP 40

Web 1.0 9–10, 21, 44
Web 2.0 6, 8, 9,-10, 19, 30, 31, 40, 44, 62, 72, 74, 106, 123, 130, 131, 149, 154, 170
WebCT 70
Wellman, B. 7, 178
Wenger, E. 32, 126
Wikipedia 4, 9, 26, 62, 92, 130, 150; issues of language 62
Wittgenstein, L. 25
Wodak, R. 14
writing spaces 16, 19, 30, 31, 36–41, 47, 51, 52, 54, 86, 90, 123, 127, 148–49

Yahoo! 149
YouTube 30, 31, 39, 40, 65, 72, 82, 134, 150, 156–57; meta-linguistic discourse on 109, 110–12; multilingualism on 53–54, 60